England Alone

Brexit and the Crisis of English Identity

by Stephen Haseler

First published in 2017 by Forumpress.

Forumpress
c/o Global Policy Institute
84 Moorgate
London EC2M 6SQ
United Kingdom

ISBN: 978-1-9071440-6-6

A catalogue record for this book is available from the British Library.

Design by Ben Eldridge www.bitmap.co.uk

Printed by Lightning Source www.lightningsource.com

Other Books By Stephen Haseler

The Gaitskellites
The Death of British Democracy
Euro-Communism
The Tragedy of Labour
Battle For Britain: Thatcher and the New Liberals
The End of The House of Windsor
Super-State
The English Tribe
The Super-Rich
Sidekick
Meltdown
Meltdown UK
The Grand Delusion

Themes

- The Brexit referendum result represents the end product of a crisis of English identity and confidence that has been building for over a century as the UK lost its role as a global imperial power.

- The Brexiteers live in a fantasy-land about our negotiating position and power in relation to the EU, and about the viability of a new 'global role'. They have consistently over-estimated the importance of the UK in the new global order.

- Brexit – the final result of a century of this delusion of grandeur – will, as we leave the world's largest Single Market, leave us much poorer. And, as separatism grows in Scotland and Northern Ireland, it will also de-stabilise the Westminster state itself, including the monarchy, as the UK breaks up.

- So devastating was the EU referendum result that the existing Parliament, where there is an anti-Brexit majority, should, as an act of real as opposed to phoney patriotism, re-align the parties and reverse Brexit in order to stay in the EU.

Contents

Author's note

I have been writing about British politics and political culture for well over four decades, and during that time I have developed a growing sense that the country was auditioning for some kind of existential crisis – of governance and identity. The vote for Brexit in June 2016 looks as though it might indeed be the catalyst for such a crisis. And this book is an attempt to look at some of the underlying causes and features of the crisis. It takes the form of a collection of essays some of which were published in earlier books of mine in chapter form and have been updated (in particular *The English Tribe*, Macmillan, 1996 and *The Grand Delusion*, IB Tauris, 2012). Others – the Introductory Essay 'England Alone' and Essays Two, Five and Six – are new. The Final Essay 'Stopping Brexit' was written after the EU referendum result, tells the story of the road to Brexit, and, no doubt controversially, argues the case for stopping or reversing Brexit.

I wish to thank my colleagues in The Global Policy Institute and The Reform Foundation who have helped with the editing of this book. A special thanks to The Federal Trust (For Education and Research) for helping with the publication, and Ben Eldridge for the design and typesetting.

Stephen Haseler
London, Spring 2017

Introduction
England Alone

The British electorate's decision to leave the European Union, announced in the early hours of June 24th, 2016 has, seemingly at least, ushered in a new phase in the country's elusive search for a role in the world.

Immediately after the Second World War, and living in a twilight world of the afterglow of empire, we tried, fancifully, to resurrect our world role by creating a 'British Commonwealth'. Then, during the exigencies of the Cold War we lived, uneasily, within the growing American empire, becoming a somewhat resentful junior partner to 'Uncle Sam'. And then, as the Cold War wound down, we joined, half-heartedly, the European project, becoming a semi-detached and awkward partner. And now, after over forty years, we have voted to leave. For some this is a story of a country regaining its 'independence', 'taking back control'; for others, though, it is a story of a country clinging to past glories, and obsessing over out-of-date ideas like 'sovereignty'.

Yet, whichever it is, the fact remains that well into the twenty-first century we British are still not been able to shake off Dean Acheson's oft-cited, but still cutting, 1962 jibe about the country – that 'Britain has lost an empire and still not yet found a role.'

Now, though, the big question is whether, after over 40 years in the European institutions, and as the dust settles upon the people's decision to leave the EU, can we, so to speak, look Acheson in the eye and say we have finally found a role?

During the referendum campaign leading Brexiteers insisted that should they be victorious then Britain, shorn of its misguided membership of the European project, would find this elusive role. And, they argued, that role would not be isolationist or inward-looking – like some kind of 'Little England' wallowing in the bravura idea of 'Ourselves Alone' and suffused with endless nostalgia for past times. Rather, they asserted, Britain outside of the EU will be free to 'go global', free to develop the 'global role' that membership of the EU had precluded.

This idea of 'a global role' sits well with many British people, particularly so with many of the country's elites. The *Daily Telegraph* journalist Charles Moore, speaks for many of his generation when he sees a 'global role' both as preferable to, and distinct from, a European role and sees the Brexit vote as reclaiming 'the freedom to strike out for the open sea.'[1] The idea of 'choosing the Open Sea' rather than the European continent has continued to appeal, evoking as it does the romanticism of empire when the Royal Navy ruled the seas. More importantly, a 'global role' also appeals to a significant section of Britain's business community who see free-market 'globalisation' as good for business – as it ensures light regulation, low costs, low taxes and low wages. Former Chancellor Nigel Lawson has been a leading advocate of such a 'global role', indeed has argued that outside the single European market Britain would be free to compete in the global economy and to de-regulate at home, thus 'completing the Thatcher revolution'.[2]

However, there is a serious, indeed fatal, flaw in this kind of thinking: for this new 'global' role of the Brexiteers, with its rejection of a continental bloc future, will take place in a very competitive world – one no longer particularly favourable to Britain. Earlier periods of globalisation took place during imperial times when Britain, through its empire, was world top dog and could rig the system in its own favour. But, post-empire, the country, shorn of real power in the world, has only survived by close alignments with larger blocs. From 1947 onwards we were the junior partner in the American empire, and from 1973 onwards we formed part of the might of the EU trading system.

And, as the good ship 'England Alone' attempts to launch itself into the global economy it is worth reminding ourselves that the elites in our former colonies, no matter the honeyed words at Commonwealth meetings and junkets, have not forgotten our role, and rule, during the colonial era and will do us no special favours. And that they will, as a price for any new trade deal, demand a visa regime which allows many more immigrants into Britain from the new Commonwealth countries – a development that many 2016 Brexit voters are not likely to welcome.

Of course, theoretically at least, once outside of a great trading bloc the country will have more manouvreability and flexibility. Even so, the only way for British commerce to compete on the global playing field – an un-level field – is to engage with our low-cost competitors in a 'race to the bottom' by pushing costs (primarily wages and taxes) lower and lower. And should London's financial services sector be precluded from full use of the EU's single market (by, amongst other things, financial 'passporting' being withdrawn) the British Treasury's tax receipts will take a serious hit. So, in order to attract money into the country London will have to become an even more ruthless tax haven – an off-shore home to excessive speculation and white collar criminality. Of course, countries like Switzerland and Singapore can, temporarily at least, thrive by developing this model, but then these countries, and others like them, have very small populations.

Also, should Brexit Britain adopt this off-shore model it must remain a possibility that the EU authorities will seek to retaliate by higher tariffs and other protectionist measures against us. Indeed, relations between Britain and the EU could significantly sour as the EU attempts to penalise Britain in order to discourage 'les autres' in the EU from following in our footsteps. A serious trade war between a country of 60 million and a bloc of 450 million is not one the smaller unit should relish.

Of course, none of this will pose a problem for Britain's super-rich who, in this environment, will probably become richer still. But for many millions of British families (many of them Brexit voters) the tax-receipt dependent public and welfare services will certainly deteriorate. Britain will become poorer and even more unequal.

There is a sense, though, in which these economic and materialist concerns were irrelevant in the referendum campaign. In the early morning of June 24th after the results were in, Nigel Farage, the true and authentic leader of the Leave campaign, proclaimed that the result showed that 'we have our country back' – a catchy phrase that echoed the main theme of the Brexit campaigners that leaving the EU would establish Britain as a 'self-governing', 'sovereign' nation again. Indeed, if the overriding national desire expressed in the referendum was, at least according to Brexit leaders, for the country to become a 'self-governing country' and to restore 'sovereignty' and 'democracy' to the peoples of the United Kingdom, then, indeed, gloomy economic warnings about economics were missing the mark.

For some supporters of Brexit the restoration of 'self-government' was an ultimate virtue – so important that it was well worth the price of taking a cut in the country's standard of living. For others, assertions of identity – often linked to the immigration issue – were paramount. In sum, the Brexiteers successfully played on the smouldering resentment held in the breasts of many Britons about Britain's declining role since World War Two – first as junior partner to the US, and then to what came to be described as 'Brussels rule'. Indeed a central weakness of the pro-EU (Remain) campaign was that it concentrated overmuch on the economic and consumerist case, ignoring the importance, and the sheer emotional resonance, of questions of identity, dignity and democracy.

Yet, for all the attractive, indeed compelling, talk of 'self-government' and 'sovereignty', of 'taking the country back', and of 'restoring power to the powerless' – which found so much favour with the population – it seems unlikely that leaving one of the world's great trading blocs will do anything much to restore this 'sovereignty' and 'self-government'. For it seems self-evident that 'Britain Alone', or, 'England Alone', no matter how emotionally satisfying an idea, will be weaker vis a vis the great concentrations of power and capital in the world than it was as a full member of the EU. And that 'Independent', 'Self-Governing' Britain, now a smallish to medium-size nation-state – 60 million people, compared to USA's 350 million or the EU's 450 million – will be at a huge disadvantage when dealing with trans-national corporations and great geopolitical blocs. In sum, it would seem obvious that only the big battalions, say the USA, China and the EU, will possess the leverage, based upon access to a large internal market, to enable them to negotiate on level terms with the Apples and Microsofts of this world. The history of globalisation surely teaches us that when great global corporations (including banks) can demand from smaller countries low taxes, low wages, light regulation and minimal labour standards, they tend to get their way.

Thus the 'voiceless and powerless' who, as the narrative goes, voted for Brexit in order to restore 'control over their lives' will likely find that in their brave new world of restored 'national sovereignty' they will, paradoxically, have even less say, and be increasingly at the mercy of global forces – without the protection that Americans and continental Europeans are afforded. My first essay 'Decline and the Myth of Sovereignty' looks at this question of 'sovereignty' and how hollow a concept it has become in the age of globalisation.

What is more, in 'independent', 'self-governing' Britain the Brexit voters will still find themselves powerless in their own country. Outside the EU these 'powerless' voters will still live as 'subjects' under a centralised and over-mighty executive, an unelected monarchy, an unelected upper house and a crookedly elected lower house. They will still live in a deeply unequal society with power and wealth concentrated in fewer and fewer hands. Indeed, rather than being 'liberated' they may well find themselves more tightly controlled, and excluded, than ever – as Britain's elites, now shorn of countervailing EU power and regulations, can be counted on to become even more selfish and remote.

So, unless Brexit can be reversed, this unanchored new era will, at the very least, lead to a period of debilitating domestic uncertainty and instability. For, in a strange paradox the great 2016 assertion of British 'national sovereignty' inherent in the Brexit referendum result may well lead not to a national, or nationalist, revival but, rather, to its opposite: a weakening of the British state, even its disintegration. At the very least Brexit will cause existing tensions to rise across the 'kingdom' as Scotland and Northern Ireland review their position in the union, as large swathes of Northern England increasingly resent London and the South, and as London increasingly sees its interests as diverging from the rest of the union. Depending on the outcome of the Brexit negotiations, and particularly the extent to which Single Market access can be secured, these tensions could easily spill over into serious calls for separatism.

The Disintegrating British State

Only a few years ago the idea that the nation-state of the United Kingdom – the 'sovereign' polity which has governed the people of the British Isles for almost 300 years – was facing dissolution would have been unthinkable. Yet since then powerful undercurrents of change – both external and internal – have intensified to the point where tensions are near the point of breaking the union. Andrew Marr, the TV presenter but also a serious analyst of Scottish politics, has argued post-Brexit that Scotland 'now simply doesn't feel like the same country [as the rest of Britain] at all', that Scotland has 'different leaders, different newspapers, different headlines, different underlying assumptions' than the South of England. Professor John Curtice of Strathclyde University, and Britain's leading poll analyst, has stated that there is a 50/50 chance that Scotland will leave the UK by 2018.[3] And a final decision by the UK government to leave the EU will make these tensions much worse – for, outside the EU, the Celtic countries will then have no countervailing EU power against English-dominated Westminster. It is a rich soil in which Celtic nationalism and separatism can only grow – and along with them other presently dormant separatist tendencies, particularly in London. The unthinkable is now simply the controversial.

In one sense none of this should be surprising. For the top-down UK state has long been living on borrowed time. This southern-dominated state and its media support system has been auditioning for a fall. The deep cultural diversity of the British – displayed not just by the nations of Scotland and Wales, by the communities in Northern Ireland, but also by the diversity of the highly distinct regions of England, including London – has never been properly represented by, or reflected in, the tightly centralised institutions of the UK. And the great undercurrents of social and economic change of the last few decades have made these UK institutions even less relevant. Quite simply, the UK state is too small to deal with the big problems of globalisation, too big and centralised to properly run cities and regions (including London), and too steeped in imperial tradition to reflect and deal with the great modern democratic, demographic and ethnic changes.

A contention of this book is that the UK – and its top-down institutions, primarily the Westminster Parliament, the Monarchy, the Church of England, and the London-centred media – is no longer fit for purpose. In my second essay 'The UK State And The Fall of The House of Westminster', I attempt to show how the UK's long-established and centralised Westminster system of government (in which I include the echo chamber of the London-based media) has lost authority and legitimacy under the twin hammer blows of Celtic separatism and public contempt for the Westminster political class. And I argue that without surgical constitutional change, involving the enactment of a written constitution, this loss of credibility, unlikely to be reversed any time soon, represents a real danger to social and economic stability.

England's Identity-Crisis

Yet, at the heart of the malaise of the UK state and its politics, and a reason for it, is a deeper crisis – the crisis of England, and English identity. After all, the UK state is essentially, and has always been, the English state – with bits, Scotland, Wales and Northern Ireland, tacked on to it. It was, still is, but an extension of England and English power. As of today the English represent about 5/6th of the peoples of the UK and about the same, perhaps more, of the country's GDP (whilst also playing host to the City of London, its most vibrant and profitable area).[4] Culturally too the English are dominant within the islands – for even after 300 years or so of cultural propaganda 'Britain' and 'Britishness' still do not have the authenticity and resonance of 'Englishness', or 'Scottishness', or 'Welshness' for that matter. (Indeed this author rather reckons himself to be a 'Londoner' first, an 'Englishman' second and a 'Brit' a very bad third).

Yet, strangely, this English dominance within the Isles has gone hand in hand, certainly over the last few decades of change, with a growing unease and loss of erstwhile confidence. In sum, an English identity-crisis has been gathering pace.

This crisis of English identity and confidence is primarily to do with the loss of empire – a loss felt more keenly in England than in Scotland, in southern England than northern England, and amongst England's elites rather more than amongst the generality of its peoples. It should not be forgotten that most English people over sixty five (a growing demographic) will have grown up whilst Britain still had an empire of sorts; and many under sixty five will have grown up under the afterglow of empire when the British Commonwealth carried forward the imperial idea. Also, many of the non-EU immigrants into Britain, those from former colonies, are as much sons and daughters of empire as indigenous Brits living in Coventry or Canterbury. Indeed notions of British pomp and power – with all the accompanying ideas of essentially imperial superiority and exceptionalism – are still propagated to younger generations by a steady stream of media propagated royal and patriotic imagery.

The sad fact is that many English people particularly in the older age groups, and amongst those with power, have simply not adapted to Britain's post-imperial reality – certainly not in the way other European peoples have already come to terms with the loss of their empires. For instance, that other great European imperial power, France, certainly experienced a serious post-imperial crisis of identity – but the trauma of occupation in the Second World War followed in 1958 by the Algerian insurgency and potential civil war in France itself forged new realistic perspectives on France's role and power – particularly in regard to Europe. The crisis of 1956 also led to radical constitutional change – as the Fourth Republic was replaced by the Fifth. By contrast, many English people continue to believe that their country is still essentially what it was in the early years of the twentieth-century – a world power, more stable and important than other European nations, even Germany and France (indeed, if some of the referendum rhetoric is to be believed, virtually on a par with the whole 27 member European Union).

This is the heart of 'the English problem': the obvious clash between our present modest reality and our overblown view of ourselves. Chief culprit in this delusion is the political class and the Westminster 'establishment' whose leaders constantly talk as though we are bigger and more powerful than we really are. This false view can be seen in the embarrassing xenophobic flag waving by Britain's hilarious but powerful comic-press; in such fatuous opinions as that of the previous Mayor of London, now Foreign Secretary Boris Johnson that we have a 'massive economy' equal to that of the EU: in what has now become the all too frequent pompous ceremonials often led by the Queen (herself representing a bygone age of grandeur); in the constant media nostalgia for lost times (exhibited by endless costume drama TV series – from *Downton Abbey* through to *Victoria* and *Poldark*); and in a national, 'Churchillian' narrative that plays up our role in the Second World War – and diminishes the role in that war of the truly decisive powers, the USA and USSR.

Yet, serious questions about ourselves, about our proper role in the world, questions that have gone unasked for decades, are now, following the Scottish and European referendums, finally beginning to be asked – and insistently so. For instance, with Scotland now asserting ideas of independence, what does 'being British' mean? And, as the UK fractures, where, in fact, does England fit in? And what about an English Parliament? And English City-Regions? What about 'the North'? Will northerners follow Scotland and seek more autonomy? And will it take the form of regional or city autonomy? And what of London, and how does the vibrant capital fit in with the rest of the country?

Englishness?

And then there is the intriguing question of what in the twenty-first century it means to be English – to be an Englishman or Englishwoman? There was a time, not too distant, when, as the self-regarding maxim had it, to be born English was to have drawn 'the top card in life'. Indeed 'Englishness' had become one of the world's strongest, most confident and most enduring stereotypes and self-images. However, with the passing of empire, and with social change and mass immigration at home, 'Englishness' is now an uncertain identity. In my fourth essay 'True Brits, Real

England', an updated version of a chapter entitled 'Identity-Crisis' that I wrote in The English Tribe which was published by Macmillan in 1996, I try to answer the obvious question arising from the regional, class and ethnic diversity of England: Is there such a thing as a common English identity?

And in my essay 'The Making and Un-Making of Englishness' I attempt to look at the historical development of English national identity and show how 'Englishness', rather than conventional categories like liberalism or conservatism, has virtually become our national ideology. I argue that the idea of 'Englishness' was always largely a southern rural conception, a product of nineteenth-century aristocratic manners and of those who aped them. It had little to do with the industrial, suburban or regional Britain that developed over the twentieth-century, let alone with the ethnic changes of the twenty-first. 'Englishness' – that is, what we think of as 'Englishness' today – was in essence an imposed identity, imposed by the cultural power of an elite groomed to run an empire.

And since the end of the war 'Englishness' as a kind of ideology – the exceptionalist idea that we are a superior and exceptional people – living in a strong economy with an enviable culture of stability, freedom and liberty – certainly compared with our continental neighbours, has become a source of illusions and myths about ourselves that have served us badly, and is wholly at odds with the reality of political and social diversity at home and with our real place in the world.

England's 'Establishment'

These myths and illusions are not just the preserve of the 'we won the war' xenophobia often exhibited amongst British football crowds (and fanned by elites in London working for big media outlets whose owners live abroad and pay no British taxes). In fact, they are nowhere more strongly held than amongst Britain's 'establishment', more accurately England's 'establishment' – although they tend to be expressed in a more sophisticated and refined way.

This book is highly critical of the mindset of the UK's 'English Establishment' as it has reacted over recent years to the changing realities of European and global politics and economics. The term 'establishment' is, of course, a rather imprecise category. It was introduced into our contemporary political language by historian Hugh Thomas and liberal Tory journalist Henry Fairlie in a book entitled 'The Establishment' in 1959 when they singled out the leaderships of certain key institutions – the established Church, the BBC, the public schools, the upper levels of the civil service and military and so on (I would have added the monarchy) – as forming this permanent 'establishment'. Today's 'establishment' is, of course, broadened out since then and needs to include leaders in the media and entertainment world and the business community – most of them living and working in London.

For me, though, today's 'establishment' is more than a list of institutions and people: for it has come to represent a mindset, a tone, and a set of values and prejudices that frame and influence the general outlook – the way we British look at ourselves and at the world. Also, I use the depiction 'English' establishment rather than 'British', because the leaders of Britain's political, cultural and media elites are indeed primarily English, and, of course, primarily male.

And it is these elites – particularly in the London media and Westminster political village – who have, over the decades, both consciously and unconsciously, propagated a conceited and provincialised world view. Their besetting sin is indeed conceit – an arrogance incubated during the country's past glories but today based upon little in the way of evidence as the English elites continue to misread the country's true power position in the world.

This conceit is not confined to any particular part of the political and class spectrum. Of course, the British right has always vastly overrated British power – as any inspection of the daily xenophobia of *The Sun* and *The Express* or the Letters page and the columnists of *The Daily Telegraph* will attest to. But the British left, too, are also guilty. Today's left, now infused with the thinking of Jeremy Corbyn, still have visions of establishing an offshore siege socialist economy which they fancifully believe will be big enough to be sustained without massive cuts in living standards. Mainstream politicians have been little better. Those from the centre-left like Tony Blair and the centre-right like David Cameron, although somewhat more realistic, have also exhibited these delusional traits. Britain's centre politicians have consistently acted in their foreign policy – particularly in the Middle East – as though Britain was still a Great Power and as though no lessons had been learnt from 1956 and the Suez catastrophe. And Britain's political class, even after the Wall Street and City of London crash, continued to buy into the heady Thatcherite rhetoric about the superiority of Britain's financial acumen – regularly lecturing our European partners about their sclerotic economies.

Of course, the country's political class tends to reflect the outlook of the broader more permanent elite. And the role of the country's media-friendly and extremely high-profile monarchy and royal family here is interesting. For instance, the Queen may not make policy but she has become, for many, the embodiment of the country and its values; and certainly plays a role in fostering the country's self-image. The whole royal show with its grand ceremonials redolent of bygone power is not without its consequences for our political and constitutional life.

The essentially 'English' conceit – and complacency – of this 'establishment' was on full display in the run up to the Scottish referendum in 2014 when it was blithely assumed that a country as 'stable' as Britain could not possibly break-up. And it was on display again in the awesome decision to risk the future of the country on an in/out European referendum. In a sense this conceit – laced with good-mannered arrogance – was perfectly represented by Prime Minister David Cameron, a graduate of Eton public school and the Bullingdon Club, a son of this 'establishment' if ever there was one, whose remoteness from ordinary lives made it easy for him to take great risks with the fabric of the country, its very direction, unity and role.

The Break-up of the Brexit State?

In the final essay 'A Federal Future' I return to the immediate constitutional crisis of the British state caused by the Scottish and European questions, and try to point a way forward. In it I argue for a clean break with the past, for a constitutional convention to replace the UK/Westminster model with a written constitution that would establish a federal design for the future British polity. This design would see Scotland (and Northern Ireland and Wales) as securing entrenched Home Rule, rather like a US state or a German 'Land', with seats in the upper house of a federal parliament. As for England, this particular federal design, and there are others, would include seats in the upper house for the English regions, each roughly the population size of Scotland. Once a constitutional convention is no longer just talk but is actually underway such a proposed new federal structure for the country might well serve to take the wind out of the sails of the SNP and persuade them to settle for less than full independence.

All of this (Plan A), of course, assumes that the Scots decide to stay in a reformed British union. Yet we live in dramatic times, and it may turn out that in the next few years, no matter how we in England respond, Scotland will decide to leave the union and the country will break up.

So I also include a Plan B that could be introduced in the aftermath of Scotland voting to leave the union. This aftermath could become very dangerous with the separation negotiations between the Westminster government and the putative independent Scottish government poisoned in an atmosphere of recriminations and threats.

In this environment the most explosive part of the Rump UK would be Northern Ireland, where the Protestant community would feel that their link to England and to 'the crown' would be fatally weakened. At the same time the Catholic community would be increasingly drawn to unity with the republic to the south. It was exactly these conflicting visions that in the past have led to a mutiny in the British armed forces at the Curragh in 1914 and a bombing campaign on the mainland in the 1970s. So the urgent need today would be to establish a sense of security which would satisfy both sides – by keeping the Protestants in a relationship with London, and giving the Catholics some kind of relationship with Dublin.

With Scotland gone, and with Northern Ireland about to return to conflict (and with other areas of the Rump UK, like London, and maybe the North of England, looking for further autonomy) the onus will be on the Westminster government to start thinking radically about how to recreate a sense of stability and security in the islands. For the truth of the matter is that the whole decades-long strategy of devolution will have failed, and with it the traditional, evolutionary, piecemeal, reformist, indeed 'Westminster', approach to constitutional change. Any Plan B would therefore need to involve nothing less than wholesale structural change – a fundamental constitutional transformation of the whole area of the British Isles and maybe too of the wider Anglo-Celtic archipelago.

Any Plan B would, of course, be full of pitfalls, and possess many variants. But its central idea would be to limit the rupture in Britain (and the consequent explosion of Northern Ireland) by a plan to include the newly-independent Scotland in what amounts to a reformulation of the polity of the whole British Isles. Such a Plan B envisages that in the aftermath of the rupture of the union the Rump UK London government would take the lead in a constitutional process that would establish a loose confederation covering the erstwhile UK. Of course, Scotland, having achieved its independence, would remain an independent nation-state (with a seat at the UN), and the Rump UK would similarly remain a nation-state (or, alternatively, might use this rupture to create three new nation-states – England, Wales and Northern Ireland.

The obvious problem with this formulation centres around Northern Ireland. For whilst Northern Ireland remains either within the Rump UK or becomes its own Stormont nation-state, tensions will rise possibly to the level of reopening the violence. A solution might well be to use the opportunity of any rupture of the British union to establish some kind of more binding relationship between Northern Ireland and the Irish Republic (to replace the relationship created by common membership of the European Union) by building on the cross-border joint institutions of the Good Friday Agreement of 1998.

In the event of a break-up of the UK, Northern Ireland might just be saved from blowing up by some kind of new, loose, 'confederation of the Isles' which as well as the mainland states would include both Northern Ireland and the Irish Republic.

This new 'confederal' approach will face huge obstacles and, even with the UK having broken up, may seem somewhat far-fetched. Yet desperate times will need desperate measures and such a 'confederation' might, just might, keep all of 'the Isles' at peace.

An Existential Crisis?

There seems little doubt that Brexit – and the linked Scottish Question – are much more than one-off constitutional crises. For this author they represent the long-delayed existential crisis of the British Isles. The structure and stability of the state, the role of these states in the world and in Europe, and what it means to be British, Scottish, English, Welsh and Irish – all are now in question. This book of essays can hopefully contribute to an understanding of how we got here, for in many ways we British have been auditioning for this crisis ever since the loss of our worldwide empire.

Notes

1. Charles Moore, *Daily Telegraph*, 7 October 2016.
2. Report in *The Financial Times*, Saturday, 3 August 2016.
3. Quoted in Andrew Marr, *Sunday Times*, 4 September 2016.
4. Population and GDP figures from Office of National Statistics, ons.gov.uk, for 2015.

One
Decline and the Myth of 'Sovereignty'

Britain had entered the Second World War as a 'sovereign' independent power. During the war the country, after standing alone, became utterly dependent upon support from the USA and upon the alliance with the Soviet Union. In the process it lost, along with its empire, this precious independence – and along with it its 'sovereignty'. The country which had 'won the war' had lost this independence because its economic base was inadequate to sustain an independent existence. Since the war, and during this period of its comparative decline, Britain has, in essence, been but a part of a larger bloc – first as junior partner to the United States and then as a member of the European Community and the EU. In these postwar years the country, far from being independent has been interdependent. It was defended during the Cold War by the US nuclear umbrella and far from maintaining a distinctive 'national culture' has become 'increasingly 'Americanised'. But as Britain's comparative decline and growing interdependence became a reality, domestic resentment, amongst both elites and public, has festered and fuelled a growing populist revolt – which finally broke out into the open in the Brexit debate when the myths of 'sovereignty' and 'national independence' have seemingly carried the day. But 'sovereignty', though 'regained', remains a myth.

Decline

A sad truth about modern Britain is that for a country on the verge of breaking up we have an exceedingly high view of ourselves. Whether it is the screaming headlines of British tabloids telling their readers about Britain's 'greatness', or whether it is Cabinet ministers lecturing foreigners on how to run their economies, or the Queen presiding over some grand pageant redolent of global empire, our power in the world could easily be over-estimated.

However, a better guide to our true position in the world – better that is than much established rhetoric and opinion – is the strength of our economy. Of course, throughout the twentieth century Britain's GNP was generally rising and the condition of her people was broadly improving, certainly so during the 1950s and 1960s – the very years when Britain was falling behind many of its continental competitors. Yet, the story here was one of comparative decline – and comparative decline was of crucial importance. If Britain had been able to match the economic performance of the United States then not only would it have been able to retain its independence of action, but (as was the case in the nineteenth century) it would have been able to construct, lead and guide a world economic system. As it was, comparative economic decline was a cruel taskmaster: for, under its sway, Britain not only ceased to remain an independent nation, an independent player on the international scene, but after the Second World War became, in all but name, a client-state of the United States. Of course, whilst a junior partner to the US we clung on to some vestige of global power; but since the end of the Cold War we have ceased to be the US's principal junior partner, a role now assigned to Germany. So, contrary to all the braggadocio, the reality is that the UK is now, in the early years of the twenty-first century, a middle ranking European power.

The comparative decline was precipitate. In 1870, at the height of Victorian power and prosperity, Britain's share of world manufactured exports was 45 per cent; by 1950 it had fallen to 26 per cent; and by 1989 to only 9 per cent. Britain's share of manufacturing output reached 22.9 per cent of the world level in 1880; by 1913, on the eve of the Great War, it was 13.6 per cent and by 1938, on the eve of World War II, it was 10.7 per cent. In 1890 Britain was second only to the United States in iron and steel production (producing 8 million tons of pig iron) but by 1913 the country was ranked third (producing only 7.7 million tons of steel, compared with Germany, 17.6 million, and the USA, 31.8 million, who were ranked second and first respectively).

One reason for Britain's rather swift fall from economic pre-eminence was that its Victorian economic performance, though impressive, was not much of a launching pad. Britain's economic growth in the nineteenth century was, by today's standards, relatively slow; investment rates were fairly paltry – particularly in education and training. As late as 1870 the average number of years of schooling for male workers was as low as 4.3, and share of GNP invested in machinery and equipment never exceeded 2 per cent. As the economic historian Nick Craft has pointed out, the basic enterprise in the growing Victorian economy was 'small-scale family capitalism rather than the joint-stock multi-divisional corporations which were to give the United States its great capitalist boost in the twentieth century.' Americans pioneered the development of the large corporation with the associated investments in highly trained management which this required 'whereas in Britain managers continued to be poorly trained and recruited from a narrow social elite'. In the new century, the conditions needed for economic success were changing, and in ways which were not good news for Britain: 'a much higher level of investment, more skilled workforce and more sophisticated management' were becoming the order of the day.[1]

On the eve of the First World War Britain still possessed a high per capita income (amongst the great powers, second only to the United States), yet the writing was on the wall. Indeed, in 1913 – when national economies still had meaning – Britain was slipping well behind its competitors in a whole range of industrial sectors. It was first in rail and shipping, but third in textiles, fourth in alcohol and tobacco, and, crucially, way behind in many of the lighter industries which were to dominate the new commercial age (eleventh in chemicals, thirteenth in books and films, fourteenth in bricks and glass, fifteenth in wood and leather and eighteenth in electricals).[2]

From its pre-eminence at the height of Empire, Britain had fallen so far and so fast that by the late 1930s it became increasingly dependent – for its very survival – upon another country: the United States. There were two phases in this unfolding dependence. The first began when the country's inter-war re-armament programme became utterly reliant upon American industry and technology. American machinery was needed to equip British industry for the production of tanks, aero-engines and weapons and 'Britain had to turn to America even for steel, the very foundation of an advanced industrial economy in peace or in war.'[3] By 1940 Britain was bankrupt, 'incapable either of waging war or of sustaining her national life. In that summer of heroic attitudes, therefore, when the English scanned the skies for the Luftwaffe and the sea for the German navy, and thrilled to Churchillian rhetoric on the wireless, England's [sic] existence as an independent, self-sustaining power was reckoned by the Government to have just four months to run'.[4] (Although the national culture – the English way of life – was about to receive a new, though short, lease of life from the war, it must indeed have seemed in 1940 that, along with its country and its nation-state, it was about to expire then and there.)

After 1940 Britain's war effort – particularly the output of guns and aircraft – would have been out of the question without the American machine-tool industry: the country's domestic machine-tool industry was simply too inefficient and unskilled to produce the quality and output of guns and aircraft needed. The design and manufacture of British tanks (particularly the Covenanter, described by Barnett as 'junk') remained a problem, and by the summer of 1942 the famous British Eighth Army was equipped with almost twice as many American (Grants and Stuarts) as British (Crusader) tanks. Even in the sensitive and crucial radar industry Britain became reliant upon North America for sophisticated parts – such as magnetrons for the airborne interception radar for night fighters. It was estimated in 1943 that annual imports of radio components and equipment from the USA equalled four-fifths of British production. As with other war technologies, British inventive and theoretical science was first rate, but production and design were often below the standards of allies and potential competitors.[5]

Britain also became reliant upon American financial goodwill. British reserves had run out by the early spring of 1941 and the country was in no position to repay America for war supplies. However, the 'Defense of the United States Act' – otherwise known as 'lend-lease' – was passed by Congress in

March 1941 and thenceforth, for the rest of the war, Britain no longer needed to wage war 'within her own means'. She became 'as dependent upon American strength as a patient on a life-support machine'.[6]

By 1944 so dependent upon the United States had Britain become that she played host to hundreds of thousands of American troops, the only foreign army to be stationed on British soil since the Norman invasion. Britain was unable to prosecute a second front without the United States, and her new subordinate relationship to her American protector was soon revealed when an American, General Eisenhower, became the supreme allied commander. And it was under his leadership that the British, from British soil, encouraged the first non-European army to set foot in continental Europe since the Mongol invasion. In such an environment the idea – central to the ideology of Englishness – of Britain as an independent, 'sovereign' nation was extremely difficult to sustain.

These American troops left Europe and Britain immediately upon the armistice. And for a time it seemed as though, the exigencies and deprivations of war over, Britain was regaining her independence, returning to a 'sovereign' state. Yet, the second phase of Britain's dependence upon the United States was about to begin. When, after the Marshall Plan and the setting up of NATO, the Americans returned to Britain and Europe – both economically and militarily – Britain became a key player (for a time, the key European player) in the American – led western system.

It was a role – soon dubbed 'the special relationship' – which was able to appease national sensibilities and pride, at least for a while. Yet, the reality was that Britain, yet again, became utterly dependent upon the United States: and more so than during the war. Whereas the wartime dependence could at least be sold as a temporary emergency, the Cold War dependence, it seemed at the time, was open-ended, even permanent. There could be no more poignant sign of the dependence of a once independent and proud (not to say arrogant) imperial English ruling class than having to shelter under the American nuclear umbrella, and seek protection – in the form of an ultimate nuclear guarantee – from a foreign government against an even more 'foreign' nation-state.

Britain's own nuclear bomb was built, originally by the postwar Labour cabinet, as an attempt to retain some independent influence and to keep a seat at the geopolitical 'top table'. Yet, the British bomb's delivery system increasingly became dependent – certainly so after the 1962 Nassau agreement on Polaris between Prime Minister Macmillan and President Kennedy – upon American goodwill. If nuclear independence was a test of national independence, then France (which under De Gaulle insisted upon a genuinely independent and self-sufficient nuclear system) remained an independent nation much longer than Britain.

The history of the early postwar years is littered with examples of reluctant British acquiescence in American policy. In January 1951 John Strachey, the British Minister of War, and other ministers including Aneurin Bevan, argued for a show of British independence during the Korean War, but was overruled by the cabinet, particularly the very pro-American Hugh Gaitskell, who argued that if Britain supported an anti-American resolution at the United Nations it could lead to the break-up of the alliance and the Americans leaving Europe.[7] And during the international crisis sparked by the Iranian nationalisation of oilfields in 1951 the British only backed away from a confrontation because the United States had determined that no force should be used.[8]

British dependence upon the United States, and subordination to her world view, became more than apparent during the 1956 Suez crisis when the British Tory Prime Minister Anthony Eden organised the Anglo-French invasion of Egypt following the Egyptian leader Colonel Nasser's nationalisation of the Suez Canal. Eden was forced to abandon the military operation in humiliating circumstances primarily because of the American government's displeasure. Even more revealing of Britain's lack of independence was the subsequent discovery that the American President had virtually conspired in forcing not only a policy change upon Britain, but possibly also the resignation of the Prime Minister.

The historian David Carlton has reported that during the crisis President Eisenhower not only refused to have dealings with the British Prime Minister but, even more brutally, bypassed him altogether and dealt separately with a selected group of pro-American cabinet ministers (Harold Macmillan, Rab Butler and Lord Salisbury). At one point the President instructed his ambassador in London to 'get the boys moving' – in other words to activate his pro-American sympathisers in the British cabinet (in much the same way as the Soviet Politburo might have activated their own supporters in their East European client-states).[9]

The Suez affair was a major blow for English national sensibility. Here was an archetypal Englishman – representing almost perfectly the culture and ideology of Englishness – being brought low not only by the American leadership but, much more piquantly, by an upstart Egyptian colonel. It was an early sign that England and Britain was no longer the centre of the world, and that 'the voice born to be obeyed' no longer carried as much authority as many thought it did. It was also a measure of American influence in the new postwar order and of the emptiness of the notion of British national 'sovereignty'.

Following the Suez adventure there were to be no further serious independent British geopolitical initiatives. The British decision to enter the EEC in 1973, although in part prompted by a residual conservative reaction against American influence over British foreign policy (an instinct shared by Prime Minister Edward Heath), had none the less been a long-term American goal. And the 1982 Falklands War, conducted by an ostensibly independent government pursuing independent foreign-policy objectives, was, in reality, virtually a joint exercise with the Americans.[10]

As it became increasingly apparent that postwar Britain was little more than a junior partner to the United States, perhaps even a client-state, those English elites who took an interest in foreign policy (some of the most fervent supporters of the culture and ideology of Englishness) formulated a face-saving formula which, it was hoped, would allow them to live with the new realities. Quite simply Britain suddenly became 'Athens' to America's 'Rome'. Drawing on a somewhat presumptuous throwaway remark by Lord Halifax, Britain, or rather its foreign-policy elites, were deemed to have 'all the brains' whilst America had 'all the power'. In a biography of Foreign Secretary Edward Halifax, Andrew Roberts reports a British diplomat as saying that during the loan negotiations in December 1945: 'Lord Halifax once whispered to John Maynard Keynes...it's true they [the Americans] have all the money-bags but we have all the brains.'[11]

Yet, these Americans, although diplomatically very courteous, hardly began to act as though this formulation was an apt one. As the Cold War progressed, and the United States began to guide and direct the West's global policy towards the Soviet Union, Britain, although remaining a major lobbyist in Washington, was increasingly supplanted as the major European ally by the emerging Federal Republic of Germany.

This more lowly role for Britain was not, though, essentially the product of a failed statecraft – for the breach with

Washington in 1956 was only a temporary one, restored quite quickly by the very pro-American, Harold Macmillan. Rather, it simply reflected Britain's economic performance. The British economy had, in the very early postwar years, achieved a very temporary boost over Germany and France, her devastated European national competitors. Yet the postwar period was to see what one leading economic historian described as the 'the acceleration of the industrial decline of Great Britain'. The country's share of world manufacturing production fell from 8.6 per cent in 1953 to a mere 4 per cent in 1980, and its share of world trade from 19.8 per cent in 1955 to 8.7 per cent – and still falling – in 1976.[12] And during the last quarter of the twentieth-century Britain's Gross National Product was to slip below that of Italy and hover around that of a resurgent Spain. Paul Kennedy, in his mammoth work *The Rise and Fall of the Great Powers*, argues that by the early 1980s Britain had become 'an ordinary, moderately large power, not a Great Power' – a development which, as it increasingly came to be understood, shook to the core the more self-important aspects of English self-image and identity.

The scene was set for the greatest challenge traditional Englishness ever faced – the invasion of Britain not by American military bases but by American culture.

Cultural Invasion: The Americanisation of Englishness

If the 1940s introduced large numbers of American troops and large amounts of American money (through the Marshall Plan) to Britain, then the 1950s saw an American cultural invasion. It was not resisted. The appeal of democratic American culture to a people slowly emerging from the embrace of Empire and hierarchy was considerable – and is still so.

This Americanisation of Britain would probably have happened anyway – even if the United States had remained a great, rather than a super, power. Indeed, some time before the outbreak of the Second World War (and America's new world role) the high priests of Englishness were already lamenting American influence.

In the mid-1930s J. B. Priestley's *English Journey* identified three Englands – the old England (where 'Englishness' had reigned supreme), the industrial north of England (intriguingly not counting as part of old England), and a 'new England'. This 'new England' of 'clean, bright, art-deco factories, palatial cinemas and eating houses and the young, anonymous people who frequented them' and of crowds 'as rootless as the car which symbolised the age' drew its 'models from sportsmen and film stars, not the old upper class'. The historian David Starkey suggests that Priestley was right in believing that this 'new England' 'wasn't really England at all' and that he was prescient in believing it to be another country altogether: 'America'.[13]

This American challenge to the culture of Englishness, well under way in the 1930s, was enhanced by the wartime role of the United States and its immediate postwar economic hegemony. And in the heyday of postwar affluence and optimism (the 1950s and 1960s) the American challenge turned into a great cultural contest – a battle in which the ideal of Englishness (essentially built around the image of the gentleman) had to compete with American culture and 'the American dream' (of prosperous property-owning families inhabiting a mass consumer society) in its own backyard – for the minds and loyalty of the British. American movies, television, mass catering, clothes, even many aspects of American music, literature and art, engaged Englishness in fierce competition, and the American dream won. Hands down.

It was hardly surprising. The American dream had some powerful advantages over Englishness. First, it was democratic. It said to anyone who would listen and aspire that they could participate in it, that 'you too' can be like this. By contrast the English ideal – essentially that of the English country gentleman – remained purposely elusive and exclusionary, a life which certainly allowed itself to be admired, but was available only to a few. It reduced the population to onlookers. In Britain, the increasingly odd – by world standards – idea of royalty set the ultimate social standard, but could not, ever, and by definition, be emulated. Whereas the American dream was providing an attractive suburban life for American women, and the possibility of upward social mobility – 'rags to riches', 'log cabin to White House' – for 'blue collar' working-class Americans, the ideal of the English gentleman or of English royalty had little to give to their British counterparts.

Also, the themes of American culture transcended national boundaries. Whereas Englishness was about one particular national cultural elite's lifestyle and approach to manners and behaviour, the American way of life dealt with the universal and accessible themes of love, ambition, money, sex and violence. And the American dream had the financial and technical power of the US economy and the propaganda arm of Americana, Hollywood, behind it.

The American dream spoke to the postwar British population in their own native language, but with the appeal of a democratic accent. Thus, the English language, for so long the preserve of the ruling culture of Englishness, conveyed to the British people an alternative, and more democratic, culture. As the twentieth century progressed, and more and more foreigners spoke English, then not only American culture, but other cultures too, would be able to transmit their values and life styles to the domestic British population. And as new information technologies took advantage of the new postwar mass market, mass-circulation newspapers, paperbacks, magazines, movies and, finally, television, brought this alternative culture to millions, arguably making Americanness even more widely diffused than had been Englishness.

The American influence on British 1960s popular culture was immense. Stephen Amidon has suggested that in the 1950s and 1960s 'Great Britain' became so Americanised that it 'became a 51st state of mind, without ceding her national identity'.[14] The sociologist Arthur Marwick, in his influential work on contemporary British Culture, *Culture in Britain Since 1945*, does not share Amidon's view of American culture being so dominant, but the overall impression received from his survey is of American influences being extremely powerful.

In the 1950s and 1960s the arrival of popular music amounted to a social revolution. On one level it was a revolution in public taste; but on another it was a revolution in sociology, as the previously dormant social category of 'the teenager' was discovered, and a mass market for this new social group was created. Both the United States and Britain (primarily New York and London) became world centres for this new, highly commercial popular art form. Yet, at the same time, much British popular music was essentially a derivative of a slightly earlier American experience. Arthur Marwick argues that British popular music's origins 'lay solidly in America, with black rhythm and blues, transmitted to Britain by the white imitators and adaptors, principally Bill Haley and Elvis Presley'.[15]

The list of British popular musicians who owe much of their inspiration to American artists is impressive. Marwick suggests that the American artists Little Richard and Chuck Berry gave birth to the British artists the Rolling Stones, while 'the great Chicago bluesmen' – and other blues singers – were the inspiration for Eric Burdon in Newcastle and for the very popular British guitarist and singer Eric Clapton. He sees the British bandleader Ted Heath as but a (poor) response to the American Swing bands, and Vera Lynn – the 'wartime forces sweetheart' – and the crooner Donald Peers as essentially imitative of the American crooners and ballad singers Bing Crosby, Guy Mitchell and Doris Day. Also, Keith Richard in London, it is argued, modelled himself on the guitarplaying of such rock 'n' roll stars as Chuck Berry.[16]

Charlie Gillett has suggested that Britain's most successful popular music group, The Beatles, were 'derivative of two American styles which had not previously been put together, the hard rock 'n' roll style like the singers Little Richard and Larry Williams, and the soft gospel co-and-response style of the Shirelles, the Drifters, and the rest of the singers produced by Leiber and Stoller, Luther Dixon, and Berry Gordy'.[17] Stephen Amidon argues that one of the main reasons that 'there was a beat on the river Mersey' in the first place was that the port of Liverpool was the arrival point for the crates of popular music record and records albums being imported from America. Apart from any direct American influence on British popular music taste in the postwar years, the propensity of generations of British pop singers to adopt American accents in their performances is another tribute to the power of American popular music.

Postwar American literature was also extremely influential, both as an inspiration for many British writers and directly with the public. American novelists, most notably Saul Bellow and John Updike, have inspired a generation of British writers. In popular literature, and the seemingly English preserve of detective stories, the American Hank Jansen catered to a huge British audience, and even Peter Cheyney 'who was English to the core…had his characters speak the weirdest kind of pidgin

American'.[18] And in the theatre the great postwar British genre of the 'angry young man' lent heavily on some of the works of Arthur Miller and Tennessee Williams.

In painting, a host of American Abstract Expressionists and 'Pop artists' have inspired a whole generation of British painters, most notably David Hockney, who left Britain to live in the United States. And American influence upon the built environment was also pronounced. Many of Britain's most prominent architects spent considerable time in the United States, where they were influenced by modernism and 'high tech' architecture.

Yet it was in the world of film – the movies – where American culture scored its greatest success with the British public. Cowboy films (heroes like John Wayne, Randolph Scott, Gary Cooper and later Clint Eastwood) provided a new frontier for the imagination of Britons. American detective stories, like Philip Marlow (by Raymond Chandler) or Perry Mason, and even some of the early gangster movies, possessed, for the postwar British a certain romantic charm. American musicals (such as *Annie Get your Gun*, *Oklahoma* or *West Side Story*) were huge box office hits.

The Hollywood star system provided role models for British youth, and for many British women the female roles in American movies – many of them strong and assertive – proved attractive and, to some extent, subversive of the lowly role assigned to women by the 'gentlemanly' ideology of Englishness. It also provided role models for some of the best British actors. In the land where the profession of Shakespearean actor still held sway, 'Albert Finney's hard man monologues in 1960s *Saturday Night and Sunday Morning* have a lot more to do with Brando and the Method than they do Olivier and the Royal Shakespeare Company.'[19]

By contrast to the democratic content of American movies, the British movies of the period were invariably about class.

The Ealing Comedies (and the films starring Ian Carmichael and Norman Wisdom) purveyed class themes, as did the 'anti-class' movies like *Look Back in Anger* and *Room at the Top* and other movies starring Richard Burton and Lawrence Harvey.

Intriguingly, in this period, British movies produced no real heroes or role models from amongst the 'blue-collar' working-class majority. (although later Michael Caine and Bob Hoskins did emerge). In the postwar British movie industry Britain's largest social group were assigned the roles of 'chirpy cockneys' or the role of joker, loyal deferential (who blurted out 'gor bless ya guvnor' as he went over the top in the First War trenches), or bitter young talents who turned into 'angry young men' as they railed at the establishment and the system. Nor were British women assigned particularly strong roles in the new mass medium of film – a reflection of the dominance of male life in the national culture. It was not surprising that 'the world of Ealing and Norman Wisdom was swept away when a new generation of film makers such as Tony Richardson and Karel Reisz, weaned on American directors such as Sidney Lumet and Elia Kazan, came to the fore.'[20]

With this huge cultural invasion it is little wonder that an Americanisation of the English language used in Britain took place. American – English increasingly interpenetrated English-English and British-English. Greetings such as 'Hi', words such as 'hike', 'wise', 'sure', 'guy' entered British-English. An Englishman, Captain Marryat, travelling in the US in 1838, singled out a number of American-English words with meanings strange to the British-English ear. Few of them are unfamiliar any longer. Amongst them were: 'reckon', 'calculate', 'guess' (colloquial synonyms for 'think' or 'believe'); 'clever' (for 'good natured'); 'smart' (for 'clever'); 'fix' (for 'repair'); 'mean' (for 'ashamed'); 'great' (for 'fine' or 'splendid'); 'stipulated' and so forth.

Other American words or phrases now in common use in British – English are: from the wild west – 'poker, saloon'; from the Gold Rush 'bonanza' – 'pan out', 'strike', 'hustler'; from the railroad era – 'in the clear', 'make the grade', 'right of way', 'off the rails'; from Mark Twain – 'take it easy', 'get over', 'a close call', 'gilt-edged'; from German-Americans – 'check', 'delicatessen', 'ecology', 'fresh' (meaning impertinent), 'hoodlum', 'kindergarten', 'yes man', 'no way', 'will do', 'let it be'; and from American-Jewish – 'enjoy' and 'I should worry'. The twentieth-century wars created some common words between the Americans and the English: such as barrage, camouflage, 'going over the top', 'digging in' and the like.[21]

With the arrival of mass television (a process largely complete in Britain by the mid-1960s), American influences upon the culture of the postwar British became ever more potent. Also, North American ownership of the mass culture industry – the American citizen Rupert Murdoch in both television and newspapers, Canadian Conrad Black in newspapers and magazines, and the large American corporate penetration of Britain's top ten publishing houses – helped propagate American cultural forms and attitudes.

Modernisation

This process of Americanisation was not, though, some kind of alien implant in the British cultural body politic. Apart from mutterings amongst some English cultural elites (many of whom were also able to accept American resources when they were offered), the American cultural invasion was hardly contentious, and certainly not resisted. There were no serious political moves (as in France) to limit its reach.

In a sense, Americanisation might more properly be defined as modernisation – a metaphor for the growth of cultural democracy and the spread of consumerism, a feature first perfected in the USA but a product of all Western societies in the post-Second World War period. Even in France, the Western society most self-conscious about its national identity and most resistant to Americanisation, it is now increasingly realised that 'Gallic accusations of materialism, social conformity, and status seeking were a caricature of America...these faults were as inherently French as they were native to America.'[22]

And in inter-war Britain this process of modernisation – producing those 'clean, bright art-deco factories, palatial cinemas and eating houses and...young, anonymous people who frequented them...as rootless as the car which symbolised the age' – owed as much, if not more, to indigenous industrialism and the first stirrings of mass democracy as it did to early twentieth-century American influences.

America was also a metaphor for globalisation. America itself was (and is) a collage of international ethnicities and cultures, a kind of forerunner – captured within the confines of a single continent-wide nation-state – of later globalisation. And it should not be forgotten that the British input into contemporary American culture is formidable. After all, it was British people who founded the nation-state and took the primary role in setting the language, the industrial system, the financial system (including modern accountancy), the original industrial management techniques, the framework of American law and politics – indeed all the 'Anglo' structures and values of the contemporary life of the United States. American culture bears the imprint of English and British rebels, of British people who left their native country before the national culture of Englishness took hold in the eighteenth century. As Alexis de Tocqueville once observed, 'the American is the Englishman left to himself.'

Thus, 'Americanisation' or 'modernisation' or 'consumerism' could, relatively accurately, be viewed as a refined and developed successor of an earlier British commercial puritanism – which, denied its full development at home, found its most perfect outlet, and internal market, in the United States. During the decades following the Second World War it had simply, like the prodigal son, returned home. J. B. Priestley was missing the point when he suggested that the 'new England' – of mass consumerism – 'wasn't really England at all'. It was as English, certainly as British, as it was American. The commercial and democratic instinct of British popular culture was simply expressing itself at last, and in modern terms – having been occluded and repressed for so long by the hold of official Englishness.

The problem though was that in the late twentieth-century the American cultural and entertainment industry – particularly its tourist sectors – increasingly needed a 'distinct' English and British culture which it could sell to its, largely American, customers. Thus it promoted its ersatz version – theme-park Englishness. This chimed in well with an indigenous militant cultural Englishness which was becoming more and more rural and more and more nostalgic, contrived and artificial. British broadcasters programmed even more re-runs of *Brideshead Revisited* and *The Jewel in the Crown*.

The Myth of 'Sovereignty'

The Americanisation of Britain – both geopolitically and culturally – was an early sign that the old nostrums of British national independence and 'sovereignty' were wearing thin.

Even so, the hold of the idea of 'national sovereignty', of British sovereignty, was still strong – especially amongst more privileged elites. It had had a centuries-long run and was firmly established.

This modern idea of 'sovereignty' was first introduced by Jean Bodin in *De la Républíque* (1576 in French and 1606 in English) during his search for what he called 'the harmony of the political community'. Thomas Hobbes also played a crucial part in the development of the idea of sovereignty 'by substituting for the Prince the abstract notion of the state'.[23]

Over time, in Britain, the idea of sovereignty became a veritable holy shrine. It was meat and drink to monarchists and to those who supported hierarchy and centralisation; and it came to represent Sir William Blackstone's 'quintessentially Anglican version of the traditional English unitary and absolutist doctrine' of governmental authority.[24]

Later, Hegel also got in on the act. During the latter part of the nineteenth century the influence of Hegel's ideas, particularly his conception of the state 'as the realisation of the moral ideal and as an absolute end, had made headway, even in supposedly liberal societies such as Britain; and this renewed interest in the sovereignty of the state went hand in hand with the rise of nationalism, and thus the "sovereign state" quite easily became interchangeable with the "sovereign nation": they were, in fact, one and the same thing.'[25]

In Britain, 'national sovereignty' became intertwined in the political mind with other ideas – the Empire, monarchy (the sovereign), Englishness, parliamentary sovereignty – which reinforced its appeal. Of these, 'Parliamentary sovereignty' was by far the most important. Invented by Albert Venn Dicey in the late nineteenth century, the idea of 'Parliamentary sovereignty', a nostrum which precluded the idea of separated powers, became the perfect legal, constitutional and 'democratic' cover for the huge centralisation of British power in the executive branch. Thus, the sovereignty of the state became the sovereignty of the nation, and, in Britain's case, also became the sovereignty of Parliament – a veritable holy concept, still being appealed to by anti-Marketeers in the 1970s and Euro-sceptics in the 1990s.

Of course, ideas of nation-state sovereignty rarely went uncontested, for they ran up against some other, contradictory English liberal beliefs. During the nineteenth century the powerful free-trade ideology and instinct rejected – mainly implicitly but sometimes openly – national sovereignty. So, too, did that aspect of liberalism which elevated individual conscience, and pacifism, over the demands of the nation-state. Indeed, Lord (Harold) Acton was very influential, though ultimately forlorn, in trying to persuade his contemporaries of the unfashionable idea that nationalism was not a liberal idea at all. And, of course, the business class was always wanting to limit the role of the state, and thus, at one remove, the nation. Scepticism came from the democratic left too. The potential for absolutism at the heart of the idea of sovereignty led the political theorist Harold Laski to argue that 'it would be of lasting benefit to political science if the whole concept of sovereignty were surrendered…it is at least probable that it has dangerous moral consequences'.[26]

Yet (as has been argued earlier) both the collectivism and the wars of the twentieth century boosted the nation-state and the idea of national sovereignty. And, strangely, so too did the rules of international law and practice drawn up by both the League of Nations and its successor the United Nations. The UN based the fundamentals of post – Second World War diplomacy on the 'sovereignty' of nation-states, only admitting to its ranks places that were deemed to be nation-states and only recognising them as the principal actors. And as far as the 'British sovereign state', the grandiosely-called United Kingdom, was concerned it was not only so recognised as an independent 'sovereign' actor, but as one with a seat on the Security Council, a favoured place which was only to be questioned in the 1990s.

In recent years, though, the idea of British national sovereignty has held less glitter. Revived somewhat during the Falklands War in the early 1980s – by some very archaic rhetoric from Margaret Thatcher and a nationalist 'amen chorus' in the tabloid press – it has nevertheless become associated, certainly amongst opinion-formers, with Empire and war, indeed being seen as one of the causes of violence.

Even more deadly for the concept of 'national sovereignty' is its increasing redundancy. Quite simply, the processes of globalisation are making the territorially-bound nation-state increasingly irrelevant. And at the very heart of the pressures forcing globalisation is the revolution in technology. Intriguingly, it may have been in the military field, traditionally the bastion of nationalism – where changing technology made a decisive breakthrough against the nation. During the 1930s in Britain the policy of appeasement was suddenly given a serious boost when it became clear that one of nationalism's great imperatives – the defence of the territory of the nation-state – was no longer possible. The frightening slogan of the time 'the bomber can always get through' displayed in vivid terms the limits of national borders. And the nuclear age, with its technology of intercontinental missiles and space weapons, opened traditionally secure national territories to instant destruction – and from thousands of miles away. There was little sovereignty – either inherent in Britain or in its 'mother of parliaments' when the Soviet politburo sitting at the other end of a continent could destroy the country in a matter of minutes.

Changing technology is also one of the primary forces behind the emergence of a global economy and the erosion of the viability of borders. For instance, the transportation, communications and computer revolution has allowed transnational corporations – the single most dynamic force weakening national sovereignty – to develop and expand on a truly global basis: 'Its [the transnational corporation's] access to knowledge is central to its success: to its production techniques, to its distribution and marketing, to its financial operations...In sectors ranging from financial services to management consultancy to commodity trading, there is no longer production as it is traditionally understood. There is only information, communicated efficiently within, between and among companies.'[27]

'Sovereign' British economic decision-making can hardly exist in a global economy in which transnational companies, many of them with financial resources the size of small nation-states, can move those resources around the world at will. Anthony Sampson suggests that 'the huge flow of foreign funds, whether from Arabs, mafias, or multinational corporations, tests the integrity of every institution to the limit' and rightly concludes that 'in the global context, national politicians or administrators begin to look more like local councillors confronting big-time developers.'[28] When meetings about investment or mergers and acquisitions in Bonn, Paris, Brussels, Washington, Riyadh or Tokyo may possess a greater purchase upon Britain's future than any decision taken in Westminster or Whitehall, then Britain's national decision makers have indeed become 'local councillors'.

'Sovereignty' is also eroded by the very institutions set up to attempt to manage this global economy, to attempt to give some order to this increasingly anarchic world marketplace. The International Monetary Fund, the World Trade Organisation, and more particularly the international meetings, both formal and informal, of national politicians, all serve to limit sovereignty even further. Indeed, it could be argued that the single most important institution affecting the economic lives of ordinary Britons in the late twentieth century was the G5 or G7 meetings of finance and other ministers, for it was often within this framework (or other ones very much like it) that Britain's so-called 'sovereign' economic destiny was co-ordinated with those of its major Western allies, that its interest-rate policy, exchange-rate policy and, ultimately, its taxation and unemployment levels were all effectively determined. Increasingly, as the European Union began to take hold, then British interest rates, exchange rates, taxation and unemployment levels were being decided in European forums (in the Economic and Financial grouping of the Council of Ministers and in the European Monetary Institute), and in the interplay between European politico-financial actors – an environment giving the British government even less room to manoeuvre than they possessed in the old, looser, Western Economic Councils. In this environment the model of a British Chancellor of the Exchequer, representing the sovereign British Crown, reporting to a cabinet which in turn reports to a sovereign Parliament, is no longer even a legal fiction.

This globalisation of the economy has enormous implications for culture. In the age of national sovereignty culture too was largely national. Public information was controlled by domestic media outlets (principally the BBC); and public taste was dictated by what amounted to a group of rather provincial upper-caste guardians. Now, though, 'sovereign' control of culture is a thing of the past. Changing technology – satellites, telecoms, computer networks – will enable a massive penetration of the domestic market by 'foreign' culture (principally, initially, American).

Also, the global economic market will allow increasing foreign control of media outlets. Traditionally, British culture (which ultimately meant 'English' culture) was supported by a nationally-owned media (including, powerfully, the mid twentieth-century Reithian BBC and the press barons of the old Fleet Street, many of them articulating patriotic, jingoistic and imperial sensibilities). Now, though, the increasing cosmopolitan character of media ownership, the increase of foreign-based satellite television, together with the increasing plethora of television and newspaper outlets, will, inevitably, take its toll upon indigenous cultural production.

In the process the culture of the British will inevitably become both more cosmopolitan and more egalitarian. There will be no turning back; the world of 'sovereign' British culture – the world bounded by 'kings and queens', by 'garden gnomes' and 'castles and cottages' – is already dissolving amidst a cloud-cover of receiving dishes from John O'Groats to Lands End.

And in the place of the old clear-cut idea – and reality – of 'sovereignty', of 'national sovereignty', of 'Parliamentary sovereignty', there is already arising a more fluid, tangential and plural theory to fit the new reality. The writer Neal Ascherson has already been reaching towards a new conceptual framework. He argues that 'sovereignty [in Europe] will cease to be a one way flow, going either downwards (as in Britain) or upwards (as in Germany). Instead it will become a sort of all permeating medium, like water in a swamp, in which clumps and floating islands of self government will relate to one another in many different ways. The 21st century will be a period not only of fuzzy logic but of fuzzy democracy.'[29] Put in another way: 'the theory of sovereignty will seem strangely out of place in a world characterised by shifting allegiances, new forms of identity and overlapping tiers of jurisdiction.'[30]

The dissolution of the sovereign British state of the United Kingdom of Great Britain and Northern Ireland – and the emergence of new, more indeterminate and malleable relationships between polities – will inevitably take its toll upon national sensibilities, upon the resilience and resonance of the idea of nation in the British psyche.[31] After all, the state itself was a major transmission agent for the idea of nation. Yet, with the state seriously weakened, rather like a croaking and sputtering radio with its message becoming fainter and obscured by other stations, national identity itself may also be on its last legs.

The Myth of National Identity

People need to identify with something bigger than themselves, and the British are no different from anyone else. For the British, as for others, sense of self can be secured, honed and developed by a relationship with others. Indeed it has been suggested that the sense of identity

> is inseparable from an awareness of ourselves as members of a particular family or class or community or people or nation, as bearers of a specific history, as citizens of a particular republic; and we look to the political realm as a way in which we can develop and refine our sense of ourselves by developing and refining forms of community with which we can be proud to identify.[32]

Yet, how important is the nation in all this? How central as a 'community' with which to identify is an old-fashioned European nation-state like Britain? How does 'belonging to Britain' compare with, say, belonging to, or identifying with, the family, the immediate locale, with the city or village, with the local sports team, with the office, with the network of friends? And, crucially, how intense is an identification with the British nation-state as compared with an identification with sub-national entities – Scotland, Wales, the English 'South', Yorkshire or Cornwall or London – or with multi – or supra-national entities like the European Union, the United Nations or even the OECD?

Certainly the nation-state used to compare extremely favourably with any of the above. Alan Milward suggests that the ultimate basis for the survival of the nation-state, including the British, 'is the same as it always was, allegiance'.[33] And the nation-states certainly appeared to generate quite remarkable levels of loyalty in their peoples. During this very century millions of British people have apparently displayed their allegiance by making serious sacrifices for their country, including a willingness to make the ultimate one.

Yet, the genuine level or intensity of allegiance, or loyalty, is very difficult to measure. The nation-state has also been the ultimate political and legal authority over the lives of its people. It could, still can, fine, tax, imprison, even take life. There was no higher appeal, and most people were powerless to leave its boundaries. In such circumstances a degree of 'loyalty' or 'allegiance' was hardly surprising, perhaps more a measure of force majeur than genuine feeling. Linda Colley has attempted to measure loyalty – by the yardstick of willingness to serve in the armed forces. She reports that by early eighteenth-century standards, 'They [the statistics organised by the government in 1798 and 1803 to find out who would serve in the armed forces] confront both those who argue on the one hand for widespread loyalty and deference throughout Great Britain...and those who claim on the other hand that the mass of Britons were alienated from their rulers.'[34]

What it is possible to measure is a real shift amongst the post-Second World War generations away from military service – perhaps the ultimate test of allegiance to nation. Fighting and dying for one's country is no longer a test of young manhood in most Western nations – and joining the military has become a job like any other. In the United States the middle-class young's resistance to conscription during the Vietnam War was in marked contrast to the kind of self-sacrifice prevalent during that earlier ill-defined bloody conflict of the First World War. And in Britain, too, the willingness of young men to risk being killed for their country, or any other abstraction, also declined. The abolition of conscription was a popular act. And the supposed war fever and xenophobia unleashed by the Falklands War was, for most of those who engaged in it, more a case of vicarious valour – the real fighting was safely distant, in colour, on television.

Today's tests of national loyalty and allegiance are much less rigorous. and dangerous. A leading nationalist Conservative politician, Norman Tebbit, declared that one test of national loyalty might be to ask whether a person supported England at cricket. National sentiment and national loyalty has indeed become an aspect of the leisure and consumer society – primarily expressed (often vociferously) through support for national sporting personalities and teams. In Britain identification with nation – in football, as it happens, with England, Scotland and Wales – becomes little more than taking sides in an entertainment. It is not ultimately serious; nor are the plethora of empty rituals – for example, the recent 'inventions of tradition' such as the Trooping of the Colour and the State Opening of Parliament – which the entertainment and tourist industries offer up as authentic 'national' experiences.

British Nationalism?

The decline in national allegiance – indeed in national identity – which has overcome the British, as it has overcome other nation-states in the West during the latter quarter of the twentieth century, still surprises many observers. The 'resilience' of the nation-state is still the currency of much comment and analysis – particularly so the 'resilience' of the British nation, which, alongside that of the French nation, is often thought of as one of the classic, centralised nation-states of the modern world.

Yet there is nothing particularly inevitable or immutable about the nation-state or nationalism. A national sensibility has only held sway over the imagination for a small portion of the time of the existence of recognisably civilised life on the territory of the British Isles. The nation-state, and a sense of nationalism, were absent during both classical times and the Middle Ages. Indeed, during medieval times 'nation' connoted 'race' (in the Cursor Mundi of the fourteenth century 'English' meant the English race).[35] Then, traditional organisations such as blood – based tribes, kingdoms and empires were the primary political units. And most of the serious analysts of nationalism agree that there was little or no nationalism in the world until the end of the eighteenth century, and that only since the French Revolution has it dominated 'the political thought and action of most peoples'.[36]

Kenneth Minogue has sought to find 'a general condition of things from which nationalism seems primordially to spring' and suggests a general answer: 'Our clue may be that nationalism in both France and Germany became the spearhead of an attack on feudalism.'[37] Ernest Gellner has also portrayed it as the inseparable ideological counterpart of modernisation, of the transition from agricultural to industrial society. He argues that the ideology of nationalism provides 'an integrative structure both assisting and easing the shocks of modernisation in all its facets – the breaking down of tribal, social and intellectual barriers, the reorientation of politics, the spread of education and literacy, the expansion of equal opportunity, the introduction of agricultural and industrial techniques'.[38] Other analysts of nationalism do not dispute its historically modernising character, its crucial role in the transition from a feudal order, but argue that the nation, and the nation-state, was not the sole transporter of modernity. Gerald Newman suggests that the modern era was formed during 'the nationless universalism of the early enlightenment, the age of Locke and Pope and Voltaire.'[39] And English, and British, nationalism was no exception. The 'integrative structure' of the new British state certainly helped absorb the exceptional dislocations ushered in by the rapid commercial, industrial and technological changes which swept over the British Isles during the late eighteenth, nineteenth and early twentieth centuries.

As well as being essentially modern phenomena, the nation-state, and nationalism, are also less than natural, or popular, in their derivation. Some experts believe that far from being a popularly rooted aspect of political life, the nationalism of modern times was all got up by the intellectuals. 'Nationalism is, at the outset, a creation of writers', argues Gerald Newman.[40] And Minogue has described the initial phase of nationalism in eighteenth-century England as being created by native intellectual 'stirrings' against French domination of literary life. There is little doubt that in the forging of English, and later British, national sensibility the role of writers, thinkers, polemicists – and others with a reflective temperament and time on their hands, what the eighteenth-century writer Richard Hurd called 'dexterous people' – was utterly crucial.[41] As was the wider dissemination of the ideas of the intellectuals that was secured by the burgeoning internal market and the advances in printing and publishing.

The idea of a new community – a 'national' or 'English' community developed by writers as part of a literary reaction against the French – fitted in well with the new political reality of the 1707 British Union state. Political and intellectual life were for a time pulling in the same direction. Together, the landed families who controlled the politics and the 'stirrings' of nationalism amongst the literati cemented the new nation-state – the realm of Great Britain, and later of the United Kingdom of Great Britain and Northern Ireland. Thus, like most of the other contemporary Western nation-states, the British variant, constructed well before the age of mass democracy, was forged by elites.

The British nation-state was born in the pre-democratic age. Therefore, not only its structures – those deriving from the compact of 1688-9 – but also its ethos was decidedly aristocratic. 'We the people' had to break into the structures, they hardly informed them – as they were to inform the late eighteenth-century Constitution of the United States. Nor was the new nation-state particularly liberal. Nationalism may have been a modern phenomenon, but it was not necessarily a liberal one. Harold Acton was one of the few nineteenth-century political thinkers who understood the inherently illiberal germ at the centre of the collectivist ideology of the nation. Thus, not surprisingly, there was no place in the body or structures of the new British state for entrenched individual rights.

The Individual and the Nation

Indeed, it was the powerful new liberal idea – involving the primacy, indeed the 'sovereignty', of the individual, and his or her autonomy and consciousness – which, over time, was to shake the very fundamentals of the collectivist nation-state – more so even than the later arrival on the scene of globalisation.

The 'sovereign individual' has always been at the centre of British liberal thought, yet Britain during the height of its nationhood has seen its liberalism constrained not only by class (of both the High-Tory and trade union varieties) but also by the collective sensibility of nationalism itself – a collectivism fuelled by two world wars. Yet, a decisive breakthrough for the idea of the individual took place in the post – Second World War era with the arrival of a mass consumer society. The industrial and commercial age, as well as fostering a technology (mass communications) which enhanced 'national' sensibility, also set in train, and more decisively so, the rise of the individual – the phenomenon most likely to destroy the idea and hold of 'nation'.

The growing political culture of individual rights met up with the economic development of mass markets catering to individual needs and desires to produce a powerful boost to assertive individualism. 'In the modern variant of capitalism, the individual's relationship to the economic system is a highly atomized one. Individualism, not collectivism, typifies consumerist society, even for those who do not possess the wealth required to fulfil their desires: I consume therefore I am.'[42] Increasingly, individuals began to count. And selflessness came to be seen as self-sacrifice or self-abnegation – whether of the mild kind like 'public service' or of the egregious kind like the sacrifices made by millions for 'country' in the First World War. In this environment the collectivities – including nation, one of the most important of collectivities – were bound to weaken.

British reactionaries – many of them fervent nationalists – saw this threat very clearly indeed. George Eliot in 1879 summed up the fear of nationalists when presented with an early glimpse of the modern consumer.

> Not only the nobleness of a nation depends upon this presence of national consciousness, but also the nobleness of each individual citizen. Our dignity [is related to] our sense of relationship to something admirable...worthy of sacrifice...a continual inspiration self-repression and discipline by the presentation of aims larger and more attractive to our generous part than the securing of personal ease or prosperity.[43]

Although such appeals to 'repression' and 'self-discipline' were not likely to advance the cause much, echoes of this anti-individualism could still be heard from horrified British Tory Lord Hinchingbrooke well into the latter part of the twentieth-century: he saw 'individualistic businessmen, financiers and speculators...creeping unnoticed...to injure the character of our people'.[44]

In this individualist environment identity itself – 'the condition of being a specified person' – begins to weaken its hold.[45] The assertive and self-conscious individual seeks to become less constrained by reference to groups – particularly to large and anonymous ones like nations. Schiller's advice to his fellow Germans: 'Do not seek to form a nation, content yourself with being men' captures this dichotomy.[46]

This 'individualistic' approach to the nation-state was intriguingly exhibited some two centuries ago when a London coachman, way ahead of his time, provided a superb description of the instrumental citizen of today. Asked whether he would fight for his country during the heightened anxiety over a French revolutionary invasion in 1803, he replied:

> No law or power under the canopy of heaven shall force me to take up arms...I pray to God, that I may never live to see my country become a province of France, but if this war is suffered to go on I know it

> will be conquered, for I am positively sure that the King, Lords and Commons…have long since lost the hearts, goodwill and affection of a very great majority of the people of this nation.[47]

National feeling, severely weakened by the rise of individualism, is also threatened by the growth of more local and regional loyalties and identities, principally the emergence of ethnic nationalisms. Since the collapse of the Soviet Union the intensity of ethnic identification that existed within the former Soviet empire has been revealed – and in the case of Yugoslavia a 'new' identity so powerful that thousands were willing to fight and die to defend it. And sub-national ethnicity may also be unleashed by the European Union as it weakens the hold of those other mini-empires – the larger European nation-states. As Neal Ascherson has argued, 'we can formulate a law of politics here. When European Union advances, so does regional autonomy.'[48] Although the Scots, unlike the Serbs or the Bosnians or the Croats, may not be prepared to die for the cause of their 'ethnic' nation, they are likely to identify with Scotland and Scottishness more intensely than any Briton will identify with Britain and Britishness.

A Rational Calculus

In western Europe, including Britain, the dramatic weakening not only of the sovereignty of the nation-state, but also of people's emotional and psychological ties to nation, will inevitably mean that a more rational view of political organisation may become possible. Publics will no longer invest sentiment in the political organisations which govern their lives. Rather, they may increasingly make what amounts to a rational calculus of functions and needs.

And, in any such rational calculus, the British nation-state, like many others in Europe, must increasingly appear as ill-equipped to perform the functions of twenty-first century government. Britain is a perfect case of this incapacity: for, like France, Germany, Italy and Spain, it is both too small and too big. It is too small to perform the functions of geopolitics and geoeconomics – the foreign, defence and strategic, international trade, international economic, environmental and transport network policies. It is also too small to properly enforce a regime of individual rights against incursions by large-scale transnational enterprises. Yet, at the same time, it is too big to provide the democratic participatory functions increasingly demanded by citizens – and more effectively provided by local and regional government.

The Last Hurrah

Thus, the loss of national sovereignty (and national identity) caused by globalisation, the rise of individualism and sub-national ethnicity, means that the eighteenth-century nation-state – the major positive force during the transition to modernity – is not only incapable and irrelevant but also ultimately doomed.

Even so, such intimations of mortality do not necessarily mean that eruptions of national sentiment are things of the past. Indeed, quite the opposite. Some of the starkest nationalist sentiment has found expression in the 1970s, 80s and 90s. Conservative politicians such as Enoch Powell made stirring and evocative nationalist speeches during the period when Britain first entered the European Community. And, later, Conservative ministers Nicholas Ridley and Patrick Nicholls gave vent to remarkably hostile anti-German and anti-French sentiments associated more with the Second World War than with life in the European Union. And, of course, the British tabloid press, even well into the twenty-first century, still exhibits a crude kind of nationalism not seen since jingo times.

Yet expressions of national sentiment often become raucous when national identity is weak, and when it is under threat either from other nationalisms or from universal forces of change. And during the latter quarter of the twentieth century British national identity, along with the British nation-state, was certainly both enfeebled and under threat.

Notes

1. Quotations from Nick Crafts, 'Managing Decline? 1870-1990', *History Today*, vol. 44, 5 June 1994, p. 38 and p. 39.
2. Figures from Crafts, op. cit., and for iron and steel production from Paul Kennedy, *The Rise and Fall of the Great Powers*, New York, 1987, p. 200.
3. Correlli Barnett, *The Collapse of British Power*, London, 1972, p. 12.
4. Ibid., pp. 14-15.
5. Correlli Barnett, *The Audit of War*, London, 1986, p. 160. The military data is also drawn from Barnett, Chapter 9.
6. Both quotes from ibid., pp. 144-5.
7. For a description of British politics during the Korean War see Callum MacDonald, *Britain and the Korean War*, Oxford, 1990.
8. See David Carlton, *Britain and the Suez Crisis*, Oxford, 1998, pp. 87-89.
9. Ibid., pp. 232-3. The quote from Eisenhower appears in David Carlton, *Anthony Eden: A Biography*, London, 1981, p. 460.
10. The ability of British forces to use US basing facilities and intelligence reports, as well as material support, was a central factor in the outcome of the conflict.
11. See Andrew Roberts, *Holy Fox: A Biography of Lord Halifax*, London, 1991, p. 297.

12. Kennedy, op. cit., p. 425.
13. The quotes are from David Starkey, 'Freedom and Responsibility', an abridged version of an article first published in *The Daily Telegraph*, *LSE Magazine*, Spring 1994.
14. Stephen Amidon, 'Overlong, Overdone and Over Here', *The Sunday Times*, 8 May 1994.
15. Arthur Marwick, *Culture in Britain Since 1945*, Oxford, 1991, p. 92.
16. Ibid., p. 92.
17. Charlie Gillett quoted in Marwick, p. 34.
18. Marwick, op. cit., pp. 56-7.
19. *Sunday Times*, 8 May 1994.
20. Marwick, op. cit., pp. 56-7.
21. Robert McCrum, William Cram and Robert McNeil, *The Story of English*, New York, 1986, Chapter 7. Also, for influence of Yiddish on British-English see Leo Rosten, *The Joys of Yiddish*, London, 1971.
22. Richard Kuisel, *Seducing the French, The Dilemma of Americanisation*, London, 1993, p. 223.
23. F. H. Hinsley, *Sovereignty*, Cambridge, 1986, p. 142.
24. J. C. D. Clarke, *The Language of Liberty 1660-1832*, Cambridge, 1994, quoted in Jack P. Greene, 'Why Did They Rebel?', *TLS*, 10 June 1994.
25. Quotation from Hinsley, op. cit., pp. 208-9.
26. Harold Laski, *The Grammar of Politics*, London, 1941, cited in Hinsley, op. cit., p. 216.
27. Mathew Horsman and Andrew Marshall, *After The Nation-State: Citizens, Tribalism and the New World Disorder*, London, 1994, p. 49.
28. Anthony Sampson, 'A Worthless World of Money', *The Independent*, 16 November 1994.
29. Neal Ascherson, 5th Sovereignty Lecture, 'Local Government and the Myth of Sovereignty', given to Charter 88 on 25 February 1994, and reprinted in *The New Statesman*, 11 March 1994.
30. Joseph A. Camilleri and Jim Falk, *The End of Sovereignty*, Aldershot, 1992.
31. The dissolution of the state referred to here need not amount to a formal act, but could effectively occur over several decades.

32. S. Mulhall and A.Swift, *Liberals and Communitarians*, Oxford, 1992, p. 67.
33. Alan S. Milward, *The European Rescue of the Nation-State*, London, 1992.
34. Linda Colley, *Britain: Forging the Nation 1707-1837*, London, 1992, p. 291.
35. This view is outlined in: *English In Use*, Gabrielle Stein and Randolph Quirk, London, 1993.
36. Quote from John Plamenatz, 'Two Types of Nationalism', in: *Nationalism: The Nature and Evolution of an Idea*, Eugene Kamenka (ed), Canberra, 1973, p. 23.
37. Kenneth Minogue, *Nationalism*, London, 1969, pp. 23-4.
38. Ernest Gellner, *Nations and Nationalism*, London, 1983.
39. Gerald Newman, *The Rise of English Nationalism, 1740-1830*, New York, 1987, p. 199.
40. Ibid., p. 87.
41. Quoted in ibid., p. 110.
42. Horsman and Marshall, op. cit., p. 253.
43. Quoted in Newman, op. cit., p. 53.
44. Quoted in W. H. Greenleaf, *The British Political Tradition*, London, 1983, p. 257.
45. This definition of identity appears in *The Oxford English Dictionary*, 7th edition, 1982. It is as good as many others.
46. Quoted in Newman, op. cit., p. 49.
47. Quoted in Colley, op. cit., p. 291, from J. R. Dinwiddy, 'Parliamentary Reform as an Issue in British Politics: 1880-1810', London University PhD dissertation, 1971.
48. Ascherson, op. cit.

Two

The UK State and the Fall of the House of Westminster

During the 2016 referrendum campaign the Brexiteers' proclaimed vision of a 'self-governing, independent nation' was a compelling vision. However, in a great historic irony this eruption of nationalist sentiment may well have the very opposite result, for the Brexit result will foster Celtic – and perhaps – London separatism within the UK which can only weaken and destabilise the British state. Of course, the British Westminster state had already being weakened before the Brexit vote by the growth of the SNP in Scotland, and Westminster had been damaged by scandals and a growing public disdain for the 'Westminster village'. This failure of the UK state, and crucially of the structure and ethos of its governance, the Westminster system, has been building for many decades. Below is a narrative of its failure.

Success

The United Kingdom was founded in 1707 by the Act of Union between England and Scotland which built upon the earlier 1603 union of the crowns of the two nations. This new kingdom, born during the war of the Spanish Succession, was, some six years into its life, to see the Treaty of Utrecht usher in an era of empire that would last right through to the middle of the twentieth-century. The new state thus 'went hand in hand with empire' and was to be forged and strengthened by an imperial mission.[1] And over the next three centuries this new state became one of the world's most impressive success stories – as it rose from the ranks of the middling European powers to become a great global power.

As the state succeeded so too did its 'constitution' and institutions. Indeed at the height of empire, in late Victorian times, Westminster's unitary state – its interlinked nexus of monarchy, Lords, established church, Privy Council and House of Commons – not only became entrenched but assumed an almost sacred standing, revered well into the present day. It was a reverence that spread abroad too as Westminster's 'Mother of Parliaments' was copied around the world. And Westminster's standing rubbed off on its political class and wider 'establishment'. Until relatively these were confident rulers for confident times.

The Westminster System: Design Flaw

That was then. Some hundred years on from the height of empire our constitution and our rulers, today's Westminster system, have been slow to adjust – both to geopolitical changes abroad and to social changes at home. In Dean Acheson's famous phrase Britain 'has lost an empire, not yet found a role', and today is no longer even a 'great power' in the old sense. Yet this middling European country has a constitution and associated institutions still redolent with imperial grandeur – 'Mother of Parliaments', monarchy, peers, established church with its world-wide Anglican community – simply do not fit the times.

At home, today's Westminster, with its highly centralised, unitary constitution, seems unconnected with the modern reality of national, regional, class and ethnic differences in Britain. As do its elites (still pompously and ludicrously calling themselves 'honourable' and 'noble') who seem, once inside the system, to become increasingly divorced from everyday lives. The old and easy arrogance and complacency of imperial times still run through many veins, qualities that nearly lost Scotland in September 2014.

In one sense modern Britain should be well-equipped to adjust to change. Our evolutionary system and our vaunted pragmatic elite should be able to react and adjust to change relatively quickly. But that is on paper. In truth, however, we still see the world through the prism of our recent past, our time in the sun, our empire. To understand the present backwardness of our constitution and institutions we need to start where the Westminster system started, in the early eighteenth-century.

Modern Westminster's Founders: 'Toffs' Born to Rule

Founded in 1707 the new nation-state, the United Kingdom, had an ignominious beginning – born out of elite corruption and double-dealing. The Scottish Presbyterian Kirk was squared by giving it a special, protected, position in any future union; and the independent Scottish Parliament was effectively sidelined by a motion in Parliament, moved at the last minute by the seemingly 'anti-union' nobleman the Duke of Hamilton, giving power over union negotiations to commissioners appointed by 'the Queen herself'. This nobleman, in a nice foretaste of the now well-established Westminster patronage system, subsequently received an English Dukedom, membership of the Order of the Thistle and the Garter, and the post of British Ambassador to Paris. Daniel Defoe reflected at the time that 'a firmer union of policy with less union of affection has hardly been known in the whole world'. And according to Norman Davies, 'The English were largely indifferent. The Scots were overwhelmingly hostile'.[2]

Born out of shady dealing, the Westminster-led union was, from the very start, a deeply unequal enterprise in which aristocrats ruled. Most of the people living in the new nation-state had nothing to say about its government – which was formed, and informed, by the dominant landed interests of the time. This new nation-state was, for all intents and purposes, a polity by, for and of the English aristocracy. And during the eighteenth and nineteenth centuries this aristocracy and the aristocratic view of governance (and its associated ideology) not only dominated the state but also permeated down into the broader political culture of the British isles.

Built For Empire: At Home and Abroad

This new nation-state (the United Kingdom of Great Britain, the Westminster-state), this aristocrat-controlled territory and polity, was to see its writ run way beyond the British Isles to reach across the Atlantic and into North America. Settlements, primarily English, in the Americas and the trading posts in East India came over time to be formalised as colonies of this 1707 union. Although Westminster lost its American colonies in the late eighteenth-century, it was to have a second imperial wind in the nineteenth. It started by blowing across the Irish Sea. Ireland was annexed by the UK in 1801 an act recognised by the Act of Union between the UK and Ireland. Although the Irish had representation in the UK Parliament they were, for all intents and purposes, part of the 'internal' or 'domestic' empire run by aristocratic Englishmen.

This 'United Kingdom of Great Britain and Ireland' was the state which saw the high-point of empire. In the process of this imperial expansion the English aristocracy, through the evolving English Parliament, extended its rule beyond the English, Scottish, Welsh and Irish natives in the British isles (few of whom had the vote) and into the colonial possessions. The Cambridge historian John Seeley could argue that 'the drift of [sic] English history' involved both an external empire 'beyond the sea' and an 'internal empire' at home (which he called the 'internal union of the three kingdoms'). Whilst rejecting 'English superiority' he nonetheless saw Britain at home and the empire abroad as one whole polity, a 'mere extension of the English race into other lands...[sic] without conquest.'[3]

This widely held view of the British at home and the colonial masses abroad united as 'subjects' under one 'Crown' (Her Majesty's subjects in Africa and the sub-continent being in some sense on a footing with Her Majesty's subjects in Britain and Ireland) had some validity. Parliament set the laws for both the domestic peoples and the colonial peoples abroad; the British government was the executive authority over both (the Colonial Office dealing with the 'colonials'); the Privy Council and the House of Lords were the arbiters of law for both peoples; and, of course, Queen Victoria and her heirs ruled as head of state, ('Empress' as far as the Indians were concerned).

When viewed in this way the British empire was not, in essence, simply a story of one 'nation' (Britain) or one 'people' (the British) dominating the masses in India and parts of Africa, Asia and the Caribbean. For the disenfranchised 'British people' at home had very little to do with the construction of the imperial system – except in the sense that they were recruited to fight and die in the wars of conquest and occupation. Rather, the imperial story was one of how a ruling group of English aristocrats and their camp followers established rulership over one third of humanity. (Only after the full franchise, some twenty odd years into the twentieth-century did the domestic peoples of this empire begin to use the vote to increase their power and place themselves in a position superior to the colonial subjects).

Of course, some form of elite rulership was the only way to run an empire as large and diverse as the British. This empire simply could not function without a ruling class which was tightly-knit, highly-disciplined, supremely confident, and possessed of a sense of superiority linked to a special mission – and, of course, ruthless. The English aristocracy was perfect for the task. England's leaders had from feudal times developed habits of rulership, what Kathryn Tidrick called a 'cult of leadership'.[4] As it happens this culture of paternalism perfected in feudal times – lord and peasant culture – was appropriate for ruling the growing number of black and brown masses that England's leadership groups controlled. The imperial ethos was redolent with 'aristocratic wisdom' about proper governance – 'firm but fair' paternalism.

Indeed this paternalistic habit of mind became the template not just for governing the colonial masses but the domestic British masses as well. Not surprisingly so. The historian

Norman Davies uses the term 'The British Imperial Isles' to describe the process in which domestic Britain and its global empire had become entwined, almost as one. He quotes *The Times of India* at the coronation of King George V to give a flavour of this idea of oneness: 'Today the eyes of the whole world will be turned towards the ancient shrine of Westminster where His Most Excellent Majesty George the Fifth will be crowned King of the United Kingdom of Great Britain and Ireland, and of the British Dominions Beyond The Seas, and Emperor of India...The Coronation then, symbolises the growth of the British Nation and the British Empire through twelve centuries.'[5]

Ruling Without Consent

The nineteenth-century – the century of empire – saw the emergence of a systematic attempt to provide this 'Ukanian' empire with a class of rulers. An educational system developed that was geared specifically for rulership over the colonial peoples (and, for good measure, over the British peoples as well).

The military historian Correlli Barnett has identified the nineteenth-century public schools as the breeding ground of this elite. '...most of the administrators of the British Empire, at home and overseas in the 1920 and 1930s, as well as many British business leaders and MPs, were products of the period of its [public schools] ripest development between 1870 and 1900.' And he makes a quite startling claim: that 'except for young Nazis or Communists no class of leaders in modern times has been so subjected to prolonged moulding of character, personality and outlook as British public-school boys in this era'.[6]

The values and lifestyle inculcated in these schools both reflected existing aristocratic life and developed it further. It was a way of thinking and living so powerful that it began to define what it meant to be 'English' – producing that most successful global brand 'The English Gentleman'. Though scornful of ideas this culture developed what amounted to an ideology: what the Scottish writer Tom Nairn called the 'Ukanian' ideology of Englishness.

Of course, the manners, values and lifestyle of this Victorian aristocratic class were reflected in the political values of the time – and, crucially, in the 'constitution' and institutions of the empire and the country. The dominant party in Parliament – the Whigs and their Liberal heirs – prided themselves on 'progressive' virtues like good governance, moderation, tolerance, and fairness. Indeed, the Whig ascendancy, these founders of the modern Westminster state, turned Britain into one of the most stable and liberal of nineteenth-century nations. Yet democrats they were not! These aristocrats saw nothing wrong with ruling, from London, indeed from Westminster and Whitehall, millions and millions of people around the globe – white, black, brown, African, Indian, British – without their consent. The mass of peoples – whether domestic or 'colonial' – were simply not fit to rule.

Colonial peoples needed a guiding hand. And best to keep governance in the hands of existing – in this time essentially landed – authority. Indeed, looking back it is striking how all sections of British elite political opinion – Tory, Whig, Liberal, even Radical and later Fabian – ultimately supported the idea of empire and imperial rule.

At home during the late Empire changes in the elite meant that business people and a new middle class were seeking a place at the table too. There began a whole century of appeasement and concessions to social change – in a series of such concessions the franchise was extended, ultimately to all adult men and then in the 1920s to adult women. The key word here is 'concession' – as new groups were appeased and the aristocratic liberals in the 'sovereign' Parliament made 'concessions'. Parliament and the Commons are pre-democratic with a pre-democratic culture. They were not forged by democracy or democratic revolutions. They have adapted to democracy; they were not formed by it. Legally and constitutionally the 'sovereign' 'Mother of Parliaments' conceded democracy, but can also take it away – as it did so blatantly when it extended the Parliament Act in 1940 and abolished the GLC in the 1980s.

A Constitution Without Rules

Therein lies the modern problem – and the modern danger. Our present 'constitution' and associated institutions are built for a guided democracy. We, unlike every other modern country, have no basis of a constitution to which we can turn in extremis. When politics go wrong there is no backstop except our good sense – or rather the good sense of the old boys and girls in Westminster. And that can sometimes let them down.

Of course there is a British 'constitution' – of sorts – handed down to us. But should a citizen or a visitor want to see it, or read it, it is simply not available. Such an enquiry will be met by the following explanation: that the constitution of Britain is made up of many things – past Acts and precedent primarily – in other words our constitution is what Westminster has done in the past and might do in the future. And to the insistent questions which modern man and woman might still impertinently ask: Is it constitutional? or What does the constitution say? Well, no way of telling! You should consult, not a document (and make up your own mind), but a sage! Such sages – normally academics like Sir Ivor Jennings or more recently Lord Blake – can only 'divine' our constitutional rules because they cannot point to a clear written rules set out in a founding document.

In the Victorian period the idea grew, particularly amongst the Whigs, that writing rules down so that we could all know them, debate them, and act within them, was far too democratic and egalitarian (indeed rather vulgar). In the eyes of the Victorian Parliamentary elite, writing a constitution was an idea born of rebellion in north America and of revolution in France. Westminster's elite was naturally suspicious of written down universal rights like the Universal Declaration of Human Rights. They were considered dangerous. Instead of written constitutional rules which we should all obey – like the Americans or the French had to do – we should, instead, leave these tiresome 'rules of the road' to be decided by the wisdom of our rulers. Our rulers should be free to react to events – even to change the constitution if they wish.

Such 'freedom' was on display some hundred years later during the Scottish independence crisis of 2014 when Westminster's three main political leaders, panicking over a potential break-up of the union, offered to completely rewrite Britain's constitution and grant 'Home Rule to Scotland'; and then, on the day following the vote the British Prime Minister decided unilaterally to propose what amounted to an 'English Parliament'. Many commentators were shocked by such momentous constitutional reforms being taken 'on the back of an envelope' and without consultation. Yet the truth is that the three Westminster leaders were acting fully in accordance with 'constitutional principles' handed to us from Victorian (and earlier) times. Like their forebears they did *in fact* have every right to change the 'constitution' in such a cavalier manner – for our unwritten Westminster system (the 'Mother of Parliaments') was designed specifically to allow its elite – without reference to the people in any way – to change the basic rules at will.

Of course in Victorian Britain, and later, it was argued by apologists that allowing our rulers to determine their own rules of government was 'nothing to worry about' because our rulers were liberal and reasonable. And, on the whole, they were – certainly by comparison with some of their opposite numbers in the tumultuous continent on our doorstep. This paternalist Victorian patrimony was fine for the *Upstairs, Downstairs* society that lasted in Britain right through to the Second World War (and which still evokes nostalgia in the *Downton Abbey* world propagated by the entertainment industry). The problem for today, though, is that 'Downstairs' has changed, and democratic ideas have broken through. In sum, old-style deference to authority has broken down, and so has trust. Quite simply, we no longer trust our rulers 'to do the right thing' – and rightly so. And without trust we need rules of the road: clearly set out for all to see.

The Three Chambers of the Aristocratic Heart: Monarchy, 'The Mother of Parliaments' and the Established Church

Deconstructing Westminster's modern unwritten constitution – our 'constitution without consent' – will reveal one central truth about the DNA of the primary institutions that rule over us: their very DNA is pre-democratic. Born in feudal times, re-animated and reformed by half-failed rebellions and by the aristocrats who ruled the Victorian empire, the great democratic revolutions that made modern countries out of our competitors have seemingly passed these institutions by.

So today, in essence, our great institutions represent a brake upon democracy not an embracing of it. Let us look at the heart of our present institutional set up – the three chambers of the aristocratic, and nostalgic, heart: Westminster's 'Holy Trinity' of Monarchy, the 'Mother of Parliaments' (Lords and Commons) and Established State Church.

Of course these institutions, dripping in the mumbo jumbo of feudal and imperial imagery (gold coaches, their Lordships clad in ermine, the Archbishop and others wearing funny hats) are part of the 'fantasy island' tourist and entertainment industry in the global city of London; it can be argued, and is, that they represent a service to a country which has lost its manufacturing industries and needs tourist income. But at the same time it is not harmless. For these three chambers at the heart of our aristocratic past represent and advance a real non-democratic, even anti-democratic ethos which permeates down – infantilising the people, keeping them in their place. How else can we explain how a major tabloid newspaper can declare a royal baby as 'person of the year'?

At the pinnacle is the monarchy. It should not be forgotten – amidst all the media public relations – that the monarch is not just a celebrity or a tourist attraction. Rather, Elizabeth Windsor is the UK's head of state, and plays a pivotal role in the unwritten constitution, has unrivalled informal political and social power and represents the country, and its subjects, to the world. Yet, this office is 'sacerdotal' – it is legitimated not by consent of the people but rather by God. This was a 'constitutional fact' revealed to us all in 2014 after the King of Spain had abdicated largely because of a fall in his popularity – and Buckingham Palace let it be known that no abdication here could be expected because Queen Elizabeth inhabits a 'sacerdotal' monarchy, with 'sacred oaths' taken to the almighty, not subject to the whims of public opinion.

This extraordinary notion (extraordinary, that is, by modern democratic standards) had also revealed itself in the 1953 coronation ceremony as it is the Archbishop of Canterbury in the name of the deity who lays the crown on the royal head and sprinkles the holy oils. In sum, in an extraordinary affront to the democratic age, the UK monarch owes no allegiance to her people. She inherits the job and holds it as long as she wishes, and is sanctified by the Almighty.

Of course, the British monarchy is not alone. For that other chamber at the heart of our establishment, the Upper House, the House of Lords, stands proudly alongside the monarchy as a blatant institutional rejection of the democratic age. Populated by a mixture of hereditary and appointed life peers and unelected bishops, this Upper House, with over 800 members, is larger in number than the Commons and, like the monarch, has a serious – though seriously under-reported – role in the Westminster state's law-making system. The unelected Queen has, formally at least, veto power over all legislation, and the unelected House of Lords can, depending on the electoral cycle, effectively hold up legislation, and frustrate the will of the Commons. 'Their Lordships' continue to play a role, informally through their parties and to some extent through the media, in setting the agenda and influencing public opinion.

If two of the UK's three law-making bodies are unelected, then the third, the House of Commons, is badly elected. Westminster's political class has consistently supported an electoral system – the 'first past the post' single constituency system – that regularly throws up quite weird election results. For instance, this Westminster electoral system consistently produces majority governments based upon a minority of the votes. Mrs Thatcher's Conservatives were able to form three majority governments, and indeed create an economic and social revolution, with the support of no more than 43% of the electorate. And in the 2015 general election 37% of the vote produced an overall majority of 12 in the Commons, enough for the government to run for a full five year term. Third parties are both severely over- and under-represented – for instance, at the 2015 general election the SNP received 4.6% of the vote but 57 seats, and at the 1983 general election the SDP-Liberal Alliance received over 24% of the vote but only 23 MPs.

The raw truth is that the Commons, our one democratic institution, has been sidelined. It has been sidelined by the powerful combination of the modern media and the modern executive (Downing Street). The modern media – a combination of newspaper and TV moguls and unknown BBC bureaucrats – has usurped the Commons in its erstwhile role of setting the agenda and the tone of British politics, and it, not the Commons, is now the 'forum of the nation'. Our media, not our elected politicians, tell us what is news and what isn't and tell us what is important and what isn't – and they are the unrivalled gatekeepers of public debate. This environment – the sidelining of the Commons by the all-powerful London-based media – has led, of course, to the spawning of the modern public relations industry and the professional manipulation of opinion which now passes for political leadership.

Just as importantly, the Commons has over recent decades been sidelined by the executive – that is, by office of the Prime Minister in Downing Street. Indeed, today's Commons is a weak institution, emasculated and dominated by the executive operating through the whips and party discipline. The powers of the Prime Minister are considerable. The PM appoints and chairs the Cabinet and government. And, alarmingly, can still exercise the Royal Prerogative Powers – for still on the books is the ability of Downing Street to make treaties and to go to war. Prime Ministers Major and Blair both contemplated their perfectly legal right to enact the Maastricht Treaty and go to war, the Second Iraq War, bypassing the Commons through the Royal Prerogative Powers. The PM is the one politician who can compete with the media in setting an agenda and mood.

All in all, modern Britain is an executive – driven country (unlike the USA, in which the power of the Congress ensures that the legislature plays an important role). And such a powerful executive is troublesome, indeed dangerous, particularly so in a country without the safeguards of a written constitution.

Making up the holy trinity that exists at the heart of the Westminster state is the established church, the Church of England. In a remarkable bravura display the bishops of the Church of England flout on a daily basis the very precepts of a modern secular democracy – the separation of church and state – as they take their seats in our legislature and help determine the laws that we all live under. No other church has such a role, and there are no reserved seats (and votes) for secularists. And this enlightenment notion of 'the separation of church and state' is, of course, consciously violated by Westminster during one of its most sacred ceremonials – the coronation ceremony. For it is the Archbishop of Canterbury, representing both the Church and God, and not the Speaker of the House representing the people, who 'legitimises' – by the act of placing the crown on the royal head – the country's head of state.

Into the Twentieth-Century: How on Earth did it Survive?

The modern Westminster system was formed by empire and sustained by empire. By the middle of the nineteenth-century Westminster ruled disparate 'nations' or peoples (Irish,

Scottish, Welsh) and an increasingly class-ridden England (with the growth of cities and industry to rival country and shires). However, empire was popular amongst the masses. Many of the bottom dogs at home – Celts in the regions and industrial masses in the towns and cities – could take succour in being top dogs abroad, with notions of superiority. They could believe that they too, alongside their imperial rulers, possessed colonies and subject peoples – with all the attendant superiority complexes. The idea that, certainly before the franchise extensions, the peoples of the British Isles were, in essence, on a moral and political par with the black and brown peoples governed by the external empire and that both peoples were governed by the same imperial elite in London, never got traction (except in Ireland).

As well as the popularity of empire, war, too, served to legitimise the Westminster state. The institutions of the country, no matter how antiquated, were worth fighting for. And the idea of British 'greatness' – symbolised by the institutions of Westminster – was given a real shot in the arm by 'victory' in two wars. Of course the fact that the Soviet Union and the USA defeated Nazi Germany did not deter 'we won the war' propaganda. In any event, if 'we' didn't actually win the war we were on the winning side; and we did stand alone against Hitler for a year or so.

Pride in the institutions of Westminster, in the monarchy, 'the Mother of Parliaments' and other institutions, benefitted from the more general pride in country and the 'British greatness' fantasy. Of course, with the end of empire, and with the fading memory of the world wars, these bonds, never particularly tightly drawn, were bound to loosen.

Still Going: Magic in the 1950s

In many respects the years following the end of the Second World War would seem to have been a great opportunity for constitutional change. The aristocracy, which had lingered into the inter-war period, was well and truly over and the general public was far less deferential, even mildly socialist, in attitude. Just as importantly the reality was of a country about to lose its world-wide empire and become a normal European power. Yet, in 1953 the coronation of Queen Elizabeth – a grand, grandiose and magical ceremony, broadcast to a global audience through the new medium of television – was a clear sign that Britain's postwar establishment (Labour and Conservative) had learnt nothing; they acted as though the country was still a great imperial state ruled by a confident imperial class. All this whilst the reality was that Britain during the Cold War sheltered under the nuclear umbrella of the USA and in security terms at least was a dependency of her former colony.

During the postwar years Britain as a 'great power' – indeed as one of the 'top three' – was a myth perpetuated across the Westminster political spectrum as was the superiority of the British constitution – envied throughout the world. Indeed during the whole postwar period right up until the turn of the millennium, the idea advanced by reformers that this oldest of old codgers of a constitution needed a thorough overhaul became a decidedly minority concern.

The British leftwing, even during its ascendancy in the 1970s, saw constitutional change as unimportant, a second or third order issue, compared to the country's pressing economic problems. And on the right the constitution and its institutions were revered; with many Conservatives suspecting that constitutional reformers, and certainly constitutional radicals, who criticised the monarchy or the House of Lords or 'the Mother of Parliaments', were in some way being unpatriotic.

Postwar Prosperity

Yet, although popular support for the empire and two world wars solidified the legitimacy of Britain's institutions. and thus the Westminster state, in the 1970s an influential section of the British socialist left began to question one of the great Whig tenets – 'parliamentary sovereignty' – arguing that social and economic change could come through mass movements as well as through 'the Mother of Parliaments'. In the 1970s as well, as the UK witnessed a deep, polarising economic crisis – dubbed in the media as a 'crisis of governability' – the institutions of the Westminster state began to lose their hold on the public, even to the point where modern institutions born in the postwar years, like the European Union (then the EEC), became more and more acceptable – even seen as a potential future for the people. However, in the late 1980s and during the 1990s, as the country came out of the sense of crisis and decline, and a general feeling of well being, at least amongst 'Middle England' was restored, so too was the standing of the Westminster system and its political class.

Now though, following the 2007-8 global financial crash, and the serious erosion of job security and living standards of many people, the legitimacy of 'the system', including the Westminster state, is once again being questioned. One of the ideas behind the campaign for Scottish independence, both before and after the referendum of 2014, was the notion that staying with Westminster, and its seemingly endless austerity programme, would weaken Scottish living standards. It is an idea which could easily gain wider traction amongst the English and Welsh.

Our 'Modern' Ancien Regime: The Myth of Sovereignty

At the turn of the millennium as Britain looked to the future it did so armed with the most backward constitution in the western world. Britain's New Labour was talking up economic modernisation and social progress but staunchly refusing to look at the fundamental framework governing the country. However, it seemed that, although constitutional change was the product of small groups on the periphery – of Charter 88, Republic and others – it was certainly going to become the wave of the future.

Yet, around this time, there was a new and growing development which ultimately would have a profound effect on Britain's constitutional debate. And this 'something else' was the growth of Euroscepticism from the margins of political life into one of today's major political forces. Modern Euroscepticism is all about 'sovereignty': that is, restoring the 'sovereignty' of the nation by either taking back powers from the EU or pulling out altogether. Restoring 'sovereignty' to Britain has its constitutional aspect – which, of course, is restoring the 'Sovereignty of Parliament' – a key nostrum of the failed Westminster state.

No question about it, the Westminster political class likes the nostrum of the 'sovereignty of Parliament' because they do not like sharing power. Never have, never will. Not with the people through a democratic constitution, and certainly not with foreigners, even those in the EU.

Yet 'Parliamentary sovereignty' in the modern world is an absurd myth. The feudal notion – of the English 'sovereign', the King – is an outmoded, medieval idea. And the related Westphalian notion of 'national-sovereignty' represents a complete misreading of the modern world, of globalisation and its interconnectedness and interdependencies. The fact is that in this day and age a 'sovereign' national Parliament is simply unable to exercise national decisions whilst the world has integrated markets, whether European or global. In today's world it is arguable that in the lives of Britons the US Fed is more important than the Treasury, and that decisions taken thousands of miles away, let alone in Brussels, have as great an import here as do decisions taken in Westminster. Everything needs to be shared and contingent. In this sense 'national sovereignty' – and the old-fashioned Westminster conception of 'Parliamentary Sovereignty' – are utterly fanciful ideas, little more than ostrich-like postures from the past!

Westminster: A Front For 'The New Establishment'

In one sense, however, Britain's half-democratic, semi-aristocratic, class-based constitution may have turned out to be – by chance, not design – a thoroughly modern construct: perfectly formed for a British elite transmuting into little more than the management apparatus for a global super-rich class and its supporters. As Britain becomes more unequal, a state which is centralised, with power concentrated at the top, and which promotes inequality through its very symbols (monarchy, peers and pomp) is a state that well suits this emerging oligarchy.

For a time, during the post-Second World War years, a serious case could be made that Westminster – although still pompous and odd – was no longer simply a front for the ruling classes of Britain. Although during the Cold War Leninists would call it 'the executive committee of the ruling class', in truth Westminster was what its protagonists argued it was: a relatively neutral state system providing a democratic forum for competing interests and ideas. And the proof was in its social composition. The Parliaments of the 1940s, 1950s,

1960s and 1970s were populated by large numbers of working class trade union MPs and also by 'the meritocratic classes' from grammar schools and the London university colleges. These new social classes rubbed shoulders with the traditional upper middle classes (from public schools and Oxbridge) who, although often in key positions, were thought of as a class of the past. Parliament was representing wider social change.

Such social mobility is now over, and parliament is again becoming a bastion of an elite, this time primarily a financial and business elite which is increasingly shutting out opposition. It is an elite that is increasingly the product of family money rather than state support, from private schooling and a few top universities. This narrowing route to the top is best exemplified by the fact that in the coalition government elected in 2010 the top four jobs in British politics, Prime Minister (David Cameron), the Chancellor of the Exchequer (George Gideon Osborne), the Deputy Prime Minister (Nick Clegg) and the Mayor of London (Boris Johnson) were all the products of top public schools and Britain's top two universities.

As well as being considered 'out of of touch' a more dangerous threat to the legitimacy of the political class is brewing – Westminster is seen as corrupt. The MPs expenses scandal which broke just before the 2010 general election, in itself not particularly egregious, was, though, nicely symptomatic of a deeper corruption at the very heart of the Westminster system. This corruption focused on the Commons but actually centres around the Upper House where seats in the Westminster legislature can effectively be bought – by judicious donations to party and party front coffers. Other peers sit in the Upper House for no other reason than their having spent a lifetime of keeping on the right side of party leaders – having, whilst in the Lower House, bent their opinions and votes to the will of leaders who could later promote them. Immersed in the phoney Lords culture of 'honour' and 'nobility' too many of our 'noble lords', who, though unelected, help make the laws of the land, are actually products of the increasingly grubby world of politics, money and influence.

The New London Establishment: Finance and Media

The political class in Westminster is, though, but the acknowledged aspect of the broader social and financial elite that run the country – an elite increasingly referred to as 'the establishment'. In the 1960s the Tory journalist Henry Fairlie made the term famous, and ever since the idea that the country is run by some kind of ruling class – 'an establishment' – has been a potent idea. Recently the radical writer Owen Jones has offered this definition: 'Today's establishment is made up – as it always has been – of powerful groups that need to protect themselves in a democracy in which the entire adult population has the right to vote.'[7]

Today's establishment, though, has seen a decided shift in its centre of gravity – away from politicians, public sector leaders (and, of course, trade union bosses) and towards the private and business sector. And as part of this process we have also seen a shift towards London. For the two newcomers to the establishment, indeed key players in the new establishment, are both heavily London-based – the finance and media industries.

There can be little doubt that the very beating heart of our new establishment is the London-based financial industry in 'the City.' Of course, the finance industry was well represented in the 1960s establishment (as pointed out by essayist Victor Sandelson in Hugh Thomas's 1959 edited book, *The Establishment*).[8] However, since then the City has grown in relative influence and power within the total economy and society – and has now drawn well ahead of the rest of the country in wealth – and consequently power. A staggering figure tells the story: Inner London's GDP per person is the highest in the whole EU at 328% of the EU27 average – and all this whilst six inner London boroughs are all in the top ten most deprived in the country. London attracts the talent and the high salaries: and migration flows from the rest of Britain into London and the South-East tell the story.

It is hardly surprising therefore that 'the City' – its collection of institutions and individuals, so dominant in the economy, should play a major role in British politics. City figures are not necessarily establishment figures themselves – although some most certainly are. Rather they work both directly – and through the wider business community – to influence the Westminster political class. Of course they are pushing at an open door. Ever since Labour Leader John Smith in the mid-1990s reversed Labour's standoffish attitude to business, and in his 'shrimp cocktail circuit' overture courted 'the City', there has been a bipartisan Westminster consensus supportive of the growth of the finance industry and thus the growth of London. Under Tony Blair and New Labour this developed into what amounted in Westminster to a 'fatal attraction' for City-based global finance, a virtual alliance with finance carried further by the coalition government following the 2010 general election.

The London Media

Another new boy on the establishment block is the London media industry, and its influential elite of moguls, managers and top journalists. Of course, media moguls were at the heart of the 1960s establishment, but at that point there was no developed media elite – of top managers and journalists – all on very high salaries who, are now part of a highly self-conscious celebrity-cum-opinion-forming culture, which helps to set the tone and agenda of national life. From the *Guardian* and BBC through to the Murdoch Press and the tabloids there is a political consensus – behind the neo-liberal values and themes of the finance industry – that was simply not present in the earlier more polarised climate of the 1970s.

This media elite – concentrated, well-off, and London and South-East based – tends to see the world through a prism that is largely southern English – to the point where the English provinces, Scotland, Wales and Northern Ireland might as well be foreign lands. It was this blinkered view that caused the London media industry to completely miss the growing Scottish rebellion against Westminster rule, causing journalists and owners alike, rather like the Westminster politicians, to wake up to the issue very late in the day.

A Failing Establishment: And Risking the Union Too

This new London-centred finance, media and political establishment – which was born under Thatcherism and flourished during Blair's New Labour years – has now lost much of its lustre and credibility. The global financial and banking crisis of 2007-8 is widely perceived to be a failure of the establishment, particularly the financial establishment – caused by mismanagement or worse. (It was difficult to blame this crisis, unlike the 1970s crisis, on trade unions and Trotskyites!). And in response to the crisis, instead of spreading the pain, Britain's rulers have been seen to preside over a sharp rise in inequality both of wealth and income. This sense that 'top people' are not only the cause of this crisis but are getting 'the rest of us to pay for it' has set off a wave of anti-establishment rhetoric; and the Westminster politicians have taken the brunt of the criticism, and the scorn.

This Westminster establishment's failure in the banking crisis was, though, to be compounded by a major political and constitutional failure. For some years, indeed decades, ideas of greater Scottish control over Scottish affairs has been growing. In the 1970s the SNP burst upon the scene as a major party in Scotland. And Westminster's response was typical. Power would not be shared, Westminster 'sovereignty' would never be conceded. Thus a federal solution to the Scottish problem – with 'entrenched' powers for regions and nations under-pinned by a proper constitution (as in Germany and the USA) – was rejected. Any alternative was just too difficult to implement, and, conveniently, Westminster would remain 'sovereign'. Should the Scots continue to be troublesome, power would be 'devolved'.

Thus 'Devolution' became the way out. 'Devolution' suited Westminster as it was rather like a leasehold. It could be 'granted', graciously of course, but also taken back should 'sovereign' Westminster so decide. Indeed Westminster took back powers when Margaret Thatcher's government abolished the Greater London Council by the simple mechanism of an Act of Parliament – an unthinkable action in mature federal states like the USA or Germany (where abolishing Texas or Bavaria, though attractive to some, would, in reality, never be countenanced).

In the 1990s as support for the SNP and Scottish nationalism continued to grow 'devolution' to a Scottish Parliament became the answer. The SNP did so well in the 1997 general election that the new Westminster government under Tony Blair decided that so important was the Scottish Question, and the potential for a build up of pressure behind independence, that its very first constitutional act would be to propose 'devolved powers' for Scotland (and Wales) to be enacted through a pre-legislative referendum. Although symbolically important, the powers granted were, though, relatively anemic. Westminster (in this case both the Treasury and the Bank of England) kept firm control, where it counted – that is control of the economy. Constitutionally the Scottish Parliament was not entrenched, leaving it in the same constitutional position as the GLC. Precious Westminster 'sovereignty' was not compromised.

However, after the crash of 2007-8, while the establishment elite presided over declining living standards, the Scottish Parliament, rather than appeasing, and thus lowering, separatist tendencies, became a launching pad for Scottish independence. And after the SNP became the government of Scotland in May 2011 the idea of a referendum on independence gained real momentum.

It was at this point that the Westminster elite yet again totally misjudged the situation north of the border. In agreeing to a referendum, the British Prime Minister David Cameron insisted on a straight 'Yes/No', 'In or Out', vote complacently confident that the 'No vote' would easily carry the day, and thus triumphantly reaffirm the union, and Westminster rule. Arguments that 'Devo Max', shorthand for 'Home Rule', should also be in the ballot paper were brushed aside.

Of course, in September 2014, as referendum polling day drew near, and it seemed that the 'Yes' campaign (for independence) might actually carry the day, the Westminster elite, in a display of panic in high places rarely seen before, reacted swiftly. The three party leaders hurriedly agreed to a seemingly united position and jointly 'vowed' to the Scottish electorate that in the event of a 'No' vote not only would the Scottish Parliament be made 'permanent' (the federal conception of entrenchment) but that it would receive extra powers in a range of policy areas (including taxation). So under pressure were the three party leaders that they enlisted former Prime Minister Gordon Brown to make the case for a 'No' vote in the light of this new 'vow'. Brown, in a major intervention in the campaign, then apparently unilaterally pledged a strict timetable for the draft legislation (on further powers amounting to 'Home Rule') that would be enacted during the following Parliament.

In sum, what happened in those mid-September days in 2014 was that the three Westminster party leaders, conspiring together over a period of hours, effectively tore up the country's existing unwritten constitution and rewrote it on 'the back of an envelope'. Their dramatic 'new' constitutional proposals were deeply confusing and contradictory. On the one hand, by offering to make 'permanent' the Scottish Parliament (a federal concept in which power cannot be taken back) they abandoned the whole devolution process – as far as the Scots were concerned, although, presumably, the rest of the British were to remain in a non-federal state. They also handed over extra powers to the Scots on a range of issues, including taxation, which amounted to Home Rule. All this without any consultation with anyone at all – not party, not parliament, not people.

As this commitment became public many English MPs complained, arguing that England should be granted the same powers as Scotland. David Cameron, just hours after the result was announced, fell into full appeasing mode, and was forced by elements in his own party into another 'back of the envelope' constitutional proposal – 'English votes for English laws', a constitutional wheeze that he asked former Foreign Secretary William Hague to flesh out and incorporate in a new Bill. Cameron had handed what amounted to the rewriting of the British constitution not to the Parliament or a constitutional convention, but to William Hague and a small cabinet committee.

Such was constitution-writing and constitution-making in twenty-first century Westminster. William Hague, for all his abilities, is no Thomas Jefferson; there was to be no deliberation by a wide section of opinion, and no ratification process; in true Westminster style, a club within the Westminster club would decide. Yet again, and drawing upon centuries-long traditions, the political class would change the constitution, such as it was, themselves. In sum, our constitution would remain unwritten and unratified – a plaything for politicians and their immediate political needs.

The situation Westminster found itself in following the Scottish referendum in 2014 was truly desperate. Scotland had voted 'No' in the referendum but only by 10% – meaning that a 5% swing would have secured a 'Yes' victory. Yet, the Westminster politicians had promised 'No' voters a major new settlement. It was clear that should Westminster be seen to renege on the promise, and break the vow, then the SNP could revive the whole independence question – by calling, at a time of its choosing, for a new referendum. A good time for such a choice would be following a UK referendum on the EU in which the majority of British people had voted narrowly in favour of Brexit (Britain leaving the EU) and a majority of Scots had voted in favour of staying. Other possible triggers for a new Scottish referendum could be an SNP landslide in any future Scottish or Westminster general election. The choice facing the Westminster politicians is now increasingly clear: Either Scotland gets Home Rule or, over time, it secures independence. And either way, England will need a new settlement too.

The English Question

The 'English Question' had been the elephant in the room during the 2014 Scottish referendum debate, and on the very morning of the result – when it was clear things would never be the same north of the border and Scotland would indeed by cashing in on 'the vow' and securing Home Rule – the Conservative Prime Minister responded by pledging to stop Westminster's Scottish MPs voting on English laws ('English MPs for English Laws'). Of course to allow only English MPs to vote on English laws is a very seductive political argument. Unfortunately, as Professor Vernon Bogdagnor has pointed out, outside of a proper federal constitution, it was well-nigh impossible to operate. First, on the questions of money you cannot divide things neatly between 'matters affecting England' and 'matters affecting Scotland'. Whilst there is one UK budget whatever English MPs decide on money questions will automatically have an effect on Scotland. Also, the 'vow' pledged to keep the Barnett formula (which set in stone the financial arrangements between Westminster and Scotland), and thus, seemingly at least, made any English law which breached the formula, redundant.

By 2015 – with Scotland now on the brink – that is in the union but threatening to leave if full Home Rule is not delivered – it has become clear that the whole 'Devolution' process engineered by Westminster since the 1970s was fatally flawed. In fact the whole programme implemented in the late 1990s now looks like a typical Westminster ad hoc fudge: another way of putting off problems rather than confronting them by real change. The key design flaw was that the 'Devolution' enacted in 1997 was essentially asymmetrical – 'granted' to some parts of the polity – Scotland, Wales, Northern Ireland and London – but not to its largest component, England. This was bound, over time, to stoke up resentment in England, particularly if the devolved powers developed into substantial Home Rule in Scotland.

And, true to form, by late 2014 the case for an English Parliament (and an English First Minister) was being made vociferously by Conservative and UKIP politicians, and by some Labour politicians as well. Under pressure from these MPs the newly-elected Cameron government in 2015 introduced proposals for EVEL ('English Votes for English Laws') which many Conservatives at least saw as a half-way house on the road to full English Home Rule and an English Parliament.

Under the existing Westminster system such an English Parliament could only come about via the 'Devolution' route – in which the Westminster Parliament would pass an Act 'granting' powers to England just as they have 'granted' powers to the Celtic nations. These powers, of course, would not be 'entrenched' and could be taken back by Westminster. And, presumably in any 'Devolution to England' Act Westminster would retain control of functions such as foreign policy, defence and macro-economic policy.

Such an Act would, of course, set up another layer of government as the Westminster Parliament would continue to operate alongside, or above, the new English Parliament. It would entail a separate election (maybe on the same day, maybe not) for each national Parliament and for the Westminster Parliament. But the West Lothian question would be resolved – that is, only English MPs would vote on English issues.

However, two fundamental problems would arise by creating an English Parliament in this 'devolved' way. First, its powers would not be entrenched, and could be taken back. And, without entrenched powers the constitutional landscape would be unclear and subject to continuing debate and conflict (as Scottish devolution has been ever since it was enacted in

1997). We might envisage for Britain a kind of 'Gorbachev and Yeltsin' scenario: in which the Prime Minister in the British Parliament (Gorbachev in The Supreme Soviet), having agreed to an English First Minister (Yeltsin in the Russian Federation) then sees the First Minister take power from him/her as a prelude to a new nation-state called England that would soon take its place in the United Nations and so forth.

Solving The English Question: A Constitutional Convention

Alternatively, the English Question, amongst others, could be solved not by the usual 'ad hockery' of the opportunistic Westminster political class, but rather by a measured constitutional reform process – that is by a constitutional convention leading to a new constitution. This well-established process would involve the drawing up, by a convention, of a draft written constitution which would set out the exact powers of an English Parliament (or, alternatively, English regions) and of the other Parliaments within the new, presumably federal, state. And the new document would then be ratified, or rejected, in a referendum of the whole people.

Yet, whenever constitutional theorists advocate a written constitution the Westminster political class backs away from the idea – not least because such a constitution would erode their own power and authority. There are, of course, genuine concerns about drawing up and ratifying a written constitutional document. It can take time; and it will be difficult to get agreement in a polarised political situation. Yet, it is surprising what a sense of crisis will do – as we saw in mid-September 2014, when the polls in Scotland predicted a possible victory for independence and the UK looked on the brink of collapse. In those crisis hours the fractious, normally warring, Westminster politicians suddenly managed to set aside differences and rewrite the UK's informal constitution – by including a 'vow' to entrench a Scottish Parliament, in double quick time.

In my view we will only finally resolve this great crisis initiated by the Scottish question when the wider British polity ratifies a whole new constitution, thus ushering in systemic and systematic change. Old Westminster habits of 'ad hoc' and 'back of the envelope' constitutional tinkering will simply not do anymore. What is more, a new constitution will be a splendid opportunity not just to restructure and modernise Britain's system of government; it could serve to bring a sense of renewal and hope to the country.

Writing such a constitution could, of course, be assigned to an elected Parliament – with the new constitution, in the form of an Act, being put to a referendum for ratification. However, giving the Westminster political class this kind of power would not be popular, and would cause legitimacy problems from the outset.

Thus it is probably best that it should it be drawn up by a constitutional convention. Such a convention might well include representatives from all three national 'parliaments' and from the great city-regions and local authorities of England. Of course, the resulting constitutional document – which would become the basic law of the land and the source of all legitimacy – would then need to be ratified or rejected, a decision, because of Westminster's low public standing, best taken by a referendum.

The Politics of 'the English Question'

Of course, behind all the arguments about an English Parliament, and more widely 'The English Question', lies the politics of it all. Many English Eurosceptic Tories see such an

English Parliament, shorn of MPs from Scotland and Wales, as likely to secure a Conservative majority – and thus continue, in England at least, their 'neo-liberal revolution'.

What About 'The North' and the 'Away Counties'

In an English Parliament the voting power of the 'Home Counties' and rural England would be strengthened as the city-regions of the Midlands and the North would become increasingly isolated and could no longer rely upon support from Scotland and Wales. Nor would the 'Away Counties' (that is non-'home counties' England) be able to resist a growing domination by the City of London. To put it in popular terms: in an English Parliament how long would Northerners put up with being ruled by a bunch of stockbrokers from Surrey. Put in party political terms, the likelihood is that in elections to an English Parliament the Conservatives (and/or UKIP) would be unbeatable. England would become a stronghold for neo-liberal economics and anti-European sentiment (a sensibility perhaps strong enough to take the North out of the EU).

Of course, a Conservative (or Conservative-UKIP) party majority in England is not guaranteed – for instance, the Labour Party has secured a plurality of the votes in England in a number of postwar general elections. Even so, in any future England shorn of the UK the Conservatives (or a combination of Conservatives and UKIP) would be the heavy favourite to win. And in the country's fraught state at the moment it is worth considering that it could well take only one Conservative or Right Wing dominated English Parliament, and one Conservative or Right Wing English First Minister, to withdraw England from the UK union – and then, presumably, from the EU (should Britain still be a member).

Does England Exist?

Much will depend on how the 'Away Counties' respond to the growing demand for an English Parliament. In other words, will 'the North' agree to continued London rule (assuming that London becomes the seat of an English Parliament)? And will Liverpool and Manchester, Leeds and Sheffield, Birmingham and Coventry, let alone the low income areas of Greater London, accept being, perhaps forever, locked into Tory England?

As in the Scottish referendum debate acceptance will in part depend on perceptions of the economy – upon how majorities in the 'Away Counties' see the economic consequences of staying with the southerners and the City of London.

But it will also depend upon how real, or unreal, is the common identity of the English people: in other words, how stands 'Englishness'. For many, 'Englishness' remains one of the world's strongest and most enduring stereotypes and self-images: as one literary critic could write in 1990 'of all the nations we have perhaps the most strongly defined sense of national identity.'[9] Yet, how real is it to think of England like this, as 'one country' (worthy of one legislature and one First Minister)? Or is 'England' simply that part of the UK that is not Scotland, Wales and Northern Ireland? In other words is there such a thing as 'Englishness'? Does, in fact, England exist? My own view is that a common English identity is hugely overdrawn – mainly by elites in the rural south of England – and is certainly far less potent than Scottish or Welsh identities.

True Brits, Real Identities

Rather than a common identity, one of the remarkable characteristics of England is the continuing strength of its regional and local identities. These identities, many of them in big city-regions – Scousers, Brummies, Cockneys, Geordies – are still very real; and in some respects are sustained by the phenomenal identification with football teams. Strong, separate identities also exist in the more rural English counties of Cornwall, Devon, Cumbria and in East Anglia. Also, the Southern English 'Home Counties' themselves have something of a common identity – and one that differentiates them from others.

Of course England remains class-ridden, perhaps more so following the global financial crash and the austerity programme. So as 'one nation' still remains something of an aspiration, class distinctions, primarily based upon wealth and income, provide another series of separated identities. As of course does recent immigration and resultant immigrant communities throughout England – even though many recent immigrants continue to integrate, with many now sharing wider social values and speaking with pronounced regional accents. Thus, when looked at this way, 'Englishness' becomes a 'tricky' topic. It obviously still means something to many people; but this, as with many national identities, is often a weakening identity drawn from the past. and in England's case from that of a particular class at a particular time. In England's case, where common identity was always fairly weak, even non-existent, there has been what might be called a manufactured common identity, imposed on the rest of us and propagated around the world through powerful media myths like that of 'The English Gentleman'.

Indeed, what common identity still exists between Bradford and Buckinghamshire or Liverpool and Littlehampton has certainly been even further weakened over the last few decades as immigration has turned the country from a largely uni-racial society into a multiracial one. Best therefore to look at England as a great patchwork of cultures and ethnicity, rather than a single common culture. I explore this idea in my chapter entitled 'True Brits'.

With regional identity still fairly strong, and in certain parts of the country arguably stronger than 'Englishness', it may seem surprising that the regions and cities of England have tended to resist moves to establish regional governments – most famously in the Northeast of England in 2004 when the idea was roundly defeated in a referendum. However, this seeming resistance may have very little to do with lack of a local or regional identity – and, still less, an attachment to the centralised Westminster state – and much more to do with popular opposition to a further level of government and taxation.

The London Question

Of course, the largest and most prosperous of all England's 'regions' is Greater London. But London is a truly global city as well; so how would such a global city – linked around the world as intensely as it is linked into the rest of Britain – fit into a new British constitution? Should further powers be devolved to Scotland (and Wales), or should we move to a federal system, London, its Mayor and Assembly, can hardly be exempted from the process. But will more power for London set in train a push for London to break free from the rest of the country? The fact is that London would be more viable than Scotland as an independent country; and in the wake of Scotland making a success of independence, a strong lobby might arise for Greater London to follow her example.

In reality, the future of London will be determined by the outcome of the parallel debate about the future of the size and role of the country's financial industry. There are two broad visions. One view sees the health and success of the financial industry in 'the City' as the rightful driver of the future direction of the country. Following the de-industrialisation of the Thatcher-Blair era, financial services has become the one success story of the UK. And if Britain stays in the Single Market then the City – providing financial services to the huge EU internal market – and the country can see a path foward for the British economy. On this reading the whole country, including the Scots, should welcome financialisation and not seek to weaken the hold of finance by loosening London's relationship with the rest.

The alternative vision sees a need to rebalance the economy away from financialisation and to re-industrialise initially primarily through New Deal-style big deficit financing or guided QE. This would go hand in hand with an attempt to revivify the industrial power houses of the North and Midlands. Such a policy might see London's financial industry taxed more heavily than it is at present as a policy of redistribution is introduced.

In a way the future of London will depend on the extent to which macro-economic policy continues to be driven from the Whitehall centre, and upon whether such macro-economic policy remains essentially neo-liberal (London will continue to aggregate power and wealth) or redistributive (in which case, after a time, London becomes proportionately less dominant). Also, in any new regional or national settlement should 'the Home Counties' be added to Greater London to form a large, perhaps too large, 'London and the South-East' (LSE) region, or should they stand on their own? The politics of this are fascinating. Greater London on its own, and in an even political year, would normally have a smallish Labour majority but the LSE region would be Conservative.

'Capacity Building'

Of course, no one should be under any illusions about the difficulties of pushing power away from London. The rest of Britain outside London is the victim of decades in which Westminster centralisation has depleted proper local administration throughout the country. In fact, 'devolution' to the regions – or, as in my case here, entrenched regional government in a new federal system – will only succeed with a concomitant commitment to what the modern management idiom calls 'capacity building' in the new regions. If more government is going to be done in these regions then the expertise and organisational acumen that used to be available in the big provincial cities of the country needs to be built up again. This will be no easy task. But if the whole of Britain is not to be dominated by London then the sooner capacity-building in the regions of England can get underway the better.

A Clean Break: A Federal Future?

As British politics get to grips with the continuing 'Scottish Question', and then the 'English Question', and then the 'London Question', the ensuing constitutional debate will finally provide us with a rare opportunity: to create a new written constitution not just for Scotland but for the whole country. Should Britain's political class be forced into creating such a new constitution, it could become about more than simply replacing bad Westminster unitary governance with good federal governance. It could also represent a new start for the country – a clean break with the sense of decline, drift and the continuing crisis of legitimacy.

Of course, over the next few years, no matter what happens in Scotland, we will see huge pressures to stick with what we have, to keep patching up a broken system through the tried and failed Westminster system of tinkering in order to survive. Yet, if we continue with the Westminster system and its elite then the crisis of legitimacy is likely to grow – perhaps even to the point where challenges to the fundamentals of democratic polity begin to emerge.

Of course, critics who support real constitutional change will need to answer the question: but how exactly do we get from A to B, how do we actually get from our present de-legitimised system to a new constitution? And who starts the ball rolling?

These are fair questions. And the answers may not be very exciting. For the only realistic way forward is to begin the constitutional change process through our existing party system – that is, by a political party placing in its manifesto a pledge, should it win a general election, to establish a constitutional convention; and then, upon winning, taking on through the existing Parliament the truly historic task of enacting the legislation that would create the convention (including its composition).

The convention should be free to go in whatever direction it sees fit – subject to some basic democratic principles – such as the democratic accountability of the institutions, the need for citizens rights, the separation of church and state and so on, and a provision should be made for amending the constitution. But within this fundamental framework there should be no sacred cows. Every institution – Parliament, government, the office of Prime Minister, the monarchy, the Supreme Court and so on – will be subject to review and the new institutions created should all be subservient to the constitution – the new fundamental law of the land.

This same Act that set up the convention could also make provision for ratification by a referendum and provision, should the referendum pass, for the handover of constitutional power. The Act could set a date, following a successful referendum vote, for Parliament and Crown to dissolve itself and vest the ultimate constitutional and legal authority of the country in the new written constitution and the newly constituted bodies of the new constitution.

This new constitution would be written – so that all citizens can read and understand it. Our fundamental rules of government will then no longer be so obscure that they need to be divined by 'constitutional experts' like Professor Bogdagnor and Lord Blake, whose tireless labours in the constitutional vineyard, would no longer be required. As in all other modern democracies a Supreme Court will interpret the rules.

This consitutional convention – like those great democratic debating sessions in Philadelphia over 200 years ago – might well be contentious, and even at times fraught, as might the European debate in the country. But at the end of the day, such a debate will give the new constitution a precious legitimacy that the old one lacked. It will be an injection of the lifeblood of democracy into our tired and corrupted system. It will allow us to do what Tom Paine always insisted we could do if we wanted to: start again.

Notes

1. Norman Davies, *The Isles: A History*, London, 1999, p. 583.
2. Ibid., pp. 582-3.
3. J. R. Seeley. *The Expansion of England*, London, 1914, p. 78.
4. Kathryn Tidrick, *Empire and The English Character*, 1992.
5. Davies, op. cit., p. 733.

6. Correlli Barnett, *The Collapse of British Power*, London, 1972, p. 24.
7. Owen Jones, *The Establishment, and how they get away with it*, London, 2014, p. 4.
8. See: Hugh Thomas (ed), *The Establishment and Society*, London, 1959.
9. Ian Ousby, *The Englishman's England*, Cambridge, 1990.

Three
The Making and Unmaking of Englishness

As the Scots move towards a new, more autonomous, relationship with England, a dynamic further encouraged by Brexit, then, as a reaction south of the border, an excessive new pride in 'England' and 'Englishness' could well take hold in a new identity politics. But questions abound. Is England one country or several? And is there such a thing as a common identity of 'Englishness'? Many people, particularly in southern and rural England, still believe a common 'Englishness' exists, indeed during imperial times an idea of 'Englishness' assumed the status of a national ideology. But, was 'Englishness' ever a truly 'common' identity, or was it imposed by a powerful southern elite, smothering the diversity not only of the UK but of the English people as well? Below is an account of its rise and fall.

Who are the English?

In the mid-fifth century three small ships – carrying no more than a few hundred barbarian soldiers – embarked from the sand dunes and pinewoods of Germany, crossed the North Sea, and fetched up on the pebble ridge of Pegwell Bay. The English had arrived in Britain.[1]

The English are, of course, German: Germans from Jutland, Germans from the 'Anglia' in Denmark (the origin of 'Anglo'), Germans from Lower Saxony. In an early display of good manners these German tribes came to Britain in the fifth century not by conquest but rather by invitation – issued by their Celtic host, the British leader Vortigern, after the Romans had left. Yet, these same English, brought in as mercenaries to help stabilise the civilised parts of the island, soon developed ambitions of their own, and when the British attempted to cut their rations, they seized land on which to raise their own food. 'These ferocious Saxons', wrote the monk Gilda, were like wolves brought into the fold, 'pretending that they were going to fight for our country, but really to fight against it'.[2]

In the resulting struggle this 'Battle of Britain' was won by the English. The rebellious English mercenaries called upon their Germanic kinsmen across the North Sea to help them, and soon a German-derived English community of warriors was established in Britain. In an early sign of superior ruthlessness the English massacred a large part of the British leadership class after having invited them to a peace conference.

England was born as the English established a beachhead in the eastern part of the island (in East Anglia and Kent). After the British leader Arturius (King Arthur?) died, and the British (the Celts) dissolved in warring factions and warlordism, the English – reinforced by a wave of English immigrants

– mopped up most of the rest of the island south of Scotland and east of Wales. And as England took hold, the British retreated to the 'Celtic' regions of the island and across the sea to Brittany.

For four hundred years these Germanic tribes which called themselves English, and spoke dialects of what they called *English*, spread out into the new polity of England, the Saxons into south-east England and Wessex ('West Saxons') and the Angles into the rest.

The English were really Germans. They were also provincial and heathen; until, that is, Christianity came to the German tribes during the sixth and seventh centuries, bringing with it a continental influence – primarily through the increased use of Latin. These Germans, now the early English, were also rather standoffish. They did not intermarry with the local Celts, nor did they adopt or inherit any of the local institutions (either Roman or Celtic) of the lands they occupied.

Yet they increasingly consolidated their hold on the lands south of Scotland and east of Wales. They also managed to accommodate, and finally incorporate, a major new tribe (again of Germanic origin), the Vikings (or Danes), following the series of Viking raids which ended in the eleventh century with a Danish king on the throne of a more or less united English polity. Thus, on the eve of the Norman invasion, the answer to the question 'who were the English?' remains fairly straightforward. Essentially, by today's standards, they were hardly much of an ethnic mix – basically Germans of one form or another, with more than a touch of Germanic Danish thrown in!

In the first decade of the eleventh century another continental tribe (the Frenchified Normans – like the Germans, also of Indo-European descent) was to add itself into the mix (if not, yet, the melting pot) that was England. Unlike the Germans, the Normans came to the island – in 1066 – uninvited, and by superior technology and organisation clearly established an ascendancy. Thus, some eight hundred and seventy-eight years before another cross-channel invasion (D-Day), German tribes (calling themselves English) were fighting Frenchified Normans (another highly mobile Germanic tribe) on English soil for the soul of England and Englishness. And 'the French' won, though not in the same way that the original Germans had prevailed over the British (who either left or were expelled).

The old Germanic tribes took some time to accommodate themselves to England's new rulers. A powerful myth developed in which the true English (the Germans) were portrayed as living under an oppressive regime – the 'Norman Yoke'. Yet, the Norman addition to English gave it a more literate dimension (as well as giving the English language many hundreds of new, French and Latin, words). And, politically, England's new ruling class united the peoples in a way that the Germanic tribes (including their famous leader King Alfred) were unable to do.

England's ethnic mix settled down somewhat after 1066. So the country (England could just about be called 'a country' by then) entered the second millennium not only as a decided part of the European continent (as it had been under the Romans) but primarily populated, as were large swathes of the continent itself, by the descendants of an identifiable Germanic culture and ethnicity. As the English developed and evolved there were to be no further dominating continental additions to the population to compare with the events of the fifth and sixth centuries and 1066. There were to be no further 'invasions' to rank with 1066. There was a Dutch (Orange) political coup, aided by a section of the English nobility, in 1688, but this amounted to a political change not a cultural or ethnic one; and the American troops who entered Britain in waves from 1942, of course, went home a few years later. Also, there were no wholesale changes in ethnic dominance – over the centuries Flemish, Huguenots, Jews, Welsh, Scots, Irish, West Indians, Indians and Pakistanis and other immigrants to England, would join the ranks of the settled English and would somewhat alter, though not (yet) transform, the meaning of Englishness. Nor were there to be any new mutations of the basic character of the language (English retained its fundamental Germanic structure even though the country was dominated by French-speaking Normans for several centuries).

Origins

A serious idea of Englishness – a self-awareness of England and its people as a sharply separate and distinctive cultural entity – did not begin to cohere until the eighteenth century, alongside the emergence of nationalism.

Yet, some historians locate a self-conscious Englishness much, much earlier. Some point to the Normans as England's nation-builders, the creators of a united people, and thus as the founders of Englishness. They point to the fragmentary quality of life before the Normans, of disparate tribal loyalties, of divisions between chieftains. Norman Cantor, perhaps the premier American medievalist, even calls the administration of Anglo-Saxon England 'the government of the absurd', agreeing with F. W. Maitland that England only developed through the centralising political genius of the Normans.[3]

The historian Geoffrey Elton, on the other hand, locates 'the effective creation of the Kingdom of England' some hundred and forty years before the Norman Conquest, in AD 927 – the year the King of Wessex established control over the Danish and English parts of Northumbria. Indeed it was these same Northumbrian English who produced that 'decisive maker of the English people' the Venerable Bede. It was the Bede who suggested, even as early as the late ninth century, before a single country of England had a single English king, that there was 'a remarkably precocious sense of common "Englishness", and not just in politically interested circles.'[4]

Elton comes down firmly in favour of a pre-Norman view of the origins of Englishness. He argues that what the Normans inherited, following their decisive victory in 1066, was an 'English kingdom peopled by an English nation' which was 'united to a degree unknown at this time in either France or Germany'.[5]

Part of Elton's argument is that the early English kings and the English Catholic church were both unifying factors. However, monarchy and religion as agents for the founding of England arc two-edged swords. The early English kings (like Offa of Mercia or Ine of Wessex) certainly established some laws of rulership which would later serve to impose a state upon the peoples of England, but these early kings remained, in reality, chieftains of regions, contributing to the political fragmentation of the islands. Also, there is considerable evidence that the most famous of all the early English kings, Alfred the Great (reigning in the late ninth century) attempted to re-unite the English and the continent through a flowering of learning and scholarship (specifically, by translating Latin scripts into English). And, although the church could also be viewed as an agency 'turning the settled bands of peasant warriors into a people', it was also, until the late sixteenth century, a decidedly anti-national force – the 'one universal church' limiting the development of separatist Englishness by its transnational character and loyalties.[6]

So some argue that it was the thirteenth century, almost two hundred years into Norman-controlled England, that saw a decisive step towards an identifiable sense of Englishness. The baronial revolts against royalist Norman power that peppered the thirteenth century finally gave forth, during the reign of Henry III, to what Elton has described as a 'communitas Angliae' – a real English community, embodying an English nation, which increasingly spoke for that nation, or collectivity of peoples, (often against kings more interested in military conflicts in France) through parliamentary meetings. Certainly, by the time Henry III's son Edward took over he was recognising the new reality, and playing to a new national gallery when he stirred up patriotic feelings against the French king: 'it is his detestable purpose, which God forbid, to wipe out the English tongue'.[7] Others believe that the Hundred Years War between England and France (which broke out in 1337) created an English national consciousness. Indeed, so successful were the English – they seemed to win most every battle they entered, against a much larger military force (at Crecy they were outnumbered by three to one, at Poitiers by five to one) – that 'perhaps for the first time, though certainly not for the last, the English began to suspect that God was an Englishman'.[8]

Even more than war, however, the physical separation of an island people from the continent was always a powerful factor separating the Germanic tribes in England from those in the rest of northern Europe. And language, too, was also beginning to play a vital role; indeed the story of the development of the English language – and its battle with French and Latin after the Conquest – may present us with a key to unlocking the mystery of the emergence of this early phase of English identity.

Although, following the Norman invasion, French became the official language of government – of court, society and the educated classes – it always remained a minority language. Georges Bourcier argues that 'the peasantry were barely touched by any cultural revolution' although French remained 'a badge of good social standing'.[9] And Robert Claiborne reports that 'by 1300, in fact, nearly everyone in England spoke English', what today we describe as 'Old English'.[10] And for most of the people English was their only language. As a poet in the reign of Edward I wrote:

> Common men know no French
> Among a hundred scarcely one.

And these 'common people' – as some historians have continued to call them – increasingly saw French as a mark of foreignness.[11]

There was certainly an English consciousness alive in the heartfelt words of the thirteenth-century introduction to the famous biblical poem *Cursor Mundi*, a book 'translated into English for the love of the English people, English people of England, and for the common man to understand'.[12] Yet, as late as the fourteenth century, the universities and the upper classes were still resisting English – preferring French and Latin – and thus the English peoples remained linguistically divided, a major limitation on the growth of national consciousness.

The English language made its great breakthrough in the late fourteenth century. English was adopted as the official language of government (Henry V was the first king to use English in the court documents) and the great storyteller-poet of the English language, Geoffrey Chaucer, appeared on the scene. The communications revolution in printing and publishing (led by William Caxton) which took hold in the fifteenth-century established the hegemony of English amongst the English and within England; and Caxton chose English (in fact, London English – the brand of English prevalent in London – there being several modes of English) as his published language. In an intriguing sign of the times the association of London brewers decided in 1422 to make English the 'official' language of their written documents.

And then there was William Shakespeare. When his chronicle plays appeared English was transformed from a primitive form of communication into the language of a new learning, a process helped forward too by the publication and wide dissemination in 1604 of the King James Bible – published in English! Some one hundred and fifty years later, by the time of the publication of Dr Johnson's seminal English Dictionary (1755), the English language was fast becoming not only a major language but the primary cultural agency for the spread of English manners and ideas – of Englishness.

Of course, this emergence of an increasingly popular and standardised English was crucial to consciousness of being English. Yet, even whilst this standardised English was destroying French and Latin in Britain it remained seriously fragmented by dialect, a diversity which, intriguingly, has lasted well into the television age of the twenty-first century.

In fact the age of Shakespeare (and Marlowe), the late sixteenth century, saw not only a flowering of the popularity and usage of the English language (what is now called Medieval English) but also a confluence of great events. It was the age of the Reformation, arguably a seminal event in the building of the English nation-state. The Reformation (guided by Thomas Cromwell) saw an increment in the growth of English national sensibility, caused by an increasing sense of separateness resulting from the religious differences between the English state and the continental religious system led by Rome. This debate concerning the authority of the English king and common law over that of the Pope and canon law was tailor-made for incipient nationalists.

It was also the age of the Renaissance – which added thousands of new words to the English language, thus further enhancing its unifying potential. And, at the same time, England and the English were becoming a serious maritime power and people, a process which, by bringing a warrior people into contact with 'foreigners', enhanced their sense of identity and separateness, and also their sense of exceptionalism. No wonder Shakespeare could talk of a 'sceptred isle set in a silver sea' which was 'the envy of less fortunate lands' – the Shakespearean braggadocio which, without a hint of irony, was, incredibly, recycled as late as 1994 as part of a television advertisement for tea.

Some decades later, the second (Oliver) Cromwell would add to the work of the first (Thomas) Cromwell. Ideologically, the parliamentary forces in England's Civil War were suffused with nationalist sentiment. The idea of a 'chosen people' – albeit possessed by a liberal, anti-authoritarian, rationalist mentality – runs through much parliamentary proselytising. The militant protestantism of the Parliamentary forces had, after all, tended to advance the idea of the English as 'chosen'. Bishop Aylmer had declared 'God is an Englishman' as early as 1558! And the Stuarts, by enlisting Irish and Scots on the side of the King, only served to reinforce this growing English sensibility not only amongst the victors of the Civil War, but amongst the broader English radical tradition.

However, there remained strict limits to the growth of English self-consciousness. Even as late as the early eighteenth century, life in England was still very cosmopolitan – specifically in its higher reaches. In his seminal work *The Rise of English Nationalism*, Gerald Newman provides an intriguing insight into how aristocratic supremacy in Britain in the eighteenth century was a source of cosmopolitanism. His argument is, basically, that landed aristocrats consolidated and enhanced their position during this period – with huge profits – but also culturally differentiated themselves from the rest of the population by a cosmopolitanism (particularly an affectation of Frenchism in manners). They were a confident, international elite, in Newman's words, 'Fine Fellows travelling in the age of cosmopolitanism'.

But the French-speaking English aristocracy also contributed to the emergence, below the surface of the landed elite, of a reaction amongst the 'common people' – as the 'lower orders' began using their common use of English to assert what was beginning to amount to a somewhat aggressive underground national patriotism. This patriotic sensibility clustered around the English language was not, though, to burst forth until some time alter the revolutionary events in France at the very end of the eighteenth century. (Although, for a time, the aristocracy was beginning to look somewhat politically isolated, after the French Revolution and the French revolutionary wars they too adopted, indeed led, the cause of national patriotism.)

In the meantime, during the early part of the eighteenth century there developed something of a contest between aristocrats and bourgeois as to who was the purest cosmopolitan:

> The aristocrat defended his superiority by ridiculing the upstart, and by exaggerating the purity of his own cosmopolitan tastes. In travel as in dress he was driven to devise 'modes more exclusive'. The unmistakable sign of this was the founding in the late 1760s of the Macaroni Club, whose members distinguished themselves by gulping pasta from their butler plates. While thousands were now rattling across the channel for their 'brief round of travel', the Beau Monde, brandishing spaghetti, showed that they had gone all the way to Italy.'[13]

Cosmopolitanism was more, though, than 'gulping pasta'. It had a decidedly cerebral dimension. Eighteenth-century England saw England's elites (many largely traceable to the Normans) still seriously imbued with French cultural and intellectual influences. Anglo-French intercourse was routine. The rationalism of Voltaire – which was a powerful intellectual force amongst some English elites – empowering the growth of universalist notions and thus limiting English (and, just as important, French) consciousness.

Also, during the previous century, north-western Europe (and not least the British Isles) had witnessed a veritable scientific revolution which respected no national boundaries or emerging national cultures. And this new respect for science, together with the growing penchant for global exploration, served to secure the idea of the underlying unity of mankind – and so inhibit the developing sense of national identity.

Thus, in the early decades of the eighteenth century, it was by no means certain that what was later to become a strong (indeed fierce) national consciousness would indeed emerge. The British Isles was still a decidedly plural place. Although all the trends pointed towards unification and commonality, the sheer diversity of the country was still evident: peasants co-existed uneasily with aristocrats and a growing bourgeoisie (both of which possessed serious cultural links to the continent); identities were fragmented, linked to a thousand locales, and perhaps a few regions, there was a wide diversity of ethnicity (including fragmented Celts, Huguenots, Jews, as well as varieties of English); and there were two, sometimes three languages spoken in the land. None of this augured well for the development of a unified national consciousness. The only unifying clement – potentially working against all this diversity – was the English landed aristocracy. Yet, as we have seen, they were, because of their cosmopolitan interests, to discourage a unified national sensibility – at least for a while!

The Incubation: 'Land, Class and Race'

Yet all of this was soon to change. In the space of a few short decades in the latter part of the eighteenth century the idea of England began to form, contributing one of the world's strongest national identities to the age of nationalism.

Some historians are quite precise about this birth of national consciousness. Newman argues that 'the English quest for National Identity began around 1750 and was subsequently complete by 1830'.[14] And Linda Colley, in her weighty and comprehensive account of the birth of the nation, also suggests that it was during the eighteenth-century that a sense of British national identity was 'forged'.[15] Geoffrey Elton also locates the pivotal period in what he describes as 'the long eighteenth century'.

Yet, the eighteenth century saw more than the emergence of a national sensibility. It also witnessed the making of the form – or character – that such an English identity would possess. It was, thus, the incubation in which the *culture* of Englishness was born. And the culture nurtured in this incubation was to last for well over 200 years. It was to dominate the islands in which it was born, determining not only their cultural development but their politics, economics and social development as well. And it was to expand overseas and provide the culture and ideology of rule for one-third of the globe.

This Englishness, born in the eighteenth century, was, therefore, pre-modern, certainly pre-industrial. The industrial revolution was getting under way some time *after* the idea of

Englishness had been formed, and thus 'the English idea', although it used and managed industrialism, *and also survived it*, was, remarkably, hardly touched by what was perhaps the most significant contribution the English people made to modern civilisation. Instead of coming to represent commerce and democracy (as did the American idea a century or so later) Englishness was built upon a pre-industrial trinity of 'land', 'class' and 'race'.

The English idea, formed in an era of landed power, before middle-and working-class males and women even achieved the vote, was also pre-democratic. Englishness was an exclusive affair. During its formation, peoples of the islands were no part of the idea of Englishness; they were, in fact, excluded from contributing to it. Rather, Englishness was the property, and reflection, of the caste that solidified its hold on the country at a time when England (by then called Britain, and, later still, to be called the United Kingdom) was about to take off as the world's leading power.

During this crucial era land was power – economically, politically and, through private control of the emerging literary world, culturally too. And it was owned by a very small group indeed. Setting the tone for the later development of Englishness, these landowners were decidedly non-entrepreneurial – most of their ancestors had either stolen land or acquired it by nefarious practices in the politics of the court. In fact, 'these men of noble and gentle status', who 'owned virtually all the land', 'exploited it in the main by offering it on long leases to farmers who employed a paid and landless labour force'.[16] Yet, they went unchallenged by the slow and uneven development of English radicalism, and consolidated themselves into what amounted to 'a new unitary ruling class'. 'Nobles and notables closed ranks and became more homogeneous in terms of wealth, marriage patterns, lifestyles and ambition.'[17]

This historic formation of a new class was preceded by a major demographic upheaval in which a large portion of the country's elite in effect disappeared because of their inability to produce male heirs.[18] Thus distant male cousins, and sometimes even women, were to become part of this fateful landed interest. These founders of Englishness had also admitted to the fold some landed families from the Celtic peripheries, many of them, of course, originally English. During the eighteenth century Scots, Welsh and Irish landed folk moved south, some of them to be closer to the heart of the developing global trading system; and some English landowners, anticipating a profit during a period in which land prices and profitability were rising, moved into estates on the Celtic fringes.

Colley argues that this mixing of English and Celts amounted to the arrival of a new *British* landed establishment.[19] Yet, although this newly forged ethnic mix of a class was real enough (even though there were a number of supposed 'Scots' and 'Welsh' who were really English) it hardly matters. For the fact was that the English dominated this class, with most of the *arriviste* Celts being more than willing to become 'honorary Englishmen'.

Thus did English culture, manners and politics, somewhat invigorated from outside, continue undisturbed. Like a dress rehearsal for so many who were to follow them – nineteenth-century businessmen, twentieth-century professionals and the lower middle classes – these upper-class Celts (if that was what they were) were simply assimilated into the mould of Englishness.

This eighteenth-century landed elite was to fuse land and class in a manner which would create the peculiar character of the English class system – and become such a pronounced part of the cult of Englishness – for the next two hundred years. Englishness not only became virtually synonymous with a culture of class distinction, it also still stands starkly apart from other types of class systems. Whereas most of the industrialised world formed their modern classes – and thus their contemporary class sense – during the age of industrialism, producing the hierarchies of capitalism (a large middle class of business entrepreneurs and professionals, and a 'blue-collar' working class), English social hierarchy was forged by land: the ownership of it, the relationship to it. And this, essentially feudal, perspective of social hierarchy – infused with, overlaying, and underlying the more normal capitalist classes of the nineteenth century, is what has made the English class system seem both so intriguing and so perverse.

At the heart of this newly-created Englishness was the remarkable and resilient English social idea of the 'Gentleman'. So powerful was this new social form that two centuries later it was a recognised social type for the twentieth century's worldwide media audience. 'The English gentleman' had established itself in the global culture in a manner which simply cannot apply to a 'French gentleman' or an 'American gentleman' (or, for the contemporary English, 'Indian gentleman', which still has a patronising tone about it!).

'I was by birth a gentleman' said Oliver Cromwell in a speech to Parliament in 1654, 'living not in any considerable height, nor yet in obscurity.' Yet, this idea of 'the gentleman' as a middling kind of middle-class person did not last. In eighteenth-century England the notion of 'the gentleman' emerged from the idea that civilised life and manners were the product of a propertied, landed existence. This idea derived from the lifestyle of 'the gentry' – the property-owning medieval middle class of thanes and knights who, in return for enjoying the property of their social betters, paid off their feudal lords and kings – as it developed in earlier centuries. The gentry, and gentlemen, though, were essentially an officer class existing under the nobility, but acting as another layer of authority placed above the rest of the, non-landed, population.

Conceptions of race, and racial superiority, also make their appearance in this formative period for Englishness. The eighteenth century saw a dramatic expansion of research by the English into the origins of the English, and the growing understanding of common ethnic origins led to an interest in the racial background of the people of the islands, racial classification, and inevitably, in racial braggadocio and ranking. This was the time when the first 'stirrings' of an idea of distinction between 'French' and 'Gallic' on the one hand, and 'Anglo-Saxon' on the other.

Much literary sentiment in the late eighteenth century was decidedly racist. Not only was the white man superior to the black, brown and yellow (an unshakable assumption at this formative time in British colonial life) but the English – or Anglo-Saxon – was also considered to be superior (in particular, more honest and trustworthy) to the white 'foreigner' from the continent. 'It was no accident…that John Bull himself, largely an invention of the 1750s (though with roots earlier), was already by the sixties acquiring definition in English periodical literature as a "very worthy, plain, honest old gentleman, of Saxon descent".'[20]

These racist ideas were relatively tame compared with the scientific racism to come later in Victorian times; however, they formed part of a more general belief in the superiority of the English. God became an Englishman (intriguingly he was never a Briton) not by revelation but rather by stages. In Plantagenet England the elite had developed a good line in propaganda in which anti-foreign sentiment was mixed with a view of the English as 'God's elect', an idea which was still alive and well as it infused much of the puritanism and parliamentarianism of the seventeenth century. Indeed, Oliver

Cromwell saw the English he led as almost divine – putting this awesome thought in a declaration in 1654: 'the dispensations of the Lord have been as if he has said, thou art my first born, my delight amongst the nations'.

Much other literary rhetoric, if not exactly seeing the English as divine, none the less saw them as inherently exceptional and superior. In the fifteenth century, in the grandly titled *The Governance of England*, Sir John Fortescue had given 'lasting currency…to two English convictions: that every other realm groaned under despots and that everywhere else the peasantry had to live on mere vegetables, while in England Kings governed with the active consent of their subjects and people ate good red meat'.[21] This 'currency' certainly lasted into the eighteenth century and beyond. But the eighteenth century was to focus and legitimise this innate notion of exceptionalism – in a nation-building anti-French consensus.

This eighteenth-century ideology of Englishness had as its unifying feature – paradoxically – a very non-ideological notion: a disdain for abstract ideas and theories. 'Land, class and race' meant familiarity and tradition. Reason, by contrast, became suspect. It undermined the social order, which was the primary concern of the new landed class.

Subversive ideas of universal rights had appeared during the Civil War amongst some of the more extreme supporters of the Parliament. Closer to home, eighteenth-century radicals were beginning to set their demands for change to the existing order in terms of abstract principles, such as 'liberty'. Eighteenth-century England's most prominent radical, John Wilkes, was developing a potentially combustible mix of patriotism and universal rights – 'O sweet liberty! Wilkes and Liberty! Old English Liberty!' went the refrain.

Englishness defined in these terms would have taken a very different course. It would have become an essentially revolutionary ideology – rather in the manner of 'Americanness': which had set out on its own separate journey during the eighteenth century, and was indeed revolutionary, being based upon abstract ideas of political equality and freedom, principles which would cohere into the powerful twentieth-century ideology of democracy.

Englishness, though, fell under the guiding hand of an establishment which, viscerally hostile to both the French and American revolutionary traditions, remained sceptical not only about reason, and about first principles, but about intellectuals too. Thus, Englishness came to embrace an anti-intellectualism, and intellectuals were perceived as being hostile to established order, essentially creatures of the city – proselytising their urban values and seeking to undermine the settled culture of the rural swathes of landed England.

Thus did Englishness – as it echoed down the centuries to the present time – come to elevate the traditional, the familiar and the practical (indeed 'the practical man' assumed a special place in the national roll-call of honour). And in the process, Englishness subtly, and not so subtly, devalued the intellect, the imagination, indeed creativity itself. In England 'too clever by half' becam a term of mild derision.

Englishness's theorists have always denied that their conservative ideas amount to anything as 'crude' as an 'ideology'. Instead, they are described as 'instincts', 'views', or, as High-Tory theorist Ian Gilmour suggests in one of the most comprehensive accounts of English conservatism, 'themes'.[22] Indeed, many adherents of Englishness would hardly dissent from Keith Thomas's half tongue-in-cheek depiction of its guiding idea: as 'Parliament, Magna Carta, roast beef, and plum pudding' (as against, as he puts it, 'the wooden-shoes of downtrodden, ragout-eating, Catholic French').[23]

The ideology of Englishness was not, like many other ideologies, based upon universal rules. It was, in fact, like all nationalisms, particularist rather than universal. But it was an ideology none the less as powerful and influential in its time (and its time is still, just, with us) as Liberalism, Socialism or Fascism. And it has held the British in its sway as much as Democracy has held the Americans – and longer and more completely than Communism has held the Russians.

Building the Nation

This 'non-ideological' ideology of Englishness – the mix of 'land, class and race' – was to become the official ideology of a new nation-state. As the eighteenth century progressed, the idea of the nation-state (of nationalism) progressed with it. If the later seventeenth century was the time when the patriotic sentiment became firmly established in English political rhetoric then the middle to late 1770s was the time when this patriotic sentiment became national, and nationalistic, in tone.[24] It was during this eighteenth century that the patriotic anti-French hero Jack Tar appeared on the scene, as did the pugnacious cartoon character John Bull (who was to remain a symbol of England even as late as the Second World War). Also, an early version of 'God Save the King' was first performed in 1745, and the nationalistic sea-song 'Hearts of Oak' (written in 1759) was widely heard.

This new nation-state was, of course, not England, but rather Britain – created by the Act of Union of 1707 – a Union which, in itself, probably gave something of a boost to nationalist sentiment, as there was now a political institution, as well as a well-defined landmass surrounded by sea, to rally around.

Yet even more important was the role played by the aristocratic leadership of the new nation-state. This landed aristocracy, no matter its changing character, was the one great over-arching, or truly 'national', social force in the England and Britain of the eighteenth century – thus always potentially able to impose its ideas upon the rest of the population. However, as we have seen, the cosmopolitan fancies of many aristocrats and 'gentlemen' were somewhat at odds with the 'stirrings' of eighteenth-century nationalism. And cosmopolitanism – or pretensions to it – died hard. After all, French manners and Latin words had helped set these elites apart from 'the common people' in the first place; and ideas of national identity (and national exceptionalism) were, ultimately, socially unifying and even democratic (as they applied to all, not just to the few).

So, with much of the anti-aristocratic dissent, protest and radicalism of the period taking on a very distinctive patriotic tinge, the English nobility faced a choice: between embracing patriotism and nationalism (and siding with the lower orders and the burgeoning bourgeoisie) or, by keeping themselves distinct, allowing radicals to stir up nationalist sentiment against them.

In what amounted to one of the most momentous social developments in British history, the landed leaders of England chose patriotism, and, inevitably, nationalism. And not surprisingly so. For, as the eighteenth century came to its close, Britain was becoming a home for aristocrats – a stable island of privilege in a world of revolutionary upheaval. French revolutionary ideas were seen as posing a direct threat to the social order – to the aristocracy – in Britain. The fear was growing that the British aristocracy might go the same way as the French. So, many aristocrats stopped flaunting French clothes and speech, and instead placed themselves at the head of what amounted to a nationalist cultural revolution – the effects of which are still with us well into early part of the twenty-first century. (Intriguingly, the landed English were never again to return to cosmopolitan ways, to a transnational lifestyle or sympathy, not even in the late twentieth century when many of their heirs and imitators became ostentatiously provincial!)

By compromising with the new age of nationalism, the English aristocracy's ideology of Englishness was not only preserved, it expanded – embraced by many amongst the broader population. Thus, the growth of national sentiment in this crucial eighteenth century acted as a transmission belt for these landed-class ideas of Englishness – carrying them not only to the lower orders but also through to the next century and beyond. Every ratchet upwards in national consciousness reinforced the ideas of land, class and race formed in this period of incubation.

The threat of revolution which turned aristocracy to nationalism was part of a more general awareness of 'foreignness'. A sense of being English (and political support for England, or Britain) was induced not so much by militant domesticity as, with all nationalisms, but an emerging rejection of 'alien' *otherness* – in this case the twin 'othernesses' of Catholicism and Frenchness.

Ever since Henry VIII the idea of a Protestant England set against a Catholic continent had been a subtle, though powerful, image in the forging of national identity. Yet these religious roots of Englishness have rarely been given the recognition they deserve. Perhaps one of the reasons is that, until recently, historians have tended to concentrate less upon divisions between Protestants and Catholics and more upon the conflicts within Protestantism. Also, the role of religion in creating an English national identity – which centred around the idea that England's Protestantism separated her from

Catholic Europe – was increasingly mixed up with a more political hostility towards France. France, and Frenchness, perhaps even more than Catholicism – which was often seen as France's agent – became the primary symbol of the alien 'other'.

It is hardly surprising that France and the French should figure prominently in the building of English nationalism. For the nationalist English this gnawing fear of the French was always understandable. The turbulent events of revolutionary England in the seventeenth century had led to the exile of the Stuarts, and for the next sixty years or so the country was faced with a series of invasion scares and insurrections orchestrated from France by the ousted dynasty. They tried an invasion of Scotland in 1708, and in 1715 there was a serious uprising throughout Scotland and parts of northern England in favour of James Edward Stuart (seeking to become James III), who some thirty years later was still at it, launching an invasion which came close to capturing the capital. Of course, the ideological battles and political loyalties which swirled around the Hanover-Stuart feud will have fed a growth in hostility to France, but by far the most significant reaction came from those – not least the traders and merchants – whose life would have been severely disrupted by the upheavals of a Stuart revolution and restoration.

Also, the events of 1789 in France – that 'other' identity by which Englishness could be measured, encouraged, and honed – posed both a revolutionary and, later, a geopolitical threat to the British state. 'More than twice as long as the First and Second World Wars added together, the wars against Revolutionary and Napoleonic France were almost as geographically extensive as far as British involvement was concerned.'[25] And in order to prosecute this bitter world-wide conflict, the London government employed a kind of patriotic propaganda and ceremonial which could only intensify the already growing sense of Englishness, a conscious identity which was even further enhanced by the taking up of arms, and the spilling of blood, by the English masses in the anti-French cause.

And, of course, the sea helped. In these conflagrations with the French, in which real threats existed on the other side of the water, 'England' became an island, a splendid, isolated island, cut off from continental troubles, an image which could only but reinforce the critically important idea of English separateness.

In this very conducive political environment the idea of Englishness was given a huge shot in the arm – certainly among the literary classes – by the Irish High-Tory Whig Edmund Burke. He flattered to instruct. For Burke, English politics was indeed distinctive: unlike that of France, English stability was based upon a superior understanding of the importance of unbroken organic national development. The English he argued were a practical people, quite properly resisted theorising, and did not proceed from first principles. By comparison, Burke's great intellectual opponent, the English radical Tom Paine, set – not least by his own example – a completely different notion of Englishness. For Paine, an active participant in the two great revolutions of his time, the American and the French, the English were not special or exceptional; they were governed by the same – universal – rules as anyone else. If anything the English, during their seventeenth-century revolution, had been amongst the pioneers of this universalist rational liberal thinking.

Yet, with the defeat of France, Tom Paine was to lose his battle with Edmund Burke. Paine was burnt in effigy in his homeland, and died abroad. For almost two centuries his works (and, as importantly, his political activities) have been devalued and marginalised by the dominant literary forces in the royalist kingdom which he had tried to overthrow.

(Only recently has a statue to the great man been erected in his native Thetford – and his own, decidedly *outre* universalism begun to become somewhat appreciated.) Burke's ascendancy was a prelude to two centuries in which the English world of letters would exhibit, somewhat perversely, an innate suspicion of 'French' reason and universalism together with an unswerving belief in the exceptional nature of the English.

In the building of the nation-state, these cultural and ideological clashes – between Catholicism and Protestantism, between France and England, between the universalism of Paine and the nationalism of Burke – were central. Yet so too was the changing economic and technological environment of the eighteenth-century British Isles.

In pre-industrial times, with most of the British people linked to the land and existing in isolated village communities, the development of 'national' consciousness, nationalism and nation-building was limited. It was the revolution in industry, technology and communications which changed all this. The eighteenth-century industrial revolution broke down the boundaries set by rural locales.

The communications and travel revolution of the eighteenth century – allowing the development and spread of commerce into a new national single market – was the real radicalising, nation-state building, agent. It opened up the frontiers, breaking down the barriers of locale (of village and community) as it established a national mass market for goods and services.

Caxton had introduced the printing press into England around 1476, and the printed word (he published the works of Chaucer) became both a boundary breaker and social unifier. And, in the eighteenth century, with a quantum leap in the technology of communications, not only was London able to reinforce its political ascendancy, but the ideas and images, the manners and codes which were to serve as the common culture of the new nation-state were transmitted from one end of the islands to the other. This was the age when 'John Bull' and 'Britannia' were being honed for a national audience, when the rules of cricket (1744) and whist (1745) were drawn up and printed, when Samuel Johnson, Jonathan Swift, David Garrick, and cartoonists James Gilray and Robert Newton, as well as an array of pamphleteers were at work.[26]

Industrialisation was a terrific boon for the literary classes, the writers, artists and clerics. Early capitalism may indeed have been too materialistic for some of the intellectuals of the day, but the technology it carried in its baggage allowed their messages to be carried to an ever wider public. And their message was increasingly nationalistic.

There had indeed been a scholarly and literary revolution during the latter half of the eighteenth century, in which a nationalist historiography and literature had emerged. It was hardly surprising. After all, writers communicated by language and increasingly, now almost totally, the language – the 'tool of the trade' – was English. The ever-increasing importance of the English language, and its history as separate and distinct from French and Latin, was bound to fuel a wider literary political and cultural separatism.

Yet, these new literary classes were not helpless, simply corks on the water drifting with a growing nationalism. They were to play their part, too, in the building of a nation-state. In fact, the role of the writing and arguing classes was crucial: for they performed no less a role than that of creating and producing the images – what Gerald Newman has called the 'artistic projections' – that helped define and describe a new national identity – the idea of Englishness. Indeed, as Newman argues provocatively, they may have created it,

> for the concept of national identity, though presented as a finished product to *das Volk* as if it were a single distillation of characteristics deeply embedded in all true countrymen, is originally simply an artistic projection, an image deliberately fashioned by a single group in the age of 'stirrings' and national awakening. Qualities *chosen* by frustrated intellectuals and projected as *national* traits.[27]

And, of course, these 'artistic projections', these 'national traits', were then copied and, over time, became established.

It is always difficult to allocate the exact responsibility for intellectual change, like that of ideas and images of identity: how much is caused by the creative writer, by the use of his or her media, or by broader forces including the resonance the image and idea receive amongst elites and the generality of the public? Yet, whatever the exact hierarchy of influences, the fact was that the character of Englishness put into words and cartoons during this crucial period formed a mould that remarkably has only changed at the margins since.

The defining characteristic of this invented Englishman was his moral elevation. This moral aspect of the ideal Englishman was drawn from the earlier notion of the honour and uprightness of 'nobility', but it also reflected a morally pretentious period in the country's history. Great literary figures were praised as much for their moral as for their technical and dramatic achievements. Politicians – even in the afterglow of the age of Newcastle – were to be respected, not only for their statecraft but also for their moral worth. 'Honour' was a serious idea taken extremely seriously. Above all, always important in England, morality supposedly set you above the common folk – who were morally lax and without civilisation. Thus, any Englishness constructed during this time was bound to be ladled in goodness.

Sincerity also emerged as a key moral attribute of this new Englishman. And by 'sincerity' was meant an amalgam of innocence, honesty, originality, frankness, above all truthfulness and moral independence. 'This was the "sincerity" that became the legendary characteristic of that English-Virginian gentleman, the first President of the United States, who would "never tell a lie".'[28] And these characteristics came to be known, over time, as 'character': a man of 'character' was *assumed* to be of *good* character. The character given to this new Englishman has lasted down the centuries, and can even help explain the unique forms (and pomposities) of British public life in the twenty-first century exhibited by the extravagances of English official life: 'honourable gentleman', the 'honourable and noble gentleman', the 'honourable and noble lady', and, of course, 'Your Majesty'.

'Character' ('sincerity' and 'truthfulness') was not, though, quite enough for the ideal, and idealised, Englishman. He also needed to possess social position and a modicum of power – and, inevitably, to be linked to the life of the land. It was here that the figure of 'the gentleman' emerges. Fashioned by the literati in the eighteenth century (from the raw material of the gentry), 'the gentleman' arrived centre-stage during Victorian times and was still going strong in inter-war Britain, although by the late twentieth century he, alongside older national stereotypes, had degenerated into a stage Englishman for the tourist trade.

'Great Britain' or 'Greater England'?

During the fateful era when English national identity was born there emerged a new dimension to the new nationalism. England – and Englishness – was expanding to cover more and more of its adjacent territory. By the end of the eighteenth century not only had a new, and enlarged, nation-state – of

Great Britain – taken hold on the islands, but the ideology of Englishness held sway within it. And through the agency of this new state – *Great Britain* was later to become the *United Kingdom* and further expand its political authority through imperial expansion – the English idea would be transmitted to the world.

Intriguingly, the idea of Britain had never died out. The early modern English memory had carried within it notions and images of Celtic Ancient Britons, who, long before the English arrived, had probably given the islands the name of Britain. Celtic leaders, such as the fierce anti-Roman warrior Boudicca, and Arturius (King Arthur of Colchester, or 'Camelot'), were also becoming legendary.

These Celts spoke a tongue – called British – named after the island, and they occupied the land until the first serious Roman invasion in the first century AD. As the wars with the English dragged on, the British people were divided: some left the country altogether, to settle in Brittany, and others formed a *British* resistance to the English, based in the west and north of the country. Over the next few centuries the British became a conquered people, and, although Britishness continued to exist in the outlying areas of the islands, mainly through Celtic tongues, it formed a peripheral existence. It was to stay that way, even after the English reinvented themselves by reviving the terms Britain and British in the early eighteenth century.

Peter Scott has called Britain an 'invented nation', 'not so much older than the United States'.[29] It was, to be precise, only 70 years older. Britain was born in 1707 – by the Act of Union between England and Wales (England had annexed Wales in 1536) and Scotland. The idea of a British nation-state had been mooted for some time, and as early as 1603 James VI of Scotland (James I of England) had adopted, for the purpose of diplomacy only, the title 'King of Great Britain'.

After the union the term 'Britain' caught on. By the 1770s the new country had its martial music – Rule *Britannia* (1740) and God Save the King (1745) – its *British* Museum (1753) and its Encyclopedia *Britannica.*

The expansion and reconstruction of the English nation-state, its transformation from England to Britain, was a series of essentially political, and military, acts – starting with the 1707 Act of Union and ending with the defeat of the Jacobites at Culloden in 1746. Yet, as the eighteenth century progressed, the islands were indeed becoming more culturally and ethnically homogeneous. English aristocrats had moved north of the border to take possession of new estates which they reckoned, in this era of rising land prices, would bring them serious profits. More importantly, Scottish landowners (and some Welsh and Irish too) had moved south to be nearer to the capital with its financial acumen and trading links to the world.[30]

The English ruling landed elite, their confidence badly shaken by the loss of the American colonies and by what they saw as the humiliating defeat of 1783, were, in consequence, quite keen to revivify the country by 'growing the nation' and absorbing the Scottish aristocracy. They used the Scots to somewhat reform their patrician style, turning themselves into 'a less frivolous, harder-working and publicly more responsible class'.[31] They also wanted help, both military and financial, with their increasing world role.

Even so, many English people feared this transmutation into Britishness. One such, the leader of the English resistance to the British idea, was John Wilkes. Wilkes, and his Wilkesites, represented the true canon of the newly-minted ideology of Englishness which sprang upon the scene as the self-confidence of the English elites grew apace during the late seventeenth and early eighteenth centuries. They believed the English were uniquely free and uniquely prosperous. The Scots, on the other hand, were divided between a nobility who were 'tyrants' and 'the common people who are slaves'.[32] And union with these people would pauperise the English.

It is Wilkes's rhetoric of freedom and liberty, linked to his political support for the out-groups of his day – the middle-class businessmen and professionals, the gentlemen manques who were using patriotism to improve their social position – which has placed him amongst the country's foremost radicals, indeed as a founder of English radicalism. Yet his message, like so much of English 'leftism' before and after, was essentially reactionary. Unlike Paine, his passion for liberty was not universal or based upon principles; rather, it stopped at the Straits of Dover and Hadrian's Wall. Englishness, not freedom, was his ultimate belief-system.

Yet, as it turned out, Wilkes had nothing to fear from the British idea. 'Great Britain' was always a misnomer; 'Greater England' would have been better. After all, the English aristocracy had built the new state. They forged its constitution and ideology in 1688 at the time of the Glorious Revolution, and in 1707 – there was, intriguingly, no written constitution (except the Act of Union itself) – all they did was extend the whole 1688 settlement north of the border. London, not Edinburgh (nor, as in a new federal system, some small town or city in a border area) became the capital. Furthermore, their ideology of Englishness was the only serious contender to be the governing culture. It had no competitors.

English landowners – and their supporters – dominated the new superstate's aristocracy, not least by the sheer power of financial resources. And the Celtic landowners who joined this new British aristocracy added little in the way of cultural pluralism: they were simply absorbed into the ruling group as they adopted – like millions who would come later – the lifestyle and manners of official Englishness. This grouping, by mixing land with industry and finance (primarily finance), came to form the ruling class of the United Kingdom – exhibiting the distinctive life style and culture which is still discernible into the twentieth-first century.)[33] And it was a class of people whose heirs, inheriting an empire as well as land, would – literally – rule the world.

As for the Celtic 'common people', they, like the Germanic-derived English 'common people' before them, were simply added to the rolls (though not, of course, the electoral rolls!), their descendants becoming the middle and working classes of later centuries.

In essence, England and the English colonised Britain and the Celts. Michael Hechter, in his major work on the subject, outlines the early stirrings of this state from the Kings of Wessex outward under the title 'the expansion of the English state'. He also argues that Ordinary Celts in the British state – unlike many of the landowning Celts – did not, ultimately, meld into the larger ethnic group of Anglo-Saxons and thus create a homogeneous ethnic Britishness. There was no such 'diffusion'. Rather, the pattern of development between English and Celts in the new Britain (and then later United Kingdom) was essentially 'colonial' (or, as he calls it, 'internal colonial'). Conflict continued, separate consciousness did not dissolve, and Celtic nationalism remained a relatively serious force. As Hechter puts it:

> the union of the Celtic periphery with England, unlike the earlier unification of English counties during the Anglo-Saxon period, did not establish state-wide legitimacy for the government in London. The periphery's weapon of resistance to English authority was the nineteenth-century development which came to be known as 'Celtic culture', Though in many ways this had little in common with its ancient

> counterpart. The renaissance of Celtic culture, the beginnings of Celtic nationalism, and the distinctive electoral behaviour of the Celtic territories were all responses to a situation which may usefully be described as colonial.[34]

Certainly many English people have always seen England and the English not only as the dominant force, but the only force, in the new nation. This perspective – embarrassing and insensitive though it may be – has often slipped out in public. There are a million examples. When George Orwell wrote his great paean of praise to the people in these islands who were winning the war his title was 'Socialism and the genius of the *English* people'. And in the Penguin Catalogue of Books (1994), under the heading 'History of *England*', there appears a number of books that are more properly 'History of Britain' books, for instance one entitled *Task Force: The Falklands War, 1982* and intriguingly *Pax Britannica*. Even careful scholars like Correlli Barnett, in the inscription to his work on British history, *The Pride and the Fall*, writes: 'in the hope that *England* may yet prove stronger than the storms'.[35] Of course, Orwell and Barnett are probably right, calling it 'as it is' – but it still must be disconcerting for the Scots and Welsh to become unpersons and invisible.

Yet the English elite's takeover of Scotland, like its earlier takeover of Wales, did not mean that there was to be no popular, indigenous support for the new Britain or Britishness. Following the Reformation, Scotland, like England and Wales, became a Protestant nation. Thus, although Scotland would continue to flirt politically with the Stuarts, it shared with its English coreligionists an opposition to Catholic France.

And anti-Catholic sentiment (whether of the mainstream Anglican kind or of the Scottish Knoxian variety) could always be counted on, certainly during the nineteenth century, to unite majorities within the two nations.

However, it was the Empire, more than religion, which, over time, helped to somewhat reconcile Scots to England and Britain. After all, many Scots were to play a seminal role in both the creation and the administration of the British Empire.[36] And every time an English politician – whether Pitt the Elder during the Seven Years War, or Walpole as he tried to consolidate Whig popularity, or, later, Joe Chamberlain – stirred up imperial sentiment amongst the English, he was, at least by implication, including the Scots as part of the national imperial family.

So, as the eighteenth century came to its close almost a century after the Union between England, Wales and Scotland the technology-driven blurring of frontiers within the islands, and the literary 'amen chorus' for Englishness, were helping to increase national sentiment – and with it, in some measure at least the sensibility of Britishness or UKness.

National sentiment and national identity are asserted much more than they are ever measured. Yet, one way to measure them is to attempt to assess sacrifice, indeed the ultimate sacrifice. The willingness of young men to die (or to put themselves 'in harms way') for their country must represent some kind of test of national consciousness. Thus, patterns of responses (as between urban and rural, village and town, north and south) to voluntary military service may be a key to some kind of measurement of the power of British nationalism. Linda Colley has broken new ground in attempting such a measurement. By analysing the response of Britain's manpower (what she calls 'the map of war patriotism') to the survey of volunteers called for by the Defence of the Realm Act of 1798 – at the height of the country's reaction to post-revolutionary France – she concludes that 'the nation's call for large numbers of men to defend it after 1798 was answered, not indeed unanimously but certainly abundantly'.[37]

But she also concludes that nation-building – certainly a unified national consciousness – still had some way to go. Her results told her that 'the more industrialised and urbanised a region was, the more likely it was to produce a high level of volunteers'.[38] (If indeed urban areas were more responsive than the rural and peripheral to a call to arms then it provides two intriguing insights. First, and obviously, it critically revisits the old saw that rural life and values are more patriotic than the cosmopolitan values of cityfolk. And secondly, it reinforces the notion that nationalism was, then at least, a function of modernity influencing those, primarily in urban centres, who were in the catchment areas of the new communications.)

Yet, all in all, the makers of Britain had seemingly succeeded; for by the late eighteenth-century, probably earlier, the UK-state was a going concern with a stable political order and even some popular support. This new, successful UK (the term *United Kingdom* was in normal usage by the late 1790s) became a perfect instrument for the English ruling classes. It enhanced their power base as well as broadening and reinvigorating them. And, perhaps most crucially of all, it resolved potential conflicts on the periphery of a nation which was increasingly wanting to concentrate upon its world role. It was almost as if the UK-state had been built specifically for imperial expansion.

The Liberal Idea Defeated

Yet, there was an alternative idea of England at work during the eighteenth century. It was the idea of England as the homeland of liberty. John Wilkes built his career on this idea. His political struggles (which included trial for sedition and expulsion from the Commons) built him into the English nationalist hero as he 'became the personification of liberty, and liberty was the hallmark of Englishness'.[39]

Wilkes's Englishness, like the nationalism of other radicals before him, harked back to the idea of an ancient constitution of the English in which the 'historic rights of Englishmen' were enshrined. This 'lost democracy', so the legend had it, was, though, overthrown by the Normans as, after 1066, they established 'a Norman Yoke' over the honest, freedom-loving English.[40]

The seventeenth-century Levellers mixed their early democratic and radical ideas with more than a whiff of nationalism, as in this harrowing account:

> And the last enslaving conquest which the enemy got over Israel, was the Norman over England. And from that time Kings, lords, judges, bailiffs, and the violent bitter people that are freeholders, are and have been successively: the Norman bastard William himself, his colonels, captains, inferior officers, and common soldiers, who still are from that day to this day in pursuit of that victory, imprisoning, robbing, and killing the poor enslaved English Israelites.[41]

This mixture of nationalism and liberty, although a favourite of radicals, was also adapted by those conservatives who developed the so-called 'Whig interpretation of history' – in which a past golden age of liberties becomes part of the 'entailed inheritance' of the 'long continuity of British institutions'. Edmund Burke became a proponent of this idea when he argued that there was an essential continuity 'from Magna Carta to the Declaration of Right…derived to us from our forefathers…transmitted to our posterity' – a notion not without its contemporary adherents.[42]

The idea (or myth) of continuity is not without its powerful, withering, critics. Jeremy Bentham savaged the idea of an ancient constitution of liberty as 'the wisdom of barbarian ancestors'; Tom Paine evoked the 'rights of *man*' not the rights of '*Englishmen*'; and, more recently, Ferdinand Mount has also questioned the validity of the idea of England's liberal exceptionalism.[43]

Even though the notion of a special English relationship to liberty may have been somewhat overdone by nationalist radicals, the English, of all the European national identities, can certainly lay some kind of serious claim to a uniquely powerful liberal heritage. The English certainly led the way in clipping the wings of monarchy while the rest of continental Europe was still living under various forms of absolutism. England did, in fact, experiment with a republican form of government at a very early stage in the story of the evolution of European democracy. And the 1688 settlement, although a fatal compromise between Parliament and Crown (which over the long term served to legitimise one of the most powerful executives in the Western world), was, for its time, a great democratic advance. Also, the offshore islanders can surely count amongst their number the principal theoretical architects of the modern conception of individual freedom – Thomas Hobbes and John Locke.

This English radical tradition can also be credited with many of the radical ideas which expressed themselves in dramatic, and concrete, form during the American Revolution – arguably a classic example of the struggle (carried on thousands of miles from its home) between liberal ideas and the Tory culture and ideology represented by the aristocracy and court in George III's London.

Edward Countryman places the intellectual roots of the American Revolution within the 'British' liberal tradition. He argues, reviving the idea of a special history of liberalism, that what the colonists – primarily English, but Welsh and Scots too – shared in common was a 'Britishness'. They:

> ...may have acquired it by birth as did the Puritans of New England and the Anglican gentry of the Tidewater, or by being conquered, as did the Dutch of New York, or by migration, as did the Huguenot French... [but that] all of them were heirs to a political and cultural tradition that set them off sharply from the Creoles of Spain's American dominions or from newly-conquered Catholic French of the St Lawrence Valley...To a Chinese or a Persian, of course, all Western Europeans must have seemed much the same. But in an age when absolutism ruled in much of mainland Europe, residents of Britain and its colonies could take pride in the fact that they lived in freedom...Were they asked to define it, some colonials, like some Britons, would have answered that it lay in the security of person and property that the common law guaranteed. Others might have said that it lay in specific privileges and liberties given to the Whig settlement of 1688...They would have noted that the King could neither legislate nor tax without the consent of the people, who were represented in Parliament. They would have maintained that their own assemblies stood to them as the House of Commons stood to the people of England, Scotland, and Wales...British freedom...blended the right to be left alone under the law's protection and the right to take part in political affairs.[44]

Thus the American colonists saw this 'Britishness' as ultimately guaranteeing them some kind of historic rights – the 'rights of Englishmen' – against the Crown and its church, against arbitrary executive power. This was the heart of the political message they had taken with them during the seventeenth and eighteenth centuries as they crossed the ocean from East Anglia and the West Country, from their dissenting churches and puritan sects. It was the kernel of this cluster of revolutionary liberal ideas which built the American Revolution, the formulation of the Declaration of Independence, the Articles of Confederacy and, ultimately, the Constitution of the United States. These English-Americans and British-Americans were truly 'posthumous children of the English revolution' and the 'Good Old Cause' of some 130 years before.

And there were indeed echoes of earlier English political liberalism, if not radicalism, in the domestic British response to the American Revolution – which was widespread, even within the aristocratic British polity (Edmund Burke supported the revolutionaries). Indeed, revolution might easily have proved infectious.

Yet, it did not. For the growing domestic sense of individuality and 'rights' (the 'historic liberties of Englishmen') was always in a political contest with other homegrown more organic (and reactionary) notions of society and state. Even as ideas of *individual* freedom were gaining a toehold in British life, the eighteenth century also saw the growth of the profoundly conservative *collective* identity of nationalism and national subjecthood.

The strange English mix of political liberalism and nationalism – starting with 'the Norman Yoke', running through the republicans in seventeenth century, through to Wilkes in the eighteenth, 'Radical Joe' Chamberlain in the nineteenth, and on to aspects of Orwell, Benn and Foot in the twentieth – ultimately failed. Liberal ideas of universal rights would ultimately always be in conflict with nationalism.

Tom Paine understood this more than most. 'Britishness' or 'Englishness' could not, ultimately, be reformed, or swivelled into a progressive direction. Paine understood that liberal ideas were either universal or meant nothing. As Countryman observed 'Paine attacked not one policy or another but the whole structure of Britishness, subordination, and monarchy within which colonial America had lived. The problem was not to explain what had gone wrong in a good system; it was to explain why the system itself was a problem.'[45]

So, this intriguing *alternative Englishness* – the vision of England as a land of liberty – was simply not as compelling as the Tory Englishness of land, class and race, an idea of England which perfectly suited the new era of empire upon which the country was about to embark. If pre-nineteenth century British and English nationalism had exhibited decidedly progressive and liberal tendencies, the Victorian experience of Empire transformed British nationalism into a profoundly conservative, if not reactionary, phenomenon.

The Imperial Soul of Englishness

The Empire was a decidedly *British* affair – as Scottish involvement in commercial, entrepreneurial, trading and financial origins of the empire, as well as in its building and running, was immense.[46] Yet it was the English, not the Scots, who were to become nature's imperialists. On questions of imperial rulership and administration it was the English, rather than the Scots, who took to empire as to the manor born. And it was the ideology of Englishness which guided the civil servants, top military and clergy who later *ran* the global enterprise (but which only marginally touched the lives and thinking of the merchants, engineers and sailors who *created* the Empire). Indeed, the ideology of eighteenth-century Englishness – with its imperatives of 'land, class and race' – was perfectly suited to the task of administering, if not forging, an Empire. After all, the power of the Empire, like power at home, derived from land – the Empire being simply a territorial expansion of the land mass over which the English aristocratic-cum-political class had control.

Also, paternalism of the landed system at home was almost tailor-made for the colonial experience: a beneficent government by those who knew better would be administered to lesser breeds (whose loyalty, in return, would be demanded).

The fundamentals of the political class system, which England's rulers had established at home – where the majority of people were essentially incidental to politics (without the vote and without entrenched rights) – was simply extended to the new imperial territories.

And in the colonies political life was even easier. There was no middle class competing for power and attention, no 'working class' was becoming organised, and, because the newly-acquired peoples were racially different, no pretence had to be made about universal moral worth. Black and brown people were simply inferior.

Thus, although the imperial mentality flowed quite naturally from the ideology of Englishness, the whole experience of Empire provided a crucial new twist in the development of English identity: it added, to an already pretty elevated self-image of Englishness, the crucial ingredient of superiority.

This sense of superiority – an innate superiority accruing to the English, but particularly to the English upper classes – tended to develop amongst all imperial ruling groups, not only the English. Yet the rulers of England were presiding over the most extensive, and most powerful, of Europe's empires – essentially leading the greatest country in the world and directly politically controlling a third of the globe.

It was heady stuff, and could be expected to leave its mark. A sense of national superiority was bound to breed in that environment. And this sense of superiority was enhanced, not diminished, by the nature of the English contact with their subordinate 'foreigners'. The English did not mix, they conquered. And then they ruled. (So the colonial experience – though technically an internationalising phenomenon – hardly encouraged real cosmopolitan instincts amongst the colonisers.)

Lord Hugh Cecil, English landowner, imperialist, and High Tory, is a perfect representative of this English sense of superiority – class, national, and racial. In 1912 he proffered a view of the English mission which perfectly represented the sentiment of his fellow rulers during the height of Empire. In what was the very stuff of the ideology of Englishness he argued that 'our vocation in the world...[is] to undertake the government of vast, uncivilised populations and to raise them gradually to a higher level of life'.[47]

And another imperialist, Rudyard Kipling, revealed a similar mental framework in his famous poem:

> Take up the White Man's burden, Send forth the best ye breed
> Go bind your sons to exile, to serve your captives' need;
> To wait in heavy harness, On fluttered folk and wild –
> Your new-caught, sullen peoples, Half-devil and half-child.

Thus English superiority was not simply cultural; it was racial as well. And the era of Empire saw the emergence in England not only of a general prejudice in favour of English and white racial superiority (Lord Hugh Cecil's views would have received near-universal support) but also of strains of literary racism (in, amongst others, the works of H. G. Wells), philosophic racism (exemplified by the works of G. K. Chesterton), even systematic, scientific racism (of which Stuart Houston Chamberlain was a leading exponent).

General theories of race – like general theories of politics – did not catch on amongst the English, and scientific racism became unacceptable amongst the political class, following the experience of the 1939-45 war and Nazism. However, a profound basic racial prejudice remained,

> invigorated by the experience of Empire. As one contemporary theorist has put it with or without a theory of biological racism, whether derived from the work of Count Gobineau (1915) or some other source, a

> deep-seated unrefined belief in racial difference in performance, and in standards, probably owes its origin to the colonial relationship between white master and black subordinate...The white man's civilising presence, the need to develop backward nations, the missionaries' vocation to convert the heathen acted as powerful justification for continued imperial domination. Such ideas deeply penetrated the culture of the British population and survive to the present day.[48]

Robert Colls has made the intriguing point that the imperial experience may have changed 'Whig' and Liberal perceptions of Englishness – away from ideas about Englishness being to do with liberty and constitutional development, and towards Englishness as 'race, language and custom'. Thus, according to this new view of Englishness, 'everyone who could possibly claim to have the right skins, show the right tongues, and be identified with the right feelings, was now invited across to the Whig celebrations'.[49]

Winston Churchill, the country's last unashamedly imperial leader, possessed a decidedly racist side – one shared by most all of his contemporaries in the higher reaches of English imperial public life. The historian Andrew Roberts writes of the great man:

> Churchill's views on race did not spring up fully formed when he regained office in 1951, but were held consistently during his long political career. By the standards of today – and possibly even of his own time – Winston Churchill was a convinced racist...For Churchill Negroes were 'niggers' or 'blackamoors', Arabs were 'worthless', Chinese were 'chinks' or 'pigtails', and other black races were 'baboons' or 'Hottentots', Italians were 'mere organ-grinders'...As the great tribal leader of 1940 his [Churchill's] speeches were peppered with references to the British race...Sir David Hunt, one of his Private Secretaries during his 1951-55 period of office, recalls 'Churchill was on the whole

> rather anti-black. I remember him sending a telegram to [South African President] Dr Malan and asking me whether he should say "My dear Mr President, Alles sal rect horn [all is well]. Keep on skelping the kaffirs!'" 'Blackamoor' was also a term in normal upper class usage – indeed was used by another prominent figure of the fag end of empire, Elizabeth Bowes-Lyon (now 'the Queen Mother').[50]

This kind of 'unrefined' racial superiority existed in Britain well into the twentieth century, and was revived by the arrival of mass third-world immigration into the country, a process begun in the late 1950s.

The idea of racial and national superiority at the heart of imperial Englishness was complemented by a mild and understated anti-semitism. Victorian English society developed a certain tolerance for very rich Jews such as the Sassoons, the Rothschilds and the Oppenheimers (as its 'practical-man' persona tolerated big money from any quarter). Yet, a disdain for Jewish people still surfaced regularly amongst English leadership groups. Even as late as 1959 the then British Prime Minister, Harold Macmillan, could claim that 'the Jews, the planners and the old cosmopolitan element' were playing 'no small part in the [European] Commission'.[51] A standard view, even as late as the 1970s, would be that 'everyone knew very well that there was a gaping chasm between them and us' and that although Jewish people are 'not really Jewish here in England...of course they're not really English either'.[52]

Nevertheless, superiority had its obligations. The imperial version of Englishness, conscious that it was the English role to administer large tracts of the globe, and 'the vast uncivilised populations', developed a cult of rulership. Englishmen would be trained in the arts of leadership. They would be trusted. And, like the feudal nobility, in return for the loyalty of their subjects they would rule paternalistically – over both the brown and black races and the domestic (British) whites. They would be 'firm but fair' (incredibly, as late as 1974, this paternalist slogan of was an election message of the Conservative Party in the February 1974 general election).

And they would lead by example, setting standards of behaviour for lower ranks and lesser orders to follow. This idea that rulers needed to lead by personal example had been present earlier in English history, but came into its own during imperial rule in India – when the needs of administration coincided with the rapid growth, at home, of evangelical religion. Katheryn Tidrik has argued that

> this governing class [of India] owed much of its character to evangelical religion…It…supplied a conception of authority which, because it happened to take root in India under conditions which were highly mythogenic, was of immense importance in defining the ideal to which men of empire thereafter aspired. This conception of authority was rooted in the evangelical cult of personal example.[53]

An historian of English national character, Ernest Barker, writing in the 1920s, has gone as far as to say 'No one will ever understand Victorian England who does not appreciate that among highly civilised countries…it was one of the most religious that the world had ever known.'[54] Evangelical religion was also the key ingredient in the education of the English upper-class young – the future rulers of empire – in the public schools of the nineteenth-century. The military historian Correlli Barnett has described how these young men were systematically imbued with a culture and an ideology which was purposely constructed for imperial leadership – and how Christian morality was at its heart. Dr Thomas Arnold, Headmaster of Rugby School from 1827 until 1841, exercised, according to Barnett, 'a decisive influence'. He is quoted as saying

> ...rather than have it [science] the principal thing in my son's mind, I would gladly have him think that the sun went round the earth, and that the stars were so many spangles set in the bright blue firmament. Surely the one thing needed for a Christian *and an Englishman* to study is a Christian and moral and political philosophy.[55]

And, because these public schools were the point of entry not only to the older universities, but also to virtually every leading London establishment occupation, they became the breeding ground for a governing class. Those few young men who had not gone to public school but who, during the later nineteenth and early twentieth centuries, would get to university, would also, in all its essentials, be incorporated and absorbed into the culture of Englishness by their university environment and education. Philip Dodd makes the point that by 1900 'almost all' the history text books which were made compulsory in the secondary schools 'were written by academics', a factor contributing to what he describes as their [the ancient universities'] 'establishment as custodians of the national culture'.[56]

There was an elaborate structure of mimicry – lesser public schools mimicked 'better' public schools, and most of the newer provincial 'civic' universities which came on the scene during the nineteenth century mimicked Oxford and Cambridge. (London University would be something of an exception here. Although the London colleges were created some centuries after Oxbridge, many of them, having the advantage over Oxbridge of being located in the capital, felt able to construct a relatively independent identity. University College was an avowedly non-Christian foundation, the London School of Economics was quasi-socialist.)

So systematic was this Victorian public school education that it produced a 'public school type' who was instantly identifiable – primarily by accent, but by dress and attitudes as well. His education had purposely set him apart from the rest of his compatriots, a chasm which many found it difficult to bridge later on in life.

Diversity was not a Victorian public school virtue. The boys were 'subjected to a powerful and uniform moulding process' and the schools were able to instill such a uniform education because they were able to virtually incarcerate the young men for months on end, thus depriving them of contact with families and the wider community.[57] (It is a fascinating separate speculation as to why upper class Victorian English parents allowed this to happen.)

The educational philosophy of these schools also encouraged conformity, and positively discouraged individuality and spontaneity. 'Team spirit' was the watchword for these potential rulers of empire, 'dooming the variety, spontaneity and open-mindedness that had hitherto been the saving-graces of the British upper classes'.[58] It was something of an irony, but the liberty, freedom and, above all, individuality (and eccentricity) which were proclaimed as the hallmarks of England and Englishness, were, during the high-point of empire, being systematically drained from the minds and personalities of the country's future leaders.

The 'team spirit', conformity and orthodoxy taught in the public schools may have repressed the young men, but it served (and was meant to serve) the Empire well. A limited and predictable range of set responses to difficult situations – as opposed to random and spontaneous activity – was a necessary attribute for imperial rulers. Governing an Empire needed rules, not personality! Luigi Barzini, the Italian writer, in an essay on the English, has attempted an explanation of how this 'English' trait of imperturbability was important:

> My friend Bernardo...believed that it wasn't important for Englishmen to be intelligent (intelligence could be a hindrance) because, as I discovered, they could all behave intelligently when the need arose. This is how it worked. They all had a few ideas firmly embodied in their heads. He said 'seven ideas'...whatever the number, the ideas were exactly identical and universal [that is, to all Englishmen]. That is why in older days, in distant lands with no possibility of communicating with their superiors, weeks or months by sailing ship away from London, admirals, generals, governors, ambassadors...subalterns in command of a handful of native troops in an isolated outpost...facing a dangerous crisis had always known exactly what to do...and would have behaved in the same way in same circumstances.[59]

It was from this cradle of repression that during the last three decades of the nineteenth century a new, revised and refined, culture and ideology of Englishness was brought into the world. And the Englishness so constructed resulted in a class imbued with an ideology and culture as important and peculiar as anything that happened in Germany in the thirties or Russia after the Bolshevik Revolution. Indeed, whereas the Nazification of the upper reaches of German society was to last for only a few years – eradicated by war – and the Communist culture in Russia was to last for only a few decades before it collapsed, this culture and ideology of imperial Englishness was to last for over a hundred years, and, undefeated in war or by domestic revolution, was still hanging around into the twenty-first century.

This ruling-class, public-school cult of leadership, although it provided leadership for the Empire, did not, though, lead to an authoritarian political and social system at home. Why it didn't remains an intriguing question. It possessed all the *accoutrements* of authoritarianism: an elite conscious of its leadership role, its propaganda and educational cells, an official ideology (Englishness), and control over the centres of economic and political power. Some historians argue that Britain in the late nineteenth and early twentieth centuries was too socially plural and politically liberal for any social group or ideology (even of upper classes) to dominate. Katheryn Tidrik, in a stark commentary, is not so flattering:

> We may ask ourselves in conclusion why it was that in a country where the cult of leadership enjoyed such favour as in England, fascism itself never acquired a hold. The answer must surely be twofold. First there was the empire to act as an outlet for the very emotions which it inspired: there were always brown races waiting to be led. Second, the mechanisms which developed to ensure that the imperial demand for leadership met with an unfailing supply also operated to rivet upon the British political system a governing class through which the leadership ethos was thoroughly diffused. In a land where the public school system worked to produce Fuhrers on wholesale principle, there was no prospect of any one of them arriving with the consent of his countrymen at supreme power.[60]

As well as attempting to foster a refined ideology of Englishness – and English identity – these same public schools then helped to impose it upon the still very hierarchical and deferential late Victorian, Edwardian and inter-war British society. One way in which this imposition took hold was through the creation of a standardised upper-class accent – which would serve as the authoritative voice of Englishness, and which would mark out rulers from ruled and serve as the standard for social aspirants. Philip Dodd, in an essay on Englishness, has argued that the term 'imposed' was too strong for the method by which English national culture came to establish a hegemony over the country.[61] He suggests that there were too many groups involved and thus no common intent to impose; and also that 'imposition' is too simple a term – as the 'establishment of hegemony' involves negotiation and active consent on the part of the subordinated. However, although there were indeed many groups involved in the process, none the less they did share a common position, culture and ideology, and tended to think, act and seem as one. Also, the Englishness they represented was, in its inherent character, an imposing phenomenon: possessing a sense of superiority and rulership.

Public schools such as Winchester are reported to have attempted to eradicate regional speech; in the late nineteenth century, at Bedford Modern School, local boys with a North Bedfordshire accent 'were so mercilessly imitated and laughed at that, if they had any intelligence, they were soon able to speak standard English'; and at Oxford University it had 'become virtually a condition of social acceptance amongst the undergraduates that one speak the Queen's English with a specific accent and intonation'.[62] And in the process of creating standard upper-class English the regional accents and dialects were devalued (by the most effective method in England – making them seem 'lower-class'). Future Gladstones (William Gladstone spoke with a Lancashire 'burr') and Peels (Robert Peel had a Brummie dialect) would, therefore, speak standard English.

This standard way of speaking (which later came to be called 'RP' Received Pronunciation) emerged in the public schools of the late nineteenth century as a new 'suitable' accent for imperial rulers. In the main it was precise, ungenerous, unengaging, high-pitched, controlled, non-confrontational, precious and slightly fey. In 1913 the Society for Pure English was founded and worried about the growth of 'mongrel' versions (like the American) of the now standardised English. And Henry Cecil Wyld, Professor of English language at Oxford University, 'was clear that the dominant English language was to be identified with certain English institutions – the Court, the Church, the Bar, the older universities and the great public schools'.[63]

In the 1920s, the BBC, through its Advisory Committee on Spoken English and its media monopoly power, not only sanctioned standardisation but, by and large, made the public school kind of 'RP' standardised speech 'proper'.

Thus, the British people were asked to 'receive' the word. And a single accent of authority was born which was to last for many decades. Any social, political or even economic aspirant – and there were thousands, if not millions amongst Britain's working, lower middle and middle classes – would need to make some genuflection towards this accent should they want to advance themselves. It amounted to an Orwellian type of social control, the cultural engineering of an elite – no wonder some, like Britain's late twentieth-century prime ministers Edward Heath and Margaret Thatcher, even felt it necessary to take elocution lessons.

This newly refined imperial image of Englishness was constructed during the dawning of the 'age of democracy' – when the vote, if not the power, was being extended to more and more British males. And in this 'age of democracy' the images and values of imperial Englishness were transmitted to this broader public through the medium of this new 'official' standardised English pronunciation. We only have to hear the voiceovers of 1930's, 1940's and even 1950's Pathe News to understand the authority of these voices born to be obeyed.

It was also transmitted via the growing mass public-education system which was developing below the public-school level. Elementary education, under the Act of 1870 was, thus, a crucial aid to the spread of Englishness amongst the broader British population, as was the appearance of literature and history as core subjects in the vastly expanded schools of the period.

However, the most important factor in securing acceptance of the new ideology and culture of imperial Englishness amongst the domestic masses was the hold and allure of nationalism – what some commentators, wishing to soften the term, call patriotism. It must remain an open question as to whether Victorian society (increasingly plural, quite mobile, and, although highly class-ridden, nonetheless highly economically productive), had it been able to develop free of the force and appeal of nationalism, would have junked the culture and ideology of Englishness and developed along the American model: less class-conscious, more individualistic, more open.

Yet, Englishness was not junked: indeed it became nothing less than the country's 'official' idea of itself – to be aspired to and copied by the middle and working classes.

The selling of Englishness in Victorian Britain to the wider public was helped by the rapid growth of the nineteenth-century mass media. The sheer spread of this Victorian media is often not fully understood. Raymond Williams, the socialist cultural analyst and philosopher, has pointed out that as early as the mid-1900s a popular, and populist, mass media already existed. The 1840s saw 'the effective establishment of a popular Sunday press…the growth of new kinds of periodical, combining sensational romantic fiction with recipes… the coming of cheap fiction…the development of minor theatres…rise of the music halls…'.[64]

Also, by the mid-1800s the circulation of popular Sunday newspapers (such as *Dispatch*, *News of the World* and *Chronicle)* had reached the startling heights of nearly 300,000 copies, whilst for a somewhat more selective audience the novels of Dickens, Thackeray, Reade, Marryat, Jane Austen, Trollope, Elizabeth Gaskell and Benjamin Disraeli were also widely read.[65]

Another key to the popularisation of Englishness lay in nationalism's, and patriotism's, unifying force. Because the working and middle classes were identifying with the state and nation Englishness was not seen as a separate distinctive culture for better-off people – a problem cosmopolitanism faced during the eighteenth century. Also, Englishness rode up and down on the tide of nationalism. Nothing succeeds like success: and the British nation-state (and its world-wide Empire) – and by extension its ruling class *and their culture and ideology* – was, by any contemporary test, a world-class success story.

National sentiment succeeded in dampening down the serious class divisions of the time. Indeed these class differences at the turn of century were particularly sharp. In the period immediately before the First World War there was talk, not all of it utterly fanciful, about social breakdown, even revolution. Stark differences not only in wealth and income, but also in culture, manners and dress distinguished the classes from each other. For instance, early photographs taken on the streets of London during turn-of-the-century summers (the turn to 1900 that is) reveal a rigidly classified society – boater hats (and some bowlers) for middle classes and cloth caps for the working classes; and a segregated one too – for classes did not mix – couples or clusters of people on buses or walking and standing in the streets were uniformly restricted to their own class only. Photographs of 1900 London are quite fascinating.[66] The same sharp differences applied to women. By 1900, certainly by 1918, women were beginning to emerge from their traditional domestic roles in families into the wider world, but the class patterns seemingly remained:

> You could immediately recognise the social girl, the middle-class girl, the City girl and the factory girl...The factory girl wore a black straw hat, ear-rings, a 'Mizpah' brooch, and hair dressed in rolls over her ears.

> The City girl was neat and severe. The middle-class girl was also neat, but added a touch of the style and chic which in those days could only be had by money. The society girl was consciously and demonstrably the society girl.[67]

Not only did nationalism act as a trans-class unifier, but, just as significantly, it enlisted the active support of all the classes of Victorian and Edwardian England. One such was the new industrial working classes in the cities, organising themselves into a trade union movement which was to become the most powerful in the world. The Victorian working class was patriotic, 'lousy but loyal', and their patriotism included support for the Empire. As Ellis Bartlett, a leading late Victorian jingo, remarked after the gathering of 40,000 signatures in favour of the retention of the imperial possession of Kandahar: 'It is a great mistake, as the Radical party will soon find out, to suppose that the working men of England are destitute of patriotism…the true working man is proud of his country…*is proud of its splendid and beneficent empire.*'[68]

Yet questions remain about the depth of popular support for the Empire. H. G. Wells wrote that 'Nineteen people out of twenty, the middle class and most of the lower class, knew no more of the empire than they did of the Argentine republic or the Italian Renaissance. It did not concern them.'[69]

It may not have 'concerned' them, but no section of British life ever turned decisively against the Empire – not the Scots, Welsh, English, industrial proletariat, middle class, the nineteenth-century Conservatives or Liberals, and incredibly, not even the Radicals. There was no serious anti-colonial protest movement in the country until well into the second half of the twentieth century, not until after the Second World War made Empire economically redundant. Indeed, the Empire possessed a popular constituency right up to and beyond the

Second World War. The Conservatives remained the party of Empire right up until Winston Churchill died, and neither the Liberals nor Labour (nor even the socialist intellectuals before the Second World War) attempted any systematic rejection of the principle of Empire.

The imperial experience may not have reached deep into working-class life, certainly not for those who never saw the colonies. Yet, the Empire was a constant source of images and tales in the mass popular media. And messages about the innate superiority of white Englishmen were produced and recycled in the educational texts and popular newspapers, and by the propaganda surrounding Queen Victoria, the 'Empress of India'. And in the working-class areas of the cities – even as late as the large council-house building programmes of the 1930s – the Pretoria Avenues, Kyber Crescents and Mafeking Roads acted as a constant reminder of British (and therefore their own) superiority. Through association with Empire the working classes could feel superior to others – the black and brown races. And it was their *nationality* (the only thing they shared with the rulers of the Empire) that gave them this sense of esteem and worth.

A source and sense of worth was also at the heart of the middle-class reaction to Empire. Imperialism allowed the industrialists, the merchants, the professionals, as well as to a lesser extent the clerical grades, again because of their common *nationality*, to identify with the aristocracy who ran the Empire – after all, they were all part of the same enterprise! And through this act of identifying, the culture, manners, and dress of 'official Englishness' became part of the life of the middle class.

Also, there can be little doubt that the Empire, as well as binding the people to the leadership, also helped the nationalist (and Englishness's) cause. It gave an added dimension of magic to the great nationalist ceremonials which the late nineteenth – century political class were constructing to popularise the constitution – primarily the monarchy and Parliament. The role of the monarchy was crucial here. For it was 'the sovereign' who made the link between nation and Empire – being head of both. Disraeli – and Gladstone – helped turn Victoria into the mythical figure: 'the Doyenne of Sovereigns, the Great White Queen, the Shah-in-Shah Pad-shah, the Grand-mama of Europe, *Victoria Regina Imperatrix*'.[70]

But, there were other forces at work which also helped send nationalism alive and well into the twentieth century – and they were the very forces which limited and smothered the growth of a truly modernised liberal state and society. And they came from both left and right. Amongst the working class, and many of the middle-class intellectuals who gravitated to the nascent labour movement, the ideas of liberalism, and Liberal Party, were increasingly losing out to various strands of socialist thinking. And socialism fitted quite easily into the nationalist framework. Socialist solutions were all nationalist solutions – as every reforming idea was aimed at change prosecuted through national structures. It could hardly have been otherwise, for the idea of international change, or international revolution, was indeed a romantic fantasy. Labourists, and even left-wing socialists, were more than accepting of nationalist ideology. H. M. Hyndman, the leader of the Marxist Social Democratic Federation, could say 'patriotism is part of our heritage', and the Fabian Society could argue that it 'accepts the conditions imposed on it by human nature and by the national character...of the English people'.[71]

As liberal ideas began to wane, the new and powerful ideology of socialism made an undeclared common cause with High-Tory traditionalists to limit the emergence of what might have become a real threat to the ascendancy of nationalism (and indeed also to 'the landed interest' and its associated ideology of Englishness): a strong, self-confident, individualistic, middle class.

The historian Larry Siedentop has argued that one of the most interesting sociological insights about Britain is that even during the age of Victorian capitalism, Britain did not produce a robust and self-confident middle class. Real middle classes are radical and liberal. They also tend to be internationalist, or at least less nationalist than social groups – such as aristocrats and peasants – who are linked to the land, and workers who are restricted to their locale. This historic weakness of the English middle class has lasted right up to the present day, and Neal Ascherson puts it in a constitutional setting: 'the middle class identifies with *the ancien regime* and is unable to see the advantages of overthrowing it and advancing to a condition of politically guaranteed individualism'.[72]

The Making of the English 'Gentleman'

In Victorian Britain Englishness needed its archetype and its champion. And it certainly got one – as the contemporary idea of 'the gentleman' was born. This fellow was an 'English gentleman': for there was to be no such thing as a 'Scottish gentleman' or an 'Irish gentleman' or a 'Welsh gentleman' – except as used, by English upper class types, in a somewhat ironic and belittling way.

The idea of 'the gentleman' sprang from medieval times, based upon the feudal notions of chivalry and nobility. And his social position – linked to the land, not overly grand but certainly not associated with the lower orders – derived from 'the gentry' (or 'the mere gentry' as Hugh Trevor Roper once called them).[73] The term 'gentleman' was in general use during the Civil War – 'I would rather have a plain russet-coated captain who knows what he fights for, and loves what he knows', said Oliver Cromwell, 'than that which you call a gentleman and is nothing else.' And during the eighteenth century it was becoming established as a term describing all landed, middle, and upper-middle-class adult males.

Yet, the emergence of 'the gentleman' in Victorian times had a more moral aspect to it. As the representative of Englishness, the new 'English gentleman' gave moral worth to what otherwise was simply Britain's power position in the world and the aristocrat's power position in domestic society. During the Empire, 'power had corrupted the British', argues Katheryn Tidrik, 'by making them think it inhered in them personally rather than in the terror of their aims'.[74] And this cult of moral leadership (based upon evangelical moralism) involved no serious rupture with previous more genuinely aristocratic self-images of Englishness. In fact evangelicalism 'collided productively with aristocratic conceptions of honour to emerge as the Victorian ideal of the gentleman, acknowledged by his equals and adored by his inferiors'.[75]

Alongside this moral content 'the gentlemen' possessed a degree of power, enough to be in control of his life, but not overweaning power. And as well as moral worth, and a measure of power, the added ingredients of charm and social presence were thrown in. Charles Hampden-Turner has, from his own experience, captured the idea superbly:

> If there was one abiding theme in my upbringing – one idea that held all others in thrall – it was the necessity for a commanding social presence. To be a gentleman, or to become one of the many modernistic transformations of a gentleman, was to command the attention of others with grace, style, wit, eloquence, self-possession and infinite subtlety. The purpose of life was that stage itself, a scenario where ultimate ideas and

> great passions would play themselves out around me. And I was curiously dismissive of all those subjects which did not lend themselves to social fluency, i.e. science, technology, industry...known to make people conversationally dull.[76]

The gentleman being moulded for production during late Victorian times (and given an outing in the works of Anthony Trollope) was always somewhat reticent and discreet, and certainly didn't show off. Yet, he was able to take command and was quite intelligent, but never, never, too clever and certainly not intellectual or meritocratic. Above all, and drawing upon the eighteenth-century idea of sincerity at the heart of Englishness, he was always honest and trustworthy.

In the twentieth century, P. G. Wodehouse produced an incontrovertibly dim kind of gentleman (the 'Bertie Wooster type' managed by 'Jeeves'), but he is never selfish or malign, remaining essentially a force for moral good, a 'good egg'. As is Agatha Christie's 'Hastings', the companion to Agatha Christie's Hercule Poirot.

During the twentieth-century this 'English gentleman' had a triumphant time. He was 'the officer' who led his men in two wars, and won them. He was – like Lord Peter Wimsey – the 'gentleman' – detective, the gifted amateur, who solves the murders whilst the plodding clerk of a policeman looks on. He was the romantic hero of novels. And, through the movies, this English gentleman also reached the postwar mass-market. The British 'Ealing Comedies' saw Ian Carmichael most perfectly representing the genre. And Hollywood, too, produced its own version of the English 'gentleman' – David Niven and Rex Harrison playing the part to a tee. James Bond, although initially played by the Scotsman Sean Connery, was the epitome of the cool, commanding and charming type demanded by Englishness's central casting.

And the English gentleman also made his appearance in the real world of postwar British politics, revealing Englishness, in a less English-dominated world, as still going strong, performing well. Prime ministers Anthony Eden, Harold Macmillan (an avid Trollope reader) and Alec Douglas Home (Lord Home of the Hirsel, no less) acted the parts perfectly, providing an image of Englishness which mixed old-world charm (Home was widely acknowledged to be genuinely charming) and world-weary imperial diplomacy – a combination which the English elite had then come to represent to the wider world.

Twentieth-Century Nationalism

The English ruling classes continued to be beguiled by Empire long after the sun had set upon it. And, in consequence, the national culture of Englishness was to exhibit a decidedly imperial character well into the late twentieth century. Although H. G. Wells could assert in *Mr. Drilling Sees it Through* (in 1916) that 'the middle class and most of the lower class knew no more of the empire than they did of the Argentine republic or the Italian Renaissance', this would also have been true of their knowledge of much of their own government.[77] A direct experience of Empire was not necessary in order to feel part of a great nation which had conquered a third of the globe, to feel, no matter how inchoately, superior culturally and racially to lesser breeds (and to have fixed in the mind a fairly clear racial hierarchy), and to believe that England and Britain was the centre of the world.[78]

For most of the first half of the twentieth century the national culture was pumping out its imperial messages – particularly to the young. In the 1930s schoolchildren were being told 'We're all subjects and partakers in the great design, the British empire. The British empire has always worked for the peace of the world. This was the job assigned to it by God.'[79] And in the mid-1950s secondary school children throughout the country were still assembling for 'Empire Day' to be told that they should be proud that they were the inheritors of a world power.

Also, for most of the first part of the century the statecraft of the UK's political elite was governed by little else than the need to defend and protect the Empire – and its economic preference system. At the very beginning of the century Lord Salisbury had been deeply worried about the future of Britain once he had seen the writing on the wall for the Empire; during the 1930s Neville Chamberlain had constructed his whole foreign policy upon a last-ditch defence of empire; and, at the end of the Second World War, Winston Churchill set the victory in grand imperial terms – 'Once again the British Commonwealth and Empire emerges safe, undiminished and united from a mortal struggle.'[80]

And long after the formal demise of Empire, the imperial sensibility still lingered. Aphorisms of Empire – 'If Britain had to choose between Europe and the open sea, it will always choose the open sea', 'Britain is a trading nation or it is nothing', 'Trade Follows the Flag' – continued to dominate political debate. Winston Churchill, an avowed supporter of Empire, even during his postwar premiership, put a stop to Labour's process of decolonisation, and further colonial independence had to wait until Harold Macmillan became prime minister. Although Churchill was the last truly imperialist prime minister, Anthony Eden acted like one, and his invasion of Egypt in 1956 possessed all the hallmarks of the imperial mentality. And as late as 1962 the Labour opposition leader Hugh Gaitskell was evoking not only 'a thousand years of history' but memories of 'Vimy Ridge' and 'Gallipoli' as part of his anti-Common Market campaign.

Yet, the sun was slowly setting on this extraordinary imperial venture; and as it finally dipped below the horizon, the whole culture and ideology of British imperialism, particularly the central feature of national 'greatness' and superiority, could be expected to fall with it.

But a fortuitous rescue was at hand. For the idea of Britain – and its dominant culture, Englishness – was to be given a huge boost by the two devastating world wars which were to disfigure twentieth-century Europe. The fires of patriotism, and nationalism, were restoked by these wars as they reinforced the sensibility of not only a separate but also a virtuous English and British identity.

The sheer nationalistic fervour of 1914-18, the last time in British (and Western) history when millions volunteered to fight (and die), is, to much contemporary thinking, still inexplicable. Yet it was real, and so was the full participation of the country's ruling-class youth. Quite simply 'the great war' against Germany saw the English public-school 'Christian gentleman' go to war *en masse* – thus precluding a re-run of the eighteenth-century radical taunt that the upper classes were unpatriotic. And the 'classlessness' of this sacrifice may help explain why the ineptness and bungling of many within the senior officer corps during the carnage of the trenches provoked no revolutionary reaction once the war was over.

Yet the seeming triumph both for the British state and for Englishness didn't last too long. The sheer human toll taken in the trenches – as well as the lack of a clear ideological enmity between the Allies and Germany, propaganda about 'the Hun' notwithstanding, all conspired to somewhat dim the glow of patriotic triumph and pride. Indeed, in the two decades which followed the carnage, internationalism and pacifism came to dominate political thinking, and were also rife amongst the general public.

Although nationalism received something of a setback politically, it was nevertheless sustained culturally. The 1930s British cultural scene was dominated by a dense literary network which epitomised prewar Englishness. Elizabeth Young suggests that:

> The briefest glance will suffice. Louis MacNeice, John Betjeman and Anthony Blunt, art critic and spy, attended Marlborough. Eton's cultural litany included Harold Acton, Cyril Connolly, George Orwell, Henry Green and Anthony Powell. A variety of public school friendships were consolidated at Oxford. Cecil Day-Lewis, MacNeice, Stephen Spender, Auden, Waugh, Graham Greene and Cyril Connolly clustered beneath the gleaming spires...Valentine Cunningham makes it clear to what extent 'a small enclave of the English bourgeoisie' dominated cultural life during the first part of this century. Two out of the three main first world war poets – Rupert Brooke, Siegfried Sassoon, Wilfred Owen – were drawn from the officer class. English nationalism, the tendency to close ranks around favoured sons could ultimately militate against Celtic outsiders like MacNeice.[81]

World War Two revived national, and nationalist, sentiment. And Englishness, too, had a very good war. The country faced, alone for some time, a clear, unambiguously evil, enemy. Unlike the French, it successfully repelled an invasion. And, 'it won the war', thus providing the country and, through the glamorous lens of the burgeoning film media, the wider-world, with a number of heroes, most of them upper-class southern English types. In addition to the bulldog 'Churchill' stereotype, there was also the handle-bar moustached RAF fighter-pilot type (even though the RAF fighter pilots who, in Churchill's phrase, 'knocked the Hun out of the midday sky' were, by and large, grammar-school boys from working-class and lower middle-class backgrounds, a point recognised by Churchill himself during the war).

The month of May, 1945, provided the image of Englishness with its last serious psychological boost. Field Marshal Bernard Law Montgomery was an Ulsterman, but could easily pass – by accent and bearing – as an archetypal public-school Englishman. On 5 May, commanding the 21st Army group, he presided over the surrender of all German forces in North West Germany, Holland and Denmark. Three days later, Winston Churchill – the ultimate symbol of warrior Englishness – appeared alongside the royal family on the balcony of Buckingham Palace to salute 'Victory in Europe'. The British people could be forgiven for believing that the English governing class had pulled it off yet again; that Britain was still the most powerful nation under the sun; and the ideology of Britain's rulers, and the culture of Englishness, personified in the 'English bulldog' personality of Winston Churchill and the decent 'English reticence' of King George VI, would resonate around the globe as an emblem of eternal steadfastness, courage and ingenuity.

Following the war a major myth-making industry appeared which fed the illusion of British (normally meaning English) centrality in the defeat of the Germans. To some extent national identities serve the function of hiding awkward truths. Britain played an important though subsidiary part in the landings in Normandy in 1944, but the 'turning point of the war' was more likely to be located in the 1942 Battle of Stalingrad, or even in the first invasion of the European mainland in 1943 in Italy – under the leadership of the Americans. Even so, the postwar British cultural industry and media vastly exaggerated the British contribution, as they did the role of Winston Churchill – who, as his own records more than abundantly testify to, was very much the junior partner to Roosevelt throughout the last three and a half years of the war.

Churchill's postwar standing, particularly in America where he became a statesman and hero (and rivalled the posthumous popularity of Roosevelt) did wonders for the traditional image of upper-class England and Englishness – even though he himself was half-American. It gave it a new lease on life. For the Americans and their increasingly influential mass media, Churchill, the Englishman, was not only a war hero, he was also a political poet (in President John Kennedy's words, written by Theodore Sorenson, he 'marshalled the English language and sent it into battle').

Following hard on the heels of Churchill came Elizabeth Windsor and the 'new Elizabethan age'. Once the postwar Labour government was out of the way, the official national identity, Englishness, was most perfectly represented by the official duo of Queen and Prime Minister. Churchill was its political, and Elizabeth Windsor its cultural, face. And the 1950s – the first time the mass of working-class Britons had a taste of a consumer society – seemed to promise a country which could deliver mass 'peace and prosperity'.

Politically Britain still counted in the world as one of a 'magic circle' of Western nations – she had a seat at the United Nations, a privilege denied to Germany, and, for a while, was one of 'the big three'. Even as late as the late 1950s Harold Macmillan could, just about, get away with being considered a world leader, and, through the Commonwealth of Nations, the UK political elite (and particularly the Queen) could still present themselves as leaders of a multinational alliance of states.

Even the emergence of the USA as a world power had a rub-off effect upon the English, particularly their upper classes. The English elite would – wrongly, of course – claim pride of authorship of this newly powerful nation. In the immediate postwar period, during American world supremacy, the levers of power and culture in the USA were still largely controlled by Anglophile white Anglo-Saxon Protestants. English was the language of this new superpower and for some time, well into the 1970s, there remained a 'special relationship' between the USA and Britain. Yet, this new dawn for Englishness was really its Indian summer. It all began to fall apart in the early 1960s when it became abundantly clear that Britain had suffered a major economic defeat. It was becoming apparent that the unreconstructed British economy was not going to perform, in the long term, on anything approaching a level of parity with the country's major competitors. Britain was slipping down the various economic 'league tables' (a term, from soccer, introduced in the early 1960s by Labour leader Harold Wilson to highlight Conservative economic failure). Thus a loss of confidence in the country's economic performance compounded the political humiliation of the country's ungainly retreat from its Suez operation in 1956.

Theme-Park Englishness or 'Englishness for Export'

For many English people, even as the twentieth century drew to its close, the traditional idea of Englishness, although weakening, was still alive and well. Indeed, national self-consciousness had arguably somewhat intensified with post-1940s political and economic decline. With every passing postwar decade, almost as a feature of decline, the English appeared increasingly interested in themselves, in what Englishness meant in the modern world, in the search for the essence and deeper meaning of their nationality.

There was also a relatively clear view of what Englishness amounted to. In a recent, typical, depiction, one writer suggested that 'a group of dinner guests in their thirties' would describe Englishness as:

> A bowl of scented roses on a sunlit table and the muted thwack of leather against willow. Umbrellas clashing on city streets and felt trilbies brim to brim at the races. A cup of tea, or a pre-prandial glass of sherry. The first cuckoo of spring and the first Pimms of summer. Kipling and *Just William*. Royal Doulton figurines and talking about the weather.'[82]

In a somewhat similar vision of the meaning of Englishness, the 1990s saw the country's prime minister – John Major – evoking a nostalgic theme of nationality by quoting approvingly George Orwell at his most sentimental: '…the clatter of clogs in Lancashire mill towns…the old maids biking to Holy Communion through the mists of the autumn morning…', and a leading advertising agency – with 'voiceover' quoting from Shakespeare's 'sceptered isle' soliloquy – establishing for millions the images of cottage and countryside (set against 'less fortunate lands' with the channel 'defensive as a moat') for a television advertisement for tea.

This Englishness exists for export. It is the 'English product' which is sold around the world, particularly so in North America, but which is also aggressively marketed – mainly to upper income groups and to the international super rich – in continental Europe and amongst the third world elite, particularly in the Arab countries and East Asia. Increasingly it is becoming a key ingredient in the broader English heritage industry, which as part of the leisure and tourist industry can be expected to grow in a country increasingly relying upon the service sector. The Conservative Party under John Major recognised its importance when soon after Margaret Thatcher left Downing Street it established a 'Heritage Minister' with cabinet rank.

This 'English' product is primarily about lifestyle. Englishness is sold as a way of life. One of its flagship publications is *Country Life* (which publishes every week of the year, and could be acquired in 1995 for an annual subscription in the United States for around $200). *Country Life* tells its audience how to acquire Englishness (at a price, of course). And it suggests that the heart of the matter of Englishness is the grand house or country cottage, and the related furnishings (advertisements for which take up almost half of the magazine), the English garden and the English dog, all of which appear in a rural setting. *Country Life* presents 'A week in the country' by the Duchess of Devonshire, and in the mid 1990s developed a series entitled 'Hero of the Countryside'.[83]

Country Life culture also presents a highly self-conscious 'how to do it' kind of Englishness. In an article entitled 'How a Gentleman should dress', the Duke of Devonshire advises. 'At Cambridge I wore flannels and tweed. Cavalry twill was just coming in and it was rather laughed at as the jodhpur in June brigade.'[84] And an 'English look' is presented for parading at the races, Ascot, the Badminton Horse trials, the Royal Windsor Horse Show, Henley, and of course, polo – at 'the events which make up our summer season'.[85] In promoting this 'English look' diversity is not encouraged – for instance, the men all tend to look like Charles Windsor in corduroys and tweeds, 'dressed in the best British country style' as *Country Life* put it.[86] Similar advice is offered over a range of pursuits from sports cars (normally referred to as 'motors' or 'motoring') to the proper way to picnic – Roy Strong offers, in 'A Question of Taste', advice on the traditional English picnic 'before the corporate clients promoted conspicuous wealth'.[87]

This 'stage Englishness' has been so successful that it has caused imitation: the inventing of an 'English' personality. An extreme, and somewhat sad, contemporary example is the amazing career of Stanley Olson. During the late 1960s, Stanley Olson, a Jewish-American from Akron, Ohio, left his country in his early twenties and set about reinventing himself. He acquired what he considered to be an 'English' persona. In 1969, Olson, at the age of twenty-two, left America. He set about 'rectifying nature's error: he would create himself anew – live as if born without parents, siblings, family history and religion, midwest education and cultural trappings. He moved to London and transformed himself – thoroughly, wholeheartedly, impeccably – into an Englishman.'[88]

He adopted the accent, the clothes, mannerisms, indeed the *persona* of an English gentleman until, according to his biographer, 'Englishness [fitted] him like a glove.'[89] In his nearly twenty years in London – he died of a stroke at the early age of thirty-nine – he lived the manufactured life of an 'English Gentleman', an aesthete, a man of letters, a social lion with a circle (including, appropriately, the Duke of Devonshire) which he entertained, often lavishly, on the Akron-based Olson family fortune.

Olson's story is not so odd. It is the story of large numbers of Britons too. It is the journey taken by umpteen intelligent and aspiring working-class, lower middle-class and bourgeois young men from Britain's provincial towns and cities. Faced with so stark a chasm between mainstream British life and the life of an 'English gentleman', some have engaged in just as brutal a switch of identity as did Stanley Olson. Others have adopted the manners, lifestyle and ideology of Englishness more naturally and less abruptly. Even so, the journey from Akron to Englishness is hardly any further than the journey from Bristol or Birmingham or Manchester.

In any promotion of Englishness, of the 'English product', the upstairs-downstairs image needs to be catered to. Upstairs is covered by lashings of royalty – royal tittle-tattle primarily.

And downstairs also makes regular appearances, though normally bathed in ladles of condescension and bordering on the kitsch. Identikit servants and 'loyal working folk' appear in the pages of *Country Life* – under the title of 'Living National Treasure', a hayrake maker, a basket maker, a gypsy caravan restorer and, inevitably, a housekeeper have been profiled.[90] Of all the icons of theme-park heritage Englishness the most exalted must still be the game of cricket, particularly village cricket. No aspect of Englishness induces such sentimentality as the 'leather on willow' images:

> When the late squire of Crowcomb, Major Thomas Trollope Bellew, was buried last year, he was escorted to his grave not only by uniformed hunt servants, but also by his cricket team in their whites. The image of village cricket is enduring and endearing: it has its stock characters, its folklore, its champions, its literature and its idyllic settings – the green, with the church behind, and the pub somewhere handy...[91]

This kind of rhapsodising is, of course, not really about the game of cricket. Those who play the game, and take it somewhat seriously, are often oblivious to its mystical cult status – for many of them it remains a game like any other, though more intelligent and competitive. Rather, the game – and its 'Englishness' – has in reality become a metaphor for the celebration of the English village and rural nostalgia. It has other attributes which make it attractive as an icon of nostalgic Englishness. Of course, it was invented in England, and is largely played by Englishmen and those considered 'honorary Englishmen', from the ex-colonial lands, thus restricting it to the old imperial family. (Continental Europeans and Americans do not play the game.)

It also, particularly in the three, four or five-day game, and to a lesser extent at league or club level on Saturday and Sunday afternoons, exhibits and encourages a range of supposedly 'sturdy' 'English' qualities: perseverance, patience, 'team spirit' (although in truth, cricket, unlike soccer, is not much of a team game, involving at its heart a contest between bowler and batsman only) and, of course, 'fair play'. It is a measure of the extraordinary success of cricket as an English ritual and totem of national character that, more so than the real national game (in terms of popular support soccer would qualify for this prize), so much of the terminology of the game has entered into the mainstream of everyday usage in the language of contemporary British-English. 'Sticky wicket', 'end of play', 'stumped me', 'hit for six', 'straight bat', 'had a good innings' and the like are 'very English' phrases.

This contemporary theme-park Englishness also embraces a notion of English national character. According to the standard self-image promoted during the twentieth century the essence, the 'quintessentialness', of the Englishman and woman involved very prosaic qualities. The stereotype had it that English people were essentially practical and not overly-bright (certainly not, in the national phrase which mocks intellectualism, 'too clever by half'). Yet, at the same time, they were loyal and trustworthy ('sturdy' again suffices to describe the attribute). By contrast, foreigners (and 'foreignness'), particularly continental Europeans, were altogether more exotic: they were theoretically minded and – particularly southern Europeans – emotional, given to grand gestures and ideas, qualities which can easily make for instability.

Paul Addison has argued that it was Britain's role during the Second World War that induced this particular self-image of national character: 'On all sides publicists proclaimed that the key to victory lay in the native genius of a people who were sturdy, industrious and unimaginative – not very clever in fact – but moved by an inner spirit that expressed itself in such things as patriotism, a love of the countryside and a love of liberty.' He suggests that so powerful is this stereotype in the films and literature of the postwar period – product not simply of Dunkirk, the Blitz and the subsequent mass-media legends, but also deriving from the English elite's reaction to the French Revolution and Napoleon – that 'it remains there to this day, a massive chunk of patriotic legend that still defies the best efforts of historians to break it up'.[92]

This notion – that the essence of Englishness combines ordinariness with a 'sturdy' love of liberty (and a concomitant need for privacy) – was extolled by two wartime English writers, J. B. Priestley and George Orwell, whose influence on the contemporary image of Englishness was profound. Priestley, both a novelist and a playwright, helped make his name by evoking Dunkirk as an obvious example of this English characteristic of sturdy independence. And the essayist and novelist George Orwell virtually exalted concern for privacy and freedom (particularly from 'bossy' bureaucrats) as a unique attribute of Englishness.

Intriguingly, both Priestley and Orwell, who cornered the market in describing and evoking the life of England in the wartime and early postwar years, are themselves often both depicted as being 'very English'. One writer suggested that J. B. Priestley was so English that he still nestles 'in the nursery wing of the Anglo-Saxon mind'. And George Orwell was described by one of his leading biographers as being 'a specifically English writer and a specifically English character, both in his seeming amateurism...and in his eccentricities' (a depiction which begs the question as to whether 'a specifically English' writer can possibly be both professional and 'normal'!).[93]

To some extent this may be because Orwell and Priestley added to this contemporary idea of Englishness a certain glorification of English insularity and provincialism – an aspect, too, it is argued, of the works of the less political, though 'most English of writers', Alan Bennett.[94] They were the founders of 'Little England'. For them, England's reduced circumstances were no bad thing. No lovers of Empire and the aggrandising imperial mission, they domesticated the idea of Englishness. The true English spirit, they argued, was to be found at home, was provincial and practical – not outward looking, cosmopolitan and full of grand visions.

The domesticity of Priestley's and Orwell's Little Englandism was in part a reaction against the terrors of the grand designs of Fascism and Communism (and, to some extent, those of American Capitalism too, for both Priestley and Orwell were moderate socialists). Thus, the sheer cosiness of English life, instead of provoking a reaction against its limiting, unimaginative and unproductive qualities, was built into a virtue. And in the process one of the most revered values of Englishness became familiarity. Although current theme-park English images such as 'the muted thwack of leather on willow' or 'the first cuckoo of spring' may have been a little overripe for Orwell and Priestley – and, also too middle-class: for they were both determined to depict Englishness as a phenomenon existing beyond 'the home counties' – they nonetheless both prized familiarism. In his famous essay "The Lion and the Unicorn', George Orwell was at his sentimentalising best when describing familiar English scenes:

> English civilisation…is somehow bound up with solid breakfasts and gloomy Sundays, smoky towns and winding roads, green fields and red pillar-boxes…However much you hate it or laugh at it, you will never be happy away from it for any length of time. The suet puddings and the red pillar-boxes have entered into your soul.[95]

Little Englanders saw the country not only as cosy, but also as stable, indeed uniquely so. This idea of England as a peaceable island in a troubled world, and of Englishness as a stable pillar of cultural security, has carried itself forward from Orwell and Priestley into the contemporary debate about England's role in Europe. Nearly 40 years after the end of the Second World War one of England's, and Englishness's, leading polemicists, prolific Eurosceptic Paul Johnson, still sees Britain as uniquely stable, and continental life as somehow threatening this stability – indeed as redolent with images from the Second World War, of 'conflagrations' and of Hitler's panzers hurtling with a 'speed and intensity' through France. In an extraordinary commentary, one which is not unrepresentative of much contemporary English opinion, he argues:

> There is a feeling throughout Europe that democracy is not working and that the gap between what people want and what they are allowed by their rulers is too wide. That means trouble, and exactly how and where it starts is less important than the speed and intensity with which it will spread. A European conflagration will bring the Channel (as opposed to The Chunnel) back into fashion…as the continent slithers into anarchy – or worse – and we watch the exciting drama from our grandstand seats on the White Cliffs…[96]

So powerful is this Little England image of Englishness (stable, cosy, even twee) that it increasingly assumed the proportions of an 'official' idea of Englishness. In the latter part of the twentieth century this theme-park Englishness (with its stage Englishmen and women) has become so dominant that it has forced aside other, more realistic, images of Englishness. It remains a mental straitjacket which imposes itself upon the real world – that is the diversity and plurality of the life of the country and its peoples. And it is, of course, as illusory as any of the other stage nationalisms (Irish, French, German) that many English still laugh at.

As with any 'official' culture or ideology, Englishness presents us with problems of conformity. Inevitably, there remains a tendency to dismiss as un-English those things which do not meet the standard approved style or product – even though they may represent the life and culture of millions of people living in real England. For instance, Priestley himself once observed that the society emerging in England in the mid-1930s – clean, bright...factories, palatial cinemas...crowds as rootless as the car which symbolised the age...*wasn't really England at all*'.[97] Such a starkly narrow assessment begs large numbers of questions – some of them not wholly facetious. What about those English people who don't play cricket? Are they not to be considered English at all? Is a writer who does not write like Betjeman – that 'most English of writers' – in fact under the influence of 'foreign' canon? Are they only 'honorary' English?

This theme-park Englishness (cosy, soft in temperament, steadfast, and stable) – although perhaps unrecognisable to earlier generations of English – is, nonetheless, the end-product of some three centuries of the making, and refining, of a national identity.

Of course, the idea of what it means to be English has changed, often radically, over time. For instance, Englishness during the high-point of Empire became an imperial identity: conquering and hegemonic. Beram Sakatvala captured a somewhat romantic side of this dynamic Englishness when, in the late 1960s, he could write that:

> From their tiny kingdom lying off the northern shores of Europe the Anglo-Saxon people went out over the world taking their laws, their method of government, and their language with them. They built the

> colonies in North America, settling their farms in the white plains and green valleys of the New World. They peopled Australia and New Zealand. They went into Africa and into Asia – governing many different people to whom they taught their language and their laws.'[98]

As well as retreating into a more provincial aspect, Englishness has also recently undergone a softening process – a far cry from some of its previous images. For instance, the fifteenth-century printer William Caxton was described as a 'Thoroughly English character' possessing attributes such as 'business acumen' and 'gusto' – terms not normally appended to the English in the mid to late twentieth-century, either by themselves or by foreigners. In the nineteenth century, to be English often meant to be tough, indeed ruthless, coarsely commercial, adventurous and restless – to be world travellers (like Walter Raleigh or the explorers Richard Hakluyt and Francis Drake) or conquerors of more peaceable peoples (like Clive of India).[99]

Yet, it is hardly surprising that today's Englishness – the homely, cosy, provincial and somewhat insular Englishness of the English theme-park – is less grandiose and imperial than its strutting forebears. For Englishness, like the nation it purports to represent, is now living in considerably reduced circumstances.

Notes

1. This account is given in Beram Saklavala, *The Origin of the English People*, New York, 1969.
2. Ibid., p. 14.
3. See the great protagonist of this view: J. H. Round, *Feudal England*, London, 1895 and R. Allen Brown, *The Normans and the Norman Conquest*, London, 1969.
4. All quotes from Geoffrey Elton, *The English*, Oxford, 1992, p. 2.
5. Elton, ibid., p. 28 and p. 2.

6. Ibid., p. 14.
7. Quoted in McCrum, et al., op. cit., p. 77.
8. Robert Claiborne, *The Life and Times of the English Language*, London, 1990, p. 123.
9. Georges Bourcier, *An Introduction To The History of English Language*, London, 1981.
10. Claiborne, op. cit., p. 100.
11. Poem quoted in McCrum et al., op. cit.
12. McCrum, et al., op. cit.
13. Newman, op. cit., p. 4.
14. Newman, op. cit., p. 127.
15. See Linda Colley, *Britons: Forging the Nation, 1707-1837*, London, 1992.
16. Elton, op. cit., p. 182.
17. Colley, op. cit., p. 162 and p. 164.
18. Ibid., Chapter 4.
19. Ibid.
20. Quote from Newman, op. cit., p. 116.
21. Elton, op. cit., p. 70.
22. See Ian Gilmour, *Inside Right, A Study of Conservativism*, London, 1977.
23. Keith Thomas, 'How Britain made it', *The New York Review of Books*, 19 November 1992.
24. See: Raphael Samuel (ed), *Patriotism; The Making and Unmaking of British National Identity*, vol. 1, London, 1989.
25. Colley, op. cit., p. 286.
26. See: Madge Dresser, 'Britannia', in Samuel, op. cit.
27. Newman, op. cit., p. 124.
28. Ibid., p. 127.
29. Peter Scott, *Knowledge and Nation*, Edinburgh, 1990, p. 168.
30. For a systematic analysis of this cross-fertilisation of English, Scottish, Welsh and Irish, see Colley, op. cit., p. 155.
31. Thomas, op. cit.
32. From a column in *The North Briton*, 26 June 1763, quoted in Colley, op. cit., p. 116.

33. See James Bellini, *Rule Britannia*, London, 1981.
34. Michael Hechter, *Internal Colonialism*, London, 1975, p. 59.
35. See Correlli Barnett, *The Pride and the Fall*, New York, 1986. My italics.
36. For data regarding Scottish imperial influence see T. C. Smout, *A History of the Scottish People, 1560-1830*, London, 1970 (2nd edition).
37. Colley, op. cit., p. 293.
38. Ibid., p. 293.
39. Ibid., p. 111.
40. See for instance T. H. B. Oldfield, *The Representative History of Great Britain and Ireland*, 1816, and 'The Norman Yoke' in *The True Levellers Standard Advanced*, 1649. Also see: J. Lively and A. Lively, *Democracy in Britain: A Reader*, Oxford, 1994.
41. In *The True Levellers Standard Advanced*, 1649, quoted in Lively and Lively, op. cit., p. 23.
42. Burke's quote from 'Reflections on the Revolution in France', quoted in Lively and Lively, op. cit., p. 20.
43. See Ferdinand Mount, *The British Constitution Now: Recovery or Decline*, London, 1992.
44. Edward Countryman, *The American Revolution*, New York, 1985, p. 16
45. Ibid., p. 111.
46. See R. A. Cage (ed), *The Scots Abroad: Labour, Capital, Enterprise 1750-1914*, London, 1985.
47. See Gilmour, op. cit., p. 87.
48. Frank Reeves, *British Racial Discourse: A Study of British Political Discourse about Race and Race-related Matters*, Cambridge, 1983, p. 114.
49. Robert Colls and Philip Dodd (eds), *Englishness*, Beckenham, Kent, 1986, p. 45.
50. Andrew Roberts, *Eminent Churchillians*, London, 1994, pp. 213-4.
51. Quoted in Alan S. Milward, *The European Rescue of the Nation-State*, London, 1992, p. 432.
52. First quotation from Lady Selina Hastings in Phyllis Hatfield, *Pencil Me In: A Memoir of Stanley Olson*, London, 1944, p. 94. Second quotation from an American observer of the English scene, ibid., p. 95.

53. Kathryn Tidrick, *Empire and the English Character*, London, 1992, p. 3.
54. Ernest Barker, *National Character and the Factors in its Formation*, London, 1928, p. 42.
55. Quotation from Correlli Barnett, *The Collapse of British Power*, London, 1972, p. 25. A general description of the education of Victorian public-school children also appears in the same chapter.
56. Colls and Dodd, op. cit., p. 4.
57. Quotation from Barnett, 1972, op. cit., p. 36.
58. Ibid.
59. Luigi Barzini, 'The Imperturbable British', in *The Europeans*, London, 1972, pp. 52-3.
60. Tidrick, op. cit., p. 260.
61. Philip Dodd, 'Englishness and the National Culture', in Colls and Dodd, op. cit.
62. McCrum, op. cit., p. 24. For a study of the emergence of standardised English see Raymond Williams, *The Long Revolution*, London, 1961.
63. Dodd, op. cit., p. 16.
64. See Williams. op. cit.
65. See ibid., pp. 54-62 for a fuller analysis.
66. See Alistair Service, *London 1900*, Granada, 1979.
67. Thomas Burke, *London in My Time*, London, 1934, p. 65 about the recognisable types of girls seen on London streets around 1900.
68. Cited in Hugh Cunningham, 'The Conservative Party and Patriotism', in Colls and Dodd, op. cit., p. 286. My italics.
69. Ibid., p. 298.
70. Cited in Theo Aronson, *Victoria and Disraeli*, London, 1977, p. 194.
71. Colls and Dodd, op. cit., p. 36.
72. Neal Ascherson, *Games and Shadows*, London, 1988, p. 151.
73. See Barrington Moore, *Social Origins of Dictatorship and Democracy*, Harmondsworth, 1966, p. 16.
74. Tidrick, op. cit., p. 279.
75. Ibid., p. 3.
76. Charles M. Hampden-Turner, *Gentlemen and Tradesmen*, London, 1983, p. 3.
77. Quotation cited in Cunningham, op. cit., p. 298.

78. Intriguingly, Ernest Barker, in his 1927 book *National Character*, does not, even fleetingly have anything to say about the influence of Empire on character and culture.
79. Cited in Lively and Lively (eds), op. cit., p. 238 from George Lamming's *In The Castle of My Skin*.
80. *The War Speeches of Winston Churchill*, compiled by Charles Eade, London, 1970, vol. 3, p. 512.
81. Elizabeth Young, 'Canon Law', *The Guardian Magazine*, 4 February 1994, p. 20.
82. Stephanie Lewis, *The Times*, 'Shopping' section, 23 April 1994.
83. See *Country Life*, 11 November 1993.
84. 'Yellow Socks and Coronets', by James Knox, entitled 'How a Gentleman Should Dress: A Duke Advises', *Country Life*, 19 August 1993.
85. 'Whatever the Weather' by June March, *Country Life*, 23 June 1994.
86. *Country Life*, 23 June 1994.
87. Ibid.
88. Phyllis Hatfield, *Pencil Me In: A Memoir of Stanley Olson*, London, 1994, pp. 3-4.
89. Ibid., p. 52.
90. *Country Life*, 19 May 1994, July 1994, and 30 June, 11 November 1993.
91. David Edelstein, 'Leather on Rural Willow', *Country Life*, 12 May 1994.
92. Paul Addison, 'The Day the Dream Began to Die', *Independent*, 6 June 1994.
93. The depiction of J. B. Priestley was by Paul Taylor, 'Bennett and the Betrayal of Englishness', *The Independent*, 23 May 1994. And that of George Orwell was by Bernard Crick, *George Orwell: A Life*, London, 1980.
94. Described as such in Paul Taylor, op. cit.
95. From 'The Lion and the Unicorn: Socialism and the English Genius', in *The Collected Essays, Journalism and Letters of George Orwell*, vol. 2, London, 1968.
96. Paul Johnson, *Wake Up Britain*, London, 1994.
97. Quoted from David Starkey, 'Freedom and Responsibility', *LSE Magazine*, Spring, 1994, p. 24. My Italics.
98. Beram Sakatvala, *The Origins of the English People*, New York, 1969, p. 28.
99. Depiction of Caxton cited in McCrum et al., op. cit.

Four
True Brits, Real England

If the UK establishment – with its centralised Westminster system, its London-based media and its identity and ideology of 'Englishness' – has smothered and obscured the diversity of nations, classes and ethnicity inherent in contemporary Britain, then the question remains: what does 'the real Britain' look like?

Real Identities

In a sense our great national crisis of identity is all about power – or, rather, the loss of it. For as Britain not only lost its empire but sank down world economic league tables – from 'the premiership to top of division one' – it became extremely difficult to sustain an identity, and associated ideology, based upon superiority and confidence. It became a forlorn hope to assume the role of a 'gentleman' whilst existing on an increasingly insecure inheritance, and it was embarrassing to be John Bull whilst a junior partner – both to the United States and then to the Franco-German alliance in the European Union.

Yet there was one advantage deriving from comparative economic decline and the consequent crisis in identity. For, the realities (and thus the real identities) of Britain, and of England, and of their peoples, could, at long last, begin to reveal themselves; and, as they did so, they displayed a very different world from that conjured up by the post-imperial manufactured national ideology and identity of 'Englishness'.

The unreal character of 'Englishness' – both as identity and ideology-was as complete as it was audacious. Virtually every field in which the country and its people had excelled was denied by this official ideology. The home of the industrial revolution was devalued by an idea of Englishness which was dominated by older, landed virtues; the country's massive contribution to scientific enquiry went largely uncelebrated, certainly compared with its literary output. It was no wonder that, in Martin Weiner's words, 'in the world's first industrial nation, industrialism did not seem quite at home. In the country that had started mankind on "the great ascent" economic growth was frequently viewed with suspicion and disdain.'[1]

The powerful mix of science, commerce and industry – the defining quality of the modern English (and British) experience – was denied by a self-image which, promoted by a powerful combination of aristocracy and literati, defined Englishness in terms of its own narrow reality. And, as this literary elite controlled the images and helped form the identities, it was not surprising that England's primary contribution to the Western world came to be seen exclusively for its artistic output, its land, its country houses – and not at all for its steam engines, its industrial organisation, accountancy practices or jet engines. No wonder, too, that the world's most urban country was exalted for its countryside; and, later, one of the most suburban of nations still projected itself as a land of broad acres.

And nowhere was this inversion of image and identity more total than in the attempt to rewrite the country's philosophic traditions. Britain has been one of the most practical of nations, with the most empirical of philosophic traditions – one of the most secular and, above all, the most rational. Indeed, British thinkers helped pioneer the Enlightenment, the age of reason and science. Yet we now tend to tell ourselves that the Enlightenment was essentially foreign (principally French, therefore certainly foreign!). Quite simply this idea of Britain as a foremost intellectual champion of reason has been 'written out of history' by conservative writers such as Edmund Burke as part of the making of the myth that Britain possessed no serious radical tradition which, based upon reason, appealed to universal principles. And, in the process, this myth even succeeded in marginalising the centrality and importance of Isaac Newton, Charles Darwin and T. E. Huxley. 'Abstract theories' (or 'abstractions' or indeed 'crazed abstractions'), conservatives told us, had no roots in Britain, certainly not in England; we British stood for history, tradition and 'accumulated wisdom'.

Only lately have revisionists sought to correct this record. Richard Crossman argued that 'only a moment's serious consideration is necessary in order to see that theory and speculative thought are by no means foreign to the British mind'.[2] And in the world of contemporary commentary it has taken a foreigner, the American Irving Kristol, to attempt to set the record straight by commending the British on their contribution to the age of reason. He argued that the Protestant Reformation, 'a British mood if there ever was one', played a seminal role in advancing secular ideas by severely weakening the irrational authority of the church; that Francis Bacon 'exemplifies perfectly' the primacy of reason; and that Britons have taken the lead in 'modern scientific modes of thinking about natural phenomena'.[3]

Also, there is now an increasing understanding that an English Enlightenment predated the French. It was English radicals such as John Toland, Charles Blount and Matthew Tindal and other freethinkers – many of them setting themselves in opposition to the priestly character of the Church of England in the late seventeenth century – who developed many of the ideas later taken up by French thinkers such as Voltaire and Diderot.[4] Many of these ideas sprang from the notion that reason as much as religion should be the basis for constructing a just society.

More importantly still, official Englishness distorted the very identity of the people themselves. The official ideology insisted that the image of the Englishman – the epitome of the country's success – was an aristocrat, or at the very least an aristocratic gentleman – tied to the land. Later, during the age of Empire, this typical successful Englishman would become an imperial administrator, a person still, of course, possessed of the aristocratic, paternalist values. Yet, again, the reality was very different. Britain's success as a nation was based upon its unique economic performance in the eighteenth and nineteenth centuries, an economic lift-off engineered by the commercial prowess of a new and vibrant business class – drawn from a much wider social base than the aristocracy. As one writer put it, 'the wellspring of its unique expansion came not from the aristocracy but from more practical, less well-born men of the middle or even the working classes'.[5]

And the social attitudes of these business Englishmen were inherently commercial. Many of them came from dissenting Protestant faiths – Quakers, Presbyterians, Congregationalists, Methodists – imbued with Calvinist instincts. Joel Kotkin sees this Calvinism as utterly crucial to an understanding of the British, and their economic success. Calvinism united capitalism and religion by arguing that work had a spiritual dimension.

Work was good, not just necessary. And it was this precept that helped the new British business classes develop their famed 'work ethic'. Calvinism was also crucial in helping the business classes reject the feudal, anti-commercial ethic of Catholicism – and much of Anglicanism – which still sought to subordinate individual economic achievement to the moral authority of the church. It was also scornful of aristocrats: 'To Calvin the profits of the artisan, merchant or speculator were no less worthy than the rents harvested by the land-owning aristocracy.' Calvin himself asked 'what reason is there why the income from business should not be larger than that from landowning?'[6]

Of course, these commercial instincts of Britons and Englishmen were very much to the fore during the building of Empire (though not necessarily during its later administration). Kotkin has argued that what he calls 'the British diaspora' (the Empire) had little to do with *la mission civilitrice* (the French idea of civilising and politically incorporating the colonial peoples) and much to do with 'money, not glory', with 'the search for markets, resources and, where possible, prospective lands for new economically viable colonies'.[7]

Yet these business British – with their Protestant, work-ethic values – were to become of little account in the forging of the national identity which was proceeding during the nineteenth century and emerged as a finished product in the popular press and media world of the twentieth century. In 1863, Richard Cobden, during the height of the great British capitalist boom, could reveal his great despair that feudalism's instincts and habits were returning:

> We have the spirit of feudalism rife and rampant in the midst of the antagonistic development of the age of Watt, Arkwright and Stephenson! Nay, feudalism is more and more in the ascendant in political and social life. So great is its power and prestige that it

> draws clear to it the support and homage of even those who are the natural leaders of the newer and better civilisation. Manufacturers and merchants as a rule seem only to desire riches that they prostrate themselves at the feet of feudalism. How is this to end?[8]

It was not to end. For by the mid-twentieth century Britain, the home of the bourgeoisie, the first society to create a serious middle class, none the less evoked as its national image the life of the aristocracy. And, just as perversely, the land of the Protestant business ethic – and the broader 'work ethic' – portrayed its national virtues as upper-class leisure, effortlessness, even idleness. Working for a living became somewhat socially suspect; money should be inherited not earned, hidden not flaunted.

In the political realm the idea of Englishness also served to deny reality. By any test Britain (and earlier England) possessed a rich history of political liberalism. Magna Carta, the English Civil War and Commonwealth, the settlement of 1688 – all confirmed the country as a leader in limiting the power of kings and centralised executive authority. Indeed the politics of England, before the French Revolution, was not only considered liberal by the conservative, traditionalist European standards, but positively anarchic, even revolutionary. Britain 'had a European reputation, whether admired or abhorred, as a politically volatile people given to regicide and rebellion', indeed possessing 'a revolutionary past'.[9]

Also, any society which over the years could produce Thomas Hobbes, John Locke, Adam Smith, Jeremy Bentham, Herbert Spencer, and James and John Stuart Mill must take pride of place in the history of individual and civil rights (even though Britain has not, even yet, codified or entrenched these rights). Yet this most liberal of national histories – that same history which was to produce the great Victorian liberalism (of the

Liberal Party, free trade, and, for its time, open government) – never quite translated into a modern liberal identity for the twentieth century. As the growing United States took over the mantle of liberalism, then Britain began to pride itself not on its history of liberties and rights – far too abstract! – but rather upon the traditions of its polity and the merits of its slowly evolving constitution. Twentieth-century constitutionalists like Sir Ivor Jennings, Professor Hood Phillips and Sir Kenneth Weare have all followed in the footsteps of the nineteenth-century conservatives Walter Bagehot and Albert Venn Dicey, who perfected the notion of Britain's traditionalism and organic development as being virtuous.[10]

By the mid-twentieth century, the reality of national decline tended, for a time, to reinforce this denial of Britain's history as a dynamic, liberal, industrial culture. As the country lost its industrial, scientific and technological lead then the initial reaction was to turn even more fervently to the alternative identity of England and Englishness as essentially artistic, literary, spiritual and contemplative – the presumptuous image of 'England as Athens' to 'America's Rome'. 'England as Athens' must have seemed all that was left. Yet, by the time, in 1959, when C. P. Snow fluttered the intellectual dovecots with his 'two cultures' thesis – the great *crie de coeur* on behalf of the country's lost virtues of science and reason – the long-awaited reaction was setting in. The country, for so long force-fed with the drug of 'Englishness', was beginning to dry out.

As the contours of the real Britain began to emerge, and the British slowly began to emerge from under the conformity of Englishness, and discover their true selves, the essential diversity of Britain and the British became increasingly apparent. Instead of one identity – the single, total (totalitarian), official, conception built around the idea of 'the English gentleman' and the United Kingdom (Ukania as Tom

Nairn has incisively described it) – the real Britain possessed several identities. Instead of 'one nation' the real Britain played host to several of them.

The theory of British nationhood rests upon the proposition that Britain's unitary constitution is rooted in the foundation of a broadly uniform culture where Britons share a common identity. Those who promote this 'one nation' thesis – amongst political scientists, analysts such as Jean Blondel and Samuel Finer — argue that modernisation has created in Britain one of the most homogeneous of all the industrial nations – and that social differences based upon nationality, language and religion have virtually been eradicated.[11] 'One nation' theorists have also tended to argue that regional economic inequalities are much less pronounced in Britain than in many other industrial countries – that levels of income and social provision are broadly similar throughout Britain.[12]

Furthermore, 'one nation' proponents argue that in modern times this essential homogeneity has been reinforced by the the heavily centralised London-based mass media who provide the same messages and shared experiences to a British-wide audience. Yet, one of the intriguing aspects of this 'homogeneity' is the way in which Northern Ireland is often left out of the analysis. Because of its deep religious (and ethnic) divisions, not only between the two antagonistic Northern Ireland communities but also between the Irish of Northern Ireland (and their religiosity) and the rest of the British (with their primarily secular culture), Northern Ireland and the Northern Irish fit uneasily into the United Kingdom; their support for the Union (of Northern Ireland and Great Britain) being more to do with necessity than with a homogeneous 'one nation' common identity. So weak is the common identity between the Northern Irish and the rest of Britain that the Liberals almost succeeded in releasing the whole of

Ireland from Britain in the 1920s, only to be thwarted by a last-minute military insurrection caused by Protestant fears rather than common loyalties and identities.

In the rest of Celtic Britain, in Scotland and Wales, a 'common identity' – between Scots and Welsh and the various regional peoples of England – is also fairly weakly felt. One of the most intriguing aspects of Celtic consciousness, of Scottish and Welsh separateness, is that, after centuries of British structures and Union propaganda the last half of the twentieth century has seen Scottish and Welsh political nationalism – parties which specifically reject not only the Union but the idea of a common identity within Great Britain or the United Kingdom – on a rising curve. The two separatist parties (the Scottish National Party and Plaid Cymru, the Welsh Nationalist Party) achieved a paltry 27,288 votes between them (0.1 per cent of the total UK electorate) in the general election of 1950. By 1964 this figure had risen to 133,551 (0.5 per cent), but by October 1974 it had risen to over 1 million (1,005,938, or 3.5 per cent of the total UK population, and in Scotland providing 14 seats to the SNP). Ever since this breakthrough year of 1974 certainly the Scottish separatist political movement has always been a serious electoral player, constantly threatening to become Scotland's largest single party. And, of course, in 2014 with the referendum and again in 2015 with its spectacular landslide in the Westminster elections (when it won 58 seats out of 59) it has now become the premier party of Scotland – as the country stands on the verge of Home Rule and/or independence.

I wrote in 1996 that 'as the writ of the European Union runs ever deeper, then the Celtic nationalist parties may be expected to achieve even more significant results in the next century. One of the SNP's major electoral problems was that it lost votes because many Scots felt it would be isolated should it become independent. 'An independent Scotland Within Europe' (the slogan of the SNP in recent general elections) would seem to overcome that particular disadvantage. (Should Scotland secede from the British Union, the UK-state, there are still some unresolved questions about whether such a 'successor' nation state could automatically become a member of the European Union with all the rights that entails. There is also a question about whether, in these circumstances, England would also be a 'successor' state and thus have to reapply for membership. It was, after all, the United Kingdom – and not England, Scotland, Wales and Northern Ireland separately – that joined the European Community in 1973.)

The obvious conclusion is that the spread of industrialism, the British single market, and the later 'homogenising' consequences of the media and information revolutions, and, of course, the common nationhood which the ideology of Englishness attempted to create, were simply not able to fully forge a common identity throughout the British Isles. This failure may have several causes. One, of course, may simply be the debilitating morale-sapping effects of national decline. The Scots and the Welsh, like everyone else, prefer to back winners, and Britain and the UK can no longer deliver (as they certainly could during the Empire) success, or even much of a sense of progress. Another explanation may lie in the economic realm. Although present levels of social provision, even income, may not vary (between the regions and nations of Britain) as much as 'North-South' divide protagonists tend to suggest, the phenomenon of Celtic nationalism may, in part, be the product of regional economic and social inequalities built up during the early, and defining, era of industrialism.

But, just as importantly, the lack of a strong common identity, of an unbreakable British national sentiment, may simply be because of the colonial character of the construction of Britain and the United Kingdom.The Union between England and Scotland (and earlier between England and Wales) was not forged by mutual agreement, common affection and identity, or by votes (as was Britain's accession to the Treaty of Rome in the referendum of 1975); rather it was settled on the battlefield, a product of bloodshed and *force majeure*. According to Michael Hechter, Scotland and Wales were essentially colonised (by southern English elites and their collaborators). He suggests that two models of development can be set out to explain the historic relationship between Britain's two largest ethnic groups – the Anglo-Saxons and the Celts. First, the 'diffusion' model in which the smaller group (Celts) slowly melds into the larger, leading to ethnic homogeneity and a lasting common identity; and secondly, the 'internal colonial' model in which contact between the two groups is never completely resolved, leading to conflict and continuing separate consciousness.[13] The continuing robustness of Scottish and Welsh nationalism suggests that the latter model was the more relevant.

This cultural diversity – or lack of a common identity – also reflects itself in the racial and ethnic make-up of Britain – a make-up which has been changing for many years. The 1991 census revealed that over 2,600,000 people whose head of household had been born in the new Commonwealth now lived in Britain (433,641 from the Caribbean, 312,155 from East Africa, 149,835 from the rest of Africa, 161,179 from Bangladesh, 692,692 from India, 441,869 from Pakistan and 175,477 from South-East Asia). It also revealed that over 780,000 Britons were Irish by derivation and just under 1,500,000 were from the 'rest of the world'. By the time of the 2011 census Britain's Asian population amounted to almost 7% of the total population, and Black British had reached 3%, with Mixed or multiple ethnicities being 2%. Of course, the non-white population is concentrated in certain cities and regions. For instance, in the 2011 census the non-white population of the Northwest was 13% of the total (with Greater Manchester registering 20.2% non-white and Manchester proper totalling 40.7% non-white); in West Yorkshire the percentage of non-whites was 21.6%; in the East Midlands it was 14.6% (Leicester was 54.9%); in the West Midlands it was 21.8% (Birmingham 46.9%); and in London, the most ethnically diverse of all the regions, its non-white population was 55.1%.[14] Thus, the British Isles is unquestionably a multiracial and multi-ethnic society.

Racial and ethnic diversity in the British Isles has been further entrenched by the 'pluralistic' approach adopted by successive British governments. In essence this has meant that no serious attempt to integrate – compared, say, to the French model which seeks assimilation into 'French culture' – has been undertaken in Britain. As in the multiracial United States, so in multiracial Britain: separate racially-based societies not only exist, but have been encouraged to exist, in urban ghettos, a process further encouraged by 'faith schools'. This informal segregation of races (and religions) naturally produces separate political leaderships and a system of bargaining and manoeuvring for group benefits. Whatever the merits of this segregation a 'common identity', a sense of common Britishness, remains somewhat chimeric.

There is little that is new in this racial/ethnic diversity and separateness. Rodney Hilton suggests that

> it could be argued that since prehistoric times the country has been invaded and settled by successive ethnic groups – Celts, Romans, Angles, Jutes, Saxons, Danes, Norwegians, Normans, Bretons, French – who sufficiently kept their separate identity to deprive England, during this period, of any Englishness...[and the idea that there was no such thing

> as Englishness] could be reinforced by pointing to an indigenous population speaking one language and a ruling class [Normans] speaking another, its cultural identity still outside this newly conquered land.[15]

Later, Huguenots and Jews, like more recent immigrants seeing their port of entry as the large cities, further added to the ethnic diversity of Britain. Of course, by the time the West Indians, the Pakistanis and the Indians came to Britain – during the late 1950s, 1960s, and 1970s – the earlier ethnic immigrations had already become assimilated to the point of invisibility. These new immigrants will not be invisible in the same way – a distinctiveness, together with new religious identities, which will serve to intensify cultural diversity.

The story of British cultural diversity, though, does not end with the multiracial scene. Late twentieth-century Britain may no longer be divided by religion in the sense that sixteenth-century England was; however, a survey of religious belief (and non-belief) shows a pattern rich in diversity. By the early 1990s Roman Catholics represented the largest single Christian religious grouping (over 2.04 million church members), slightly ahead of Anglicans (1.81 million) and Presbyterians (1.24 million). More interestingly there were more Muslims (over half a million) than Methodists, more Sikhs (over a quarter of a million) than Baptists, and more Hindus than Jews. In the 2011 census 59.3% of respondents stated that they were Christians, down 12.4% from previous census, 25.1% that they had no religion, up 10%, Muslims represented 4.8% of the survey, up 18%, Hindus 1.5%, up 0.5% and Sihks 0.8%, up 0.3%. The census however needs to be read alongside less formal and official surveys – one such, from YouGov showing that only 29% of respondents claimed to be 'religious' whereas 65% claimed to be 'non-religious'. It would seem that majority opinion in modern Britain is essentially secular, that religious sentiment in the white community is falling whereas religiosity amongst non-whites is stable.[16] It would seem axiomatic that the increasing Islamic presence in some of the inner cities in the midst of Britain's essentially secular society – will hardly foster 'one nation' common identities.[17]

This racial and religious diversity often leads to violence. The idea – perpetrated by the ideology of Englishness – that the English are a peaceable people, living a tranquil and civilised existence has always been mythical. The country's history is as violent as that of any other of its kind, and even in the twentieth century its racial, religious and class divisions have often spilled over into social unrest. In August 1958 serious race disturbances broke out in London's Notting Hill district. During the 1980s – in Bristol, Manchester, Brixton and other inner city areas – the country witnessed race riots on the American model. Earlier examples of street violence, though, were hidden from view by censorship of information. In the summer of 1919 in Cardiff, Newport and Liverpool there were race riots which never reached the headlines. Mining villages saw disturbances during the 1920s and 30s. Religious differences – between Protestants and Catholics – sparked numerous instances of sectarian violence in Glasgow and Liverpool during the first half of the twentieth century. Violence erupted at football matches and at marches of unemployed people – although films of these events were regularly banned (in 1932 the violence on a hunger march was filmed by Paramount Pictures but not shown publicly). And, again in the 1930s, the regular clashes between Blackshirts and Communists often turned violent.[18]

In such a society of diversity – of national, ethnic, racial, religious (let alone class and regional) differences – what is it that unites the peoples of the British isles? What, in the twenty-first century, does it mean to be British? What is it that provides the 'common identity' so often claimed by 'one nation' theorists? The answer is: increasingly little.

Certainly, for the moment – in the early years of the twenty-first century – all the peoples of Britain share a common political and legal life. All Britons, irrespective of national ethnic, religious, class and regional divisions, live under common laws in a common political unit. Yet, this particular legal (and legalist) form – the British nation-state – is a waning reality, as both the European Union and the pressures of globalisation bear down upon it.

As well as a common legal status the peoples of Britain share a common language. Whether you are a Scot from the Highlands, a Pakistani in Bradford or a Welsh hill farmer your primary means of communication *in the public sphere at least* will be English. Yet, this commonality provided by the English language – which some Britons believed helped define them and 'separate them off' from others – is eroding fast: for this 'common language' of English is now shared with millions and millions of others outside of the home base. Today, English ranks second only to Chinese in the numbers of speakers, and its world-wide reach is increasingly hegemonic. It is the world's leading 'second tongue', it is the language of science and international business, and – because of the influence of American popular culture and media technology – the language too of the global 'infotainment' industry. Most importantly it is becoming, unofficially, the primary language of the European Union.

> Even an emerging trans-European economy will likely do little to reduce English's leadership. Already both German and French firms employ English as their *lingua franca* for international business. Similarly, German, the language of Europe's premier economic power, has not even expanded beyond the less than 100 million speakers it possessed in 1925.[19]

As with German, French seems unlikely to to be able to challenge English in the European Union – particularly amongst the peoples. The English language appears simply unstoppable; and although it no longer defines the English it begins to appear as the greatest of all gifts from the English to the world.

Does England Exist?

If the modern British do not possess the characteristics necessary to forge a strong common national identity, what of the English? What of England, the heartland, the home of 'Englishness' itself?

England is essentially a geographic unit – comprising the counties bounded in the north by Hadrian's Wall, in the south by the English Channel, in the west by the Welsh border, the Atlantic Ocean and the Irish Sea, and in the East by the North Sea. It is not a nation-state, and it is not represented at the United Nations, yet it does appear on formal governmental political documents, usually referring to laws and policies for 'England and Wales', and in a peculiar hangover, it – together with Scotland, Wales and Northern Ireland – possesses its own 'national' football team.

Yet, although 'England' has for almost three centuries been subsumed by 'Britain', many British people still think of themselves as 'English', and some viscerally so. The self-description 'English' is used by many amongst the majority white, non-Celtic population of the British Isles. A 2012 study concluded that 'The English component [of British national identity] is increasingly considered the primary source of attachment for the English' and that 'the proportion of the population that prioritise their English over their British identity (40%) is now twice as large as that which prioritise their British over their English (16%).'[20]

Does this suggested sense of common 'English' identity really exist even amongst these non-Celtic English? In England, and amongst the majority population, are there serious binding commonalities to be discovered beyond the simple assertion of being 'English'?

One problem for the 'one nation' – 'one England' – theorists is that the majority non – Celtic English population are about as diverse and fragmented a people as are the wider British. When, inevitably, the idea of England as a common singular idea has been conjured up – as in 'England Expects' – the question was always, still is: which England?

The fact is that the hold of the attempted unifying culture – of 'Englishness' – was always patchy. In large parts of the north of England it hardly existed. In the land far from London, Oxford and Stratford-upon-Avon – of chapels and industry, pit villages and working-class communities – 'Englishness' imbued little. And even in the south of England (South of a line drawn from the Wash to the Severn) its writ did not run universally. The heartland of deep Englishness was to be found in the home counties and most of the small towns, but there was less of a presence in the big cities and their suburbs. Indeed the light industrial suburban 'ribbon development' which spread out to the west of London during the interwar period was the raw material for J. B. Priestley's 'New England' – so new, he argued, that it was 'not really England at all'.

Disraeli helped to unmask the myth of a common English identity when in *Sybil* he coined the term 'two nations'. Yet, of course, England was, and is, a land not just of two but of 'many nations'. And a sign of the sheer persistence of England's 'many nations' is the continuing – right up until modern times – cultural distinctiveness of the English regions. In the very means of communication, in the markedly varied accents and dialects (with all that implies for attitudes and lifestyles) the tale is told. And are the real distinctions between Cockneys, Brummies, Scousers, Yorkshiremen and women, Geordies, East Anglians and West Country people any less marked than between any of them and, say, the populations of the more recognised 'nations' of Scotland and Wales? And, aren't some of these serious cultural distinctions amongst the English much more pronounced than those that exist amongst people in more homogeneous cultures such as the United States, Germany or Scandinavia?

These cultural regions have persisted through, and beyond, the attempted 'hegemony' of 'Englishness'; indeed they survived the massive attempt to standardise dialects following the introduction of Received Pronunciation (RP) in the early twentieth century. Developed – as we have seen – as a 'suitable' accent for an imperial governing class, RP was adopted after 1920 by the BBC which used its monopolistic power over information and manners in an emerging mass society in an attempt to standardise the way people spoke English. In the process regional accents and dialects were derided socially – as being 'lower class', even though in previous eras regional accents had possessed no class connotations;

> Sir Robert Peel (Harrow and Oxford) one of England's most famous Conservative Prime Ministers, never disguised his Midlands speech. Lord Stanley, later Eighteenth Earl of Derby (Rugby and Cambridge), spoke a 'sort of Lancashire patois'. His Liberal Opponent William Gladstone, spent his childhood in Liverpool and his Lancashire 'burr' survived both Eton and Oxford, which suggests that there was virtually no social pressure to lose it. Even at Eton, the shrine of English private education, the Revd J. L. Joynes, one of the poet Swinburne's tutors, is known to have pronounced 'died' as 'doyed', and to have attacked the 'oidle' in his sermons.[21]

Yet, the attempt to impose a standard dialect ultimately failed. This failure can be seen in the skin-deep character of RP (or 'posh') English. Those elites in Britain who speak RP often picked it up quite consciously (or even, like Margaret Thatcher, by elocution lessons), and, like Margaret Thatcher, will in moments of crisis or intense feeling often revert to their original regional accent – in her case Lincolnshire. This failure can also be seen not just in the persistence of regional accents, but in their triumph. For instance, in the southeast and the 'home counties', the supposed homeland of RP and standardised English, it is the regional accent of Cockney (or Cockney mixed with 'standardised speech') which increasingly holds sway. Cockney is the genuine dialect of London, the original sixteenth-century accent of all Londoners who were not part of the court. Its centre of gravity was the old East End – the area which runs from Bethnal Green through Limehouse to Aldgate in the City of London – but it also possesses rural, French and Yiddish roots.[22] As Cockney – under the influence of Londoners moving into the surrounding countryside – tends to crowd out both the standardised UK-wide Received Pronunciation of the upper income groups of the 'home counties' and the original accents of North Essex, South Suffolk, Kent, even Hampshire, a real southeastern consciousness – akin to that, say, of Yorkshire or the northeast, has begun to emerge.

This still powerful English cultural regionalism – with its attendant identities and loyalties – can, should a federal or devolved political system become a reality, give real meaning to new political regions in England. The North (comprising Cleveland, Cumbria, Durham, Northumberland, Tyne and Wear), Yorkshire and Humberside, The East Midlands (Derbyshire, Leicestershire, Lincolnshire, Northamptonshire, Nottinghamshire), East Anglia (Cambridgeshire,

Norfolk, Suffolk), the Southwest (Avon, Cornwall, Devon, Dorset, Gloucestershire, Somerset, Wiltshire), the Southeast (Bedfordshire, Berkshire, Buckinghamshire, East Sussex, Essex, Greater London, Hampshire, Hertfordshire, the Isle of Wight, Kent, Oxfordshire, Surrey and West Sussex), the West Midlands (the county of West Midlands, Hereford and Worcestershire, Shropshire, Staffordshire, Warwickshire) and the Northwest (Merseyside, Cheshire, Lancashire and Greater Manchester) – are all real regional-cum-cultural territories with media-centres ('capital cities') and local economies. And the loyalties and identities of their respective populations (certainly outside of the Southeast and East Midlands) are arguably more regionally-grounded than they are national and 'English'. And in London, identity as a Londoner may be just as strong as, in some cases stronger than, that of an English man or woman.

Yet as well as being divided 'horizontally' – by region and nation – the English are also seriously divided vertically – by the old-time religion of class. In modern England there remains a fairly strong relationship between 'regionality' and class – in the sense that, broadly – speaking, those people rooted in regional localities and possessed of regional identities and accents tend to be lower on the social and income scale than the transregional national elite (many of whom still tend to identify with 'Englishness' and with a national London-based culture). Britain's fundamental 'class problem' (the one which distinguishes it from the 'class problem' of most other Western societies) remains, at root, a cultural one. It involves divisions between people based as much upon corrosive social and psychological inequalities as on economic ones; and deep inequalities of dignity and worth, of aspirations and self-confidence, of education and life chances. England's private education sector (the public schools) still creates a somewhat separated and self-conscious elite (with dense social networks that provide a lifetime's advantage for their members).

Alongside these cultural class distinctions the English are also riven by striking inequalities in income and wealth, inequalities that are normally, though not always, coterminous with the cultural and psychological inequalities. Old regional distinctions created by industrialism, and sustained by more recent disparities between 'North' and 'South', have left their mark on living standards. By the early 1990s Greater London was 23 per cent better off than the average, the Southeast generally was 16 per cent better off than the average, and East Anglia was 2 per cent better off than the average; on the other hand, Yorkshire and Humberside was 7 per cent less well-off than the average, the Southwest was 6 per cent less well-off, and England's poorest region, the Northwest was 10 per cent worse-off.[23] Things have deteriorated in the last twenty years, as regional inequality within England – as measured by disposable household income in 2015 – has become 'the worst in Western Europe'. (And, intriguingly, inequality within the cities of southern England – London, Reading and Milton Keynes – is even worse than for England as a whole).[24]

The debate about how to rectify these disparities will no doubt continue; but the continuing fact of them punches a serious hole in the 'one nation' illusion. When people in the Southeast are over 30 per cent better off than those in the north, and when deep economic inequalities are appearing in southern cities, then notions of 'common identity' seem increasingly fanciful.

As well as these quite sharp regional distinctions, England has seen 'national' inequality worsen even further following the global financial crisis of 2008 and the consequent austerity policies. And by the end of the first decade of the new millenium Britain was one of the most unequal of western countries, displaying a fragmentation of the middle class and the alarming emergence of an oligarchy. Traditionally, sharp differences in income and wealth – indeed large-scale poverty – may have threatened the social fabric and the political stability of the British state, but they seemingly posed no real threat to national identity and sensibility. Now, though, the ability to appeal to patriotic or imperial glory as a means of creating a common 'national' identity and sensibility is much reduced.

The Meaning of 'Being English'

So, in such a diverse society what does it mean to be English? What is unique, and exceptional, about it? What are the commonalities that separate Englishness off from Scottishness or Welshness or Frenchness or, indeed, Chineseness? In fact is there anything more to being English than the simple fact of being born and living within the borders of the geographical unit called England?

In fact, it is easier to determine what Englishness is not. It is not, and never has been, a racial category. Thomas Sowell has argued that 'race is one of the ways of collectivising people in our minds'; yet the English cannot properly be so 'collectivised'.[25] If the non-whites living in England were excluded from calculations, then, racially, the English would certainly share the commonality of the Caucasian racial category but, crucially, they would also share being Caucasian with all the other Caucasians in Europe and North America. Thus, in this racial sense, Englishness is hardly a definition of Caucasian.

Yet, of course, the non-Caucasian populations of England cannot be excluded from the analysis. And the reality within the land called England of a multiracial (multi-ethnic) society robs Englishness not only of a racial definition, but also of a potential sense of separateness: the English are no different, in this respect, from the rest of the Western multiracial and multi-ethnic world. If race (or ethnicity) is no longer a unifying and defining 'commonality' for the English, what of the English language? Certainly the English language is a form of communication which the diversity of peoples in England share in common. Yet, as a source of unity, it should not be overstated. The still sharply divergent dialects – Cockney can probably still be understood England-wide, though not a broad version of Scouse or Brummie – remain a major source of cultural distinctiveness and continue to weaken a common identity.

Indeed language has little automatic connection with nation-states. There are certainly examples of national identity being forged out of a common language. One such is Romania – which separates itself from the Hungarian and Slavic languages surrounding it. Also, 'the use of German helped Bavarians and Saxons and Wurttembergers to see themselves as German and to identify with one another at a higher level of identity'. And Japan represents the 'clearest and most outstanding example of the type in the whole world'.[26]

But there are also numerous examples of nation-states which do not possess a common language. Switzerland is an example of the 'one nation-several languages' model. So too is Belgium (Dutch and French) and Britain (English, the various Celtic languages, and a host of Indian and Asian languages). In the USA several languages now essentially compete with English, and the US authorities still refuse to designate English as an official language.

Indeed, 'nationality may predict the language but the language will not predict nationality'. English-speakers can be British, American, Australian, New Zealanders or Irish. Arabic-speakers can be Iraqi and Egyptian. Portuguese-speakers can be Portuguese but also Brazilian. An analyst argues: 'It is because of its potential to establish identities that have nothing to do with local self, the family self, the national self, that I regard the "one language-many nations" model of language use as the most promising for the future.'[27]

Indeed the English language, although often promoted as a crucial attribute of Englishness (that is a distinctive cultural form separating us from the rest of Europe), is no longer, if it ever was, the property of the people of England only, and thus a source of separate identity.

The English people now share their English language with the world. Under the influence of Empire – and, more recently, because of the popular success of American international business, information and media, and, of course, the appeal of Hollywood, English has now emerged as the world's most influential language. A language spoken by only 1.5 million people on an off-shore island in the eleventh century 'today ranks second only to Chinese in the number of speakers, with as many as 700 million users... Most important, it is spoken commonly in more countries, and on more continents, than any other language...By 1980, nearly 100 million non-English speakers – three out of five of them Asian – were studying some variant of the Queen's English.'[28] English is the unofficial second language of the European Union; when Germans and French people wish to speak to each other they do so, usually, in English. English is increasingly the *lingua franca* of international business, and is already the language of science and technology and, crucially, information. It has been estimated that 80 per cent of the information stored in electronic retrieval systems is written in English.

This worldwide appeal of English begs the large question (around which a lively debate still swirls) of the importance of language in informing national identity.

The view that 'nationality' classifications are essentially 'cultural' ones, and that these are (or rather must be) linguistic classifications' – in other words, that 'the criterion of nationhood is language' – is broadly supported by the philosopher Ernest Gellner. Yet this view is challenged by Professor Anthony Smith in his major work on nationalism, where he casts a critical eye over the importance of language to both culture and nationality. He argues that 'culture' is a far broader concept than 'language' – 'culture includes customs, the ancestry myth, institutions, history, law, and particularly religion'. And he also questions the assumptions of some nationalist theorists (both Gellner and Elie Kedourie) that there actually exists a universal need to belong – which a common language satisfies.

> Human beings, after all, do very often feel a strong desire to return to some cosy security with a routine of habits and activities; when such a pattern has been suddenly overturned. But even here it would be rash to generalise. Some may actually feel liberated from the routine, others may fluctuate in their attitudes to it...In other words, the question of individuals' needs, desires and habits requires empirical investigation in each case. It cannot be settled from such a priori assumptions.[29]

So, if race and ethnicity, as well as language, no longer adequately serve to define Englishness as a discrete and separate identity, does culture (using the word in its broadest sense, as meaning way of life)? Is there a nationality of art, of science, of consumer goods and services? Is there such a thing as 'English science'? 'English art'? 'English consumer goods'/ Certainly, there is science, art and goods which have originated in England. Yet, to fly in a jet aircraft – even though the jet engine was first developed in England – is not a particularly 'English experience'. Nor is there anything uniquely English about watching, or acting in, a play by Shakespeare (now performed throughout the world).

Also, in the modern mass-consumer society, food, clothes, cars and consumer durables are the great artefacts of globalism, the products of a transnational interlinked and interdependent economy. National distinctions – in terms of where the product was born or indeed is made – are increasingly meaningless. Although the marketing industry likes to differentiate products on the basis of country – the 'English' examples being leather goods, rural sports equipment and clothing ('Riders and Squires'), 'country house' and 'country cottage' furniture and fabrics, and foods such as marmalade, marmite and roast beef – these so-called 'English' products are not only consumed by millions of foreigners worldwide but are also often made abroad. As of writing, Crabtree and Evelyn is owned by an American multinational.

Background Not Country

Many English people would, though, still rebel against the idea that 'being English' has little meaning, only amounting to little more than a legal and geographic notion. For them 'being English' has real content and meaning, and represents a distinctive identity – separate from that of 'other' identities.

Yet, are the believed distinctions really national ones, or are they separated identities based upon different upbringings, backgrounds and familiarities? Certainly, the sights, sounds, smells and images of youth tend to breed separate familiarities, sensibilities and identities. French, German and Chinese people will all have separate youthful 'national' experiences which make them distinctive, and which may make them feel part of one particular identity ('we') which is thought to separate them from 'other' identities.

Indeed these youthful memories and sensibilities – memories and sensibilities shared with others of the same general background – may be at the core of the very idea and feeling of 'country'. Beyond the formal issues of laws and passports this shared background (or belief in a shared background) may be the very stuff of contemporary patriotism. Patriotism – or love of country – it is suggested is a perennial part of human life whereas nationalism is a product of recent times.

However, the sense of patriotism, the idea of love of country, may have little to do with 'country' or 'nationality'. It may, in fact, be little more than a love of background and familiarity – the familiar sights, sounds and smells of youth. Background and nationality may indeed overlap, particularly in countries small enough to foster a bond of common memories. Yet England has been so sharply divided by class and region (even locality) that shared 'national' memories – the sights and sounds and smells of youth – are rather few. What common memories would unite a working-class upbringing in Manchester with an upper middle-class 'compatriot' in a public school in rural Sussex. Also, what common memories would unite differing backgrounds in the same region – say, an upbringing in urban Sheffield with that in the North Riding, or inner-city London with the rural rides of Sussex only a few miles away? Or, even, what common memories would unite same-class upbringings in different regions of England? Are an unemployed Cockney's memories and familiarities in any sense the same as those of an unemployed Geordie from Middlesbrough? And are any of these distinctive upbringings, or those of their respective ancestors in other centuries, productive of a 'common identity'?

During the industrial age, the spread of technology and mass information has, of course, brought certain 'national' events and images to England's diverse population, thus creating a degree of 'national' commonality and community. Almost every English person brought up during the 1950s would, thus, share in common certain formal or 'political' memories – the Festival of Britain, the coronation of Elizabeth II, the visit to Wembley Stadium of the victorious 1956 Hungarian football team, the first televised test matches. And most English people alive today would also have shared the films, television, radio programmes and newspapers – and all the cultural paraphernalia of the British state (and Americanised British mass-popular culture) in the postwar years.

And, as for the English of the future: it is unlikely that the consciousness of 'being English' will disappear altogether. Instead, the sense of Englishness will increasingly co-exist with other important identities, and may even take second or third place to some of them.

Notes

1. Martin Weiner, *English Culture and the Decline of the Industrial Spirit, 1850-1980*, New York, 1987, Preface.
2. Richard Crossman, *Planning for Freedom*, London, 1965, pp. 3-4.
3. *Commentary Magazine*, New York, August 1991.
4. See Justin Champion, *The Pillars of Priestcraft Shaken*, Cambridge, 1992.
5. Joel Kotkin, *Tribes*, New York, 1992, p. 80.
6. Quoted in ibid., p. 80.
7. Ibid., p. 71.
8. John Morley, *The Life of Richard Cobden*, vol. II, London, 1981, pp. 481-2.
9. Jack Lively and Adam Lively, 'Introduction', *Democracy in Britain*, Oxford, 1982, p. 27.

10. For a comprehensive modern constitutional text book see Philip Norton, *The Constitution in Flux*, Oxford, 1982, p. 27.
11. For a discussion of this view see Arthur F. Midwinter et al., *Politics and Public Policy in Scotland*, London, 1991.
12. See H. M. Drucker and Gordon Brown, *The Politics of Nationalism and Devolution*, London, 1980; and Richard Rose, *Understanding the United Kingdom*, London 1981.
13. See Hechter, op. cit.
14. Source, Census, Office of Population Statistics. 1991 and 2011.
15. Rodney Hilton, in Samuel (ed), vol. 1, p. 39.
16. Source: *Social Trends*, Central Statistical Office.
17. *Social Trends*, 1994, p. 145. The YouGov poll was published in March 2011.
18. The BBC broadcast a survey of unpublicised mass violence in Britain in 'Forbidden Britain' series, 17 November 1994, BBC2.
19. Kotkin, op. cit., p. 24.
20. Richard Wyn-Jones et al., IPPR report, January 2012.
21. McCrum et al., op. cit., p. 24.
22. See McCrum, op. cit., pp. 271-83.
23. Figures from *Social Trends*, 24, 1994, p. 79, Central Statistical Office.
24. *Inequality Briefing*, from the High Pay Centre, 26 June 2015.
25. Thomas Sowell, *Race and Culture: A World View*, New York, 1994.
26. Quotation from Professor Randolf Quirk, 'Nation Speaking unto Nation', *Sunday Times*, 17 April 1994.
27. Ibid.
28. Kotkin, op. cit., p. 75.
29. Anthony D. Smith, *Theories of Nationalism*. 2nd ed., London, 1983, p. 144.

Five
The Break-up of the Brexit State

The weakness of the unitary British Westminster state had been obvious for some decades before Brexit. But the referendum decision in 2016 to leave the EU has strengthened Celtic separatism – in Scotland and Northern Ireland – to the point where the break-up of the 300-year-old union is now on the cards. This chapter looks at what can be done to save the United Kingdom. Or, if it is over, what can be done to secure the future stability of the British Isles.

The future stability of the British Isles will depend on the dynamic unleashed in Scotland and Northern Ireland as increasing numbers of people within these two Celtic areas of the UK seek separatist futures – an independent Scotland and a united Ireland. Intriguingly, as of writing in the spring of 2017, the British Brexit government, and the British Conservative party behind it, seem to be very relaxed about Celtic separatism. And the reason is simple: British Tories see their future as very much enhanced by Scotland and Northern Ireland leaving the union – as, they believe, 'England Alone' will produce endless Tory governments and become a Tory bastion.

There are, though, two very serious, perhaps fatal, downsides for the Brexiteers as they look forward to their 'England Alone' future. First, no one should forget that the British monarchy – and Queen Elizabeth 2 and her successors – is an institution inextricably linked to the union, to the United Kingdom of Great Britain and Northern Ireland, and that should the union dissolve then the future of the monarchy itself will be weakened and may even come into question. The Queen herself has made it clear that she identifies with and has sworn allegiance to the UK and not England. In the Queen's speech to both Houses of Parliament in 1977 she pointedly reminded her audience that she was 'crowned Queen of the United Kingdom of Great Britain and Northern Ireland.' More recently, during the Scottish referendum campaign of 2014, she was reported, by Prime Minister David Cameron, to have been deeply worried about Scottish independence. Thus, the problem for Brexiteers is that the aging Queen and the stability of the monarchy are huge assets for their cause – but these great symbols of their beloved 'British sovereignty', 'British independence' and 'British Greatness' could become collateral damage as Brexit induces the break-up of the kingdom.

A more profound problem for the Brexit future is that any threatened break-up of the union will have a seriously negative effect on the global markets and on general confidence in Britain itself. If a narrative takes hold that British institutions are no longer stable, and that the UK itself could actually split, then, together with the problem of confidence generated by Brexit, international financial faith in Britain could evaporate – leading to a serious run on sterling. This kind of crisis would leave the British Brexit government with next –to – no negotiating hand with our continental neighbours; and, if the British government refuses to agree terms with the EU – or walks out of the negotiations – it could send the country's relations with its European neighbours into a downward spiral of recriminations and hostility.

Yet, until very recently this potential constitutional earthquake has been both ignored and denied by the extraordinary complacency of the English Westminster and media establishment. And thus very little work has been done on plans and contingencies to stabilise the islands in the event of these potential constitutional emergencies.

Much, though, will depend on the Scottish and Northern Irish peoples. For example, if the Scots decide – either through an SNP decision or a NO vote in a future referendum – to stay in the union for a while longer then the opportunity exists at long last to create a written federal constitution for Britain – including 'Home Rule' for Scotland, Wales, Northern Ireland and the English regions. I outline below both the possible road to such a federal constitution, and what a new written constitution might look like.

Plan A: A Federal Constitution

The idea that Britain would be in need of a new constitution, or constitutional settlement, would, some years ago, have been unthinkable. It is not so today. With the Scots on the verge of ending the UK, the British ship of state is entering treacherous waters and is already listing through a lack of balance which a new federal constitution can help put right.

Yet, even should it be willed, the act of reforming Westminster and drawing up a federal system for the British people will be no small, nor easy, exercise. The whole idea, of course, will be controversial – not least because of the public perception that such a change would involve a new level of government and new expense (and expenses). It was this fear of extra levels and extra costs that defeated the November 2004 referendum in the North East of England (when 77% of the vote rejected a North-East Assembly and what could well have been the beginning of a devolution process that would spread throughout the rest of England). As any new exercise would be taking place in the shadow of the global financial crisis and the present era of austerity, public opinion would need to be even more satisfied that ultimately any change will either involve no extra cost or, better still, will serve to cut the cost of the government apparatus.

This will be a crucial condition and a prerequisite for any constitutional change. Thankfully, though, such concerns about cost will not now be a difficult condition to meet – particularly so in the era in which the Westminster Parliament is considered far too expensive and overpopulated. If federalist reforms are placed within the context of severely cutting the large number of MPs and the huge number of peers they could even become popular.

Once the cost issue is resolved then by far the easiest and quickest way forward would be for the existing Parliament to draft a new, written, constitution. In less crisis-ridden times this might be acceptable, but to hand over such a fundamental task to politicians in the Commons, and to unelected peers in the Lords, in an era when politicians have lost so much credibility and legitimacy, would be taking serious risks with public support for the process.

So, if Parliament as the drafter will not be acceptable then the fall-back position is for Parliament to create some kind of Constitutional Convention to do the job. This Convention would need to be drawn from a wide cross section of the public: realistically-speaking this would mean leaders from the nations and regions, from business and trade unions, from the private and public sector, from universities, schools and hospitals, from

NGOs and so on, as well as the Westminster politicians.

Of course, such a Convention will likely, just like the Philadelphia convention in the USA over two centuries ago, be a contentious, even raucous, affair – with many competing interests and ideologies in conflict. In any such convention populist and creative ideas will abound, but, hopefully, they will be tempered by expertise and experience. And in drawing up this new constitution those who chair the proceedings will, thankfully, be able to draw not just on our own rich history of constitutional thinking but also on a wealth of experience from successful existing foreign federal systems.

One of the very first decisions to be taken will be over the federal issue itself. As the Convention would only have been called in order to make the change, federalism as such would not be contentious. However, the federal principle – that decision-making authority should be entrenched at various levels of government in a written constitution – would need to be set out in detail with the competences of the various levels spelt out: what powers for the central government, for the nations, regions, cities and so on.

Another very early decision for the drafters will centre around whether at 'federal level' we should opt for a Parliamentary system (with a Prime Minister) or a Presidential system. Should we go for the former – a more familiar design – then the German constitution, which British lawyers helped to draw up after the war, would be a good guide.[1] If however we opt for a Presidential system then the American federal constitution or the constitution of the Fifth French Republic could serve as more than useful guides.[2] My own view is that it would be best to opt for a Prime Ministerial system. We are used to it, and the office of Prime Minister could form a familiar core to build around in an otherwise radically changed constitutional scene.

The new design could abolish the overblown Westminster structure of Commons and Lords replacing it with a slimmed-down legislature. For instance, the curtain could finally come down on the present House of Lords – thereby removing over 800 peers and their expenses. The 26 oddly-named 'Lords Spiritual' could return to solely church duties, and the rest, the 'Lords Temporal', could, should they wish, be relocated say, to an empty theatre in London where they could debate but not legislate. Their expenses could be covered by the sale of tickets. As for the third arm of the Westminster legislature, the monarchy – which in the Westminster system doubles as the office of head of state – the drafters could, should they wish, keep the Queen, but might write into the new constitution that upon her abdication or death, the Speaker of the new Upper House would become the ceremonial head of state. (Because of their 'importance for tourism' the royal family could continue – as say, an agency under the Department of Media, Culture and Sport).

In this suggested new design the federal level of government could consist of a Lower House (perhaps still called the Commons) reduced from 650 to 400 MPs (after all the US has only 435 representatives for a population of over 300 million) and an Upper House (perhaps called the Senate) of 100 Senators drawn from the nations and regions. The Lower House of this Federal Parliament could be the main legislative chamber. The Upper House could either have powers of its own or be a revising chamber with similar powers to those of the present House of Lords, and could be given the function of concurring on treaty-making. Crucially, in this kind of structure the Prime Minister would be responsible to the Lower House of the Federal Parliament, and there would need to be provisions for resignation and so on, and for the calling of elections (fixed term

Parliaments or not?). The Prime Minister's powers should be set out clearly.

Of course, such a new design would be a perfect opportunity to relocate the centre of government, and the federal capital, outside of London. Suggestions have varied from establishing a new capital in the centre of the nation in York to developing a new Federal Capital Territory, with new government buildings and road access near the M6 around the Solway Firth. However, the most cost-effective option would be to continue to locate the two reduced Houses in the existing Palace of Westminster and the federal government offices in what would be a seriously reduced Whitehall. No grand new offices need be built.

In this suggested design there would be only two tiers of government – the federal level and a second level consisting of the national parliaments of Wales, Northern Ireland and Scotland and in England of the Regions, City Regions and Rural Regions. These Nations and Regions – which would replace the existing councils – would have their own Parliaments, their own First Ministers and cabinets (replacing Leaders and Mayors). These new second tier governments would be entrenched in the new written constitution – that is, like Texas or Hamburg, they would be permanent features, and not subject, as in today's devolved system, to being abolished should a future government and parliament wish to do so. And, to give meaning to their permanence they could be called 'states'. (Below these 'States' third-tier councils – boroughs, parishes and the like – could be established where wanted but would derive their powers from the 'States').

These 'States' would send – via election or nomination – Senators to the new Upper House – the Federal Senate. As for elections, national (that is federal) and State elections could all be held on the same day in some kind of Super-

Thursday system; or, alternatively, the Federal elections could be on one day every say five years and the State elections could be staggered as in the US Senate, with a third elected every, say, three years.

The exact number and size of these States (the Regional or City-Regional governments) would be one of the most difficult of the tasks facing any convention. There are, broadly speaking two options: first, to create a number of States based loosely upon the older regional government schemes of the past (all of which have died the death as London-centred centralisation powered ahead); or secondly, to establish a number of big City States (with those local government units outside these City-States amalgamated into bigger units). All in all, the new design could ensure that no new level of government would be established as the new States would simply be amalgams of existing local government units.

A number of designs for the second tier of government have been put forward over the years by academics, commissions and journalists. Many designs use the former Regional Development Agencies as the basis for future 'States' of England: they were as follows (with population in millions in brackets): South-East (8.6); London (8.1); North-West (7.0); Eastern England (5.8); West Midlands (5.6); South-West (5.2); East Midlands (4.5); North-East (2.5). One analyst, Ian Hackett, has suggested a radical, and no doubt controversial, scheme that, 'with due regard to history, geography and identity', could comprise as well as the three national parliaments, eleven parliaments in the new States (Regions and City-Regions) of England. His fourteen parliaments would be (with populations):

Northern Ireland (1.84m),
Scotland (5.3m),
Wales (3.1m),

Lakeland (7m; Cumbria, Lancashire, Merseyside, Greater Manchester, Cheshire; new capital: Manchester),
Northumberland (7m; Northumberland, Tyne & Wear, Durham, Cleveland, Yorkshire; new capital: Durham or York),
Middle England (15m; new capital: Birmingham),
Cornwall (0.54m; new capital: Truro),
Wessex (8m; Devon, Somerset, Dorset, Wiltshire, Hampshire, Berkshire, Surrey, West Sussex; new capital: Winchester),
Essex (12.4m; Greater London, Essex, Kent, East Sussex; new capital: Westminster),
The Isle of Man (0.09m),
The Channel Islands (0.16m).

But what of the division of powers between the Federal and the State levels? The distribution of powers between the tiers is crucially important for they will determine how centralised or decentralised the British government will be. My own preference is for a decentralised government with sufficient macro-economic control by the federal or central government to allow (should an elected government so decide for example) for extensive redistribution of wealth between London and the rest of the country. In the new written constitution the powers (functions) of the Federal government as a whole (the two Houses and the executive branch led by the Prime Minister) should be clearly set out, and could include:

Foreign and Security policy
Macro-Economic policy.
Treaty-Making.

The powers of the States (that is the three national Parliaments and the regional 'State' Parliaments) could be simply defined, as in the US constitution, as 'all those powers not allocated to the Federal government'. Alternatively, should the Convention want a different bias in the system then the powers of 'the States' could be set out and 'all other powers' could be allocated to the Federal Parliament.

The convention would need to take a view on another important, arguably the most important, institution in the country in an era when monetary policy is dominant – the Bank of England. One of the delights of constitution-making is that it will allow the British body politic to decide whether bankers should control the economy. The central bank could be returned to political control under the Treasury or kept independent but under serious democratic control, possibly through its governors and leading members selected by a committee of the Lower House and subject to recall. Of course, if neoliberal ideas are still in the ascendant when the Convention meets then it will, no doubt, be left as it is. Under any provenance it should have its role and limits clearly set out – and, of course, the amendment process also clearly understood.

The convention would also need to decide on the question of 'rights'. Constitution-making is a perfect opportunity to entrench rights and to make them inviolable. But their scope will be contentious – should we stipulate political and judicial rights only or social and economic as well? – as will be the means of interpretation. Should we leave 'rights' to law or should we elevate them to constitutional rights? And what of incorporating the European Convention into the constitution, thereby entrenching it?

Any constitution would need to clearly state where authority lies in the crucial role of interpreting the written document. This would normally fall to a Supreme Court, and such a Court could, to maintain some democratic legitimacy, be nominated by the office of the Prime Minister but ratified by the Upper House. A crucial point here, dependent upon our relationship with Europe, would be the role in the new constitution of the European Court of Justice (the ECJ) and the European Court of Human Rights.

As constitutions are living documents they should be open to change; there would need to be some constitutional provision not just for the interpretive powers of a Supreme Court but for the crucial procedure of amendment – possibly by two thirds of the Lower House and one half plus one of the Upper House or by a simple majority in both Houses and two thirds of the States.

Of course, living under a written constitution will, initially, be difficult for the English political class. Separating powers, entrenching government at differing levels, cementing citizens' rights and subordinating Parliamentary lawmaking to constitutional rules and basic rights – all of this may well be frustrating and cumbersome. Yet, it will have one great overriding advantage. In Britain's present circumstances – with social and territorial tensions rising – the great benefit of a proper constitution is that it can act as a defence against fanaticism and extremism. One of the great, often unspoken fears about Westminster's unwritten constitution – and 'old boys' constitutional culture – is that our politics are not bound by entrenched democratic rules but remain at the whim of a temporary political class; without constraint British society has no defence against an extremist authoritarian cabal taking over through the mechanism of a majority of seats in the House of Commons, a majority which can be secured with a popular vote as low as 35%.

Creating a new constitution, no matter how difficult, has one other advantage. It presents our tired and cynical democracy with perhaps a final chance for renewal.

Plan B: A 'Confederal' British Isles

If under another scenario the Scots (and possibly the Northern Irish) finally take the historic decision to leave the UK there is no way of knowing what the outcome would be. In these circumstances, Britain will urgently need a Plan B to try to stabilise an extremely dangerous situation throughout the Isles – particularly in Northern Ireland.

Thankfully, there are other possible responses – other, that is, than recriminations and division. One such – which would need an unusual degree of flexibility and humility from the English leaders in the Westminster political class – would be to immediately move towards reconciling the newly-independent Scotland with the rest of the British Isles. One way to take the potential bitterness out of the Scottish issue would be to preempt the whole process. In other words: in the event that it becomes abundantly clear that the Scots are moving to a vote for independence, Westminster should, ahead of any referendum, seek to negotiate an amicable separation settlement with the Scottish government in which both governments could recommend a 'Yes' vote.

This, though, may be far too much to hope for. Even so, the UK government would be wise to start thinking – well ahead of Scottish independence – about a radical Plan B which in the immediate aftermath of a vote to leave – would stabilise the political situation. One way to take the sting out of a Scottish vote to leave would be for the Westminster government to take the lead in post-Scottish referendum negotiations with the Scots not just about the separation settlement but also about comprehensively reformulating the totality of the governance of the British Isles in a way that can establish good future relationships between England, Wales, Northern Ireland and the new nation-state of Scotland.

For instance, Westminster could propose a new loose 'confederal' structure which includes within it the two nation-states (The RumpUK and Scotland). This new loosely confederal structure would not be an actual nation-state. Perhaps called a 'Council of the Isles' or 'The Confederation of the British Isles', this new 'polity' could be quite integrative; for instance it would likely share a currency – sterling – rather as separate nation-states share the euro. And, as a gesture from England to secure a new, separate but close, relationship between Scotland and the RUK, the Bank of England could offer a small but significant gesture – a long overdue name change: and become the Bank of Britain? Or more appropriately 'The British Isles'?

Much will depend on the political circumstances operating at the time when Scotland leaves the union. Should the UK have finally left the EU at the time of Scottish independence then the Scots might see Europe as the first priority for the newly independent state – as it seeks to enter the EU or to secure a special deal in some kind of Single Market arrangement. Unfortunately, as things stand, it would seem that the Spanish government, worried about their own separatist insurgencies in Catalonia and the Basque Country, would veto any such special deal with Scotland.

Even so, a newly independent Scotland seeking a relationship with the EU could certainly take its place as an applicant country to join in the normal way, and might be fast-tracked. In other words, the people of Scotland, as they free themselves from the UK, might be able to envisage a future life within the bloc. In any event, whatever an independent Scotland's relationship with Europe, it need not affect its membership of a 'Confederation of the Isles' and the consequent continuing relationship with London.

Although future Anglo-Scottish relations could be helped in this way, Anglo-Northern Ireland relations would be a different matter. There seems little doubt that Northern Ireland would become a serious casualty of Scottish independence: for in the aftermath of Scotland leaving the union, relations between the Protestant and Catholic communities will inevitably become extremely tense, or worse. As the UK breaks up, Northern Ireland will face a less secure, indeed an ungainly, relationship with London and the RumpUK. Further loosening of the bonds of union will cause great anxiety amongst Protestants particularly if Brexit should have led to the re-establishment of the border between the North and South. At the same time, in this insecure environment many Catholics will begin again to look to Dublin for their futures.

Should it come to violence again then this time the British government would be loathe to rerun the 70s and 80s by sending troops to police the sectarian divide. Instead, English opinion might prefer to wash its hands of Northern Ireland altogether, and induce, on top of a Scottish exit, a Northern Ireland exit. Of course, we have been here before: for at the height of the troubles, during the 1970s, all kinds of future scenarios were gamed – many of them involving an Ulster exit. For instance, the British government, at the highest level, seriously considered this radical option of removing Northern Ireland from the United Kingdom. Prime Minister Jim Callaghan toyed with the idea of creating an independent nation-state of Northern Ireland via a series of referenda in each of the six counties. The idea then, which, should sectarianism flare up again, could be resuscitated today, was that each Northern Ireland county would vote in a referendum – and the choice would be between an Independent Ulster or joining the republic to the south. The prospect then, as now, was that four counties would vote to join an independent Ulster and two for joining the Republic. There would then have to be all kinds of safeguards for the minorities left within each county – and there would be quite serious issues of relocation.

Of course, such a scenario, like all the others, seems somewhat far-fetched, but only somewhat. It makes the oft-forgotten point that Northern Ireland's stability always hangs by a thread.

In this kind of contingency the Irish Republic would inevitably re-enter the scene – and become a serious player in the great debate about the future of the British Isles.

There are two possible outcomes. One scenario envisions so toxic an atmosphere that the Protestants in the North will be in no mood for any compromises, and will veto any change involving the South. However, if the London government acts resolutely, washes its hands of a permanent Protestant link with the crown in RumpUK London, but offers to facilitate the emergence of a power-sharing arrangement in a new nation called Northern Ireland which would be in a 'confederal relationship' with both London and Dublin, then Protestant fears might, just, be assuaged.

A new 'Confederation of the British Isles' might well be a bridge too far both for Dublin and London – and could founder on a host of issues. The obstacles are very real and can quickly derail any progress. But relations between the Republic and the UK have been warming for years as the two countries have cooperated to secure peace in the North. And the desperate need to avoid a return to violence following Brexit (and a possible reinstitution of the border) could work wonders on the thinking of both governments.

The Isles and Europe: Forever Intertwined?

Ultimately the destiny of the British Isles – no matter its political structure, the number of nation-states within it, or its exact relationship with the EU – will be bound up with its neighbours in Europe and with their institutions. Even should the UK finally decide to leave the EU the country's relationship with the European mainland will still help determine the future of the British peoples – for good or ill.

The act of leaving the EU will have an immense effect upon Britain and the British. But the character of the exit is all-important. If the leaving is relatively friendly then the economic status-quo will probably prevail, and Britain would be free to carry on with full access to the Single Market and even to rejoin the EU at some point. However, if the leaving turns hostile then the terms of leaving could be harsh, leading to a serious economic downturn in the country (and maybe in the EU as well). In such a downturn British opinion could be expected to harden – both for and against Europe – into what could well become a veritable political 'civil war'. As of writing it is truly unclear to this author which side in the coming 'civil war' is going to prevail.

But one side will.

An Existential Crisis

Thus, the great 'European Question', which has dogged British politics for a generation, may well, at last, and in very grim circumstances, be on the way to being resolved – and with it our own existential identity-crisis as a people. In this sense the great 'European Question' may finally cause us British, and us English, to deal with our postimperial illusions, and finally come to terms with our real position in the world.

That is the good outcome.

Notes

1. The Basic Law of the Federal Republic of Germany can be read at www.iuscomp.org/gla/statutes/GG.html.
2. The Constitution of the USA can be read at www.archives.gov/exhibits/charters/constitution. The Fifth Republic of France can be read at its Wikipedia entry.

Six
Reversing Brexit?

In early 2017 as the Brexit government triggered Article 50, and the two-year negotiating period got underway, it was becoming clearer, at least to those who had voted to Remain, that the vision of the anti-EU Brexiteer government was in essence that of the ascendant wing of the Tory party. That is, a 'Hard Brexit' which would amount to a Thatcherite' 'England Alone' bargain basement, offshore tax haven type of country. It was a vision that millions of 'Leave' voters would have rejected.

Together with this realisation was the gnawing fear about the instability of the British state itself – as the prospects for constitutional instability in Scotland and Northern Ireland were increasingly hardened by the prospect of Brexit. The situation was beginning to have all the hallmarks of a real national emergency, and in this atmosphere questions arose about whether Brexit could be reversed.

The 2016 Brexit referendum result to leave the European Union is not just about Britain's relationship to the continent – for any rudimentary understanding of British politics over the last twenty or so years will reveal the truth that this referendum was only marginally about Europe and the European Union – a specific subject about which the British people have been largely neutral.

Rather, the outcome of the vote was determined by a mixture of issues – including stagnant living standards, job insecurity, deep inequality, the perceived failure of the Westminster political class – and, of course, attitudes, hardened by economic insecurity, to foreigners, immigration and refugees. And at a deeper level still the result may be seen against a backdrop of long-term national failure, of the failure of an establishment class and its system. Arguably a sense of national decline and failure has pervaded political thinking in the country ever since the Suez disaster in 1956 – only 'alleviated' by a succession of false 'new dawns'. Harold Wilson's 'new dawn' in 1964 ended with the 'winter of discontent'; Margaret Thatcher's 'new dawn' in 1979 certainly changed the structure of the economy and society but left a degree of division and bitterness that still resonates. And the most recent 'new dawn' – ushered in by New Labour in 1997 – ended with the Blair government's disaster in the sands of Iraq in 2003 and then in the global banking crisis of 2008 followed by the coalition government's austerity programme.

This sense of elite and national failure – which had been building for some time – meant that any referendum on any issue proposed by a government and governing elite would probably lead to a government defeat. This negative national mood, together with the lacklustre Remain campaign (mainly led by erstwhile Eurosceptics!), was a godsend to anti-EU campaigners. And the Brexiteer leadership – both in the Tory Party and in UKIP – skillfully took advantage of this populist moment to make the EU and migration the excuse and the scapegoat for the national ills.

The Road To Brexit: A Right Tory Project

On the face of it the 2008 crisis – and the near universal blame attached to the banks and to finance capital – should have led to a new lease of life for the British left. But, although the crash was a failure of neoliberal finance capitalism, from the public's perception 'the left' was in power when the banks collapsed – and Labour was blamed.

So, intriguingly and somewhat unfairly, the political beneficiary of the whole post – 2008 mess was the British Tory party. The Tory party dominated the 2010 coalition arrangement with the Liberal Democrats and it went on to win an outright majority in the 2015 general election as its primary political opponent, Labour, was in structural meltdown – particularly in its erstwhile bastion in Scotland where in 2015 it won only one seat.

As the Tory party came centre stage in British politics, so too did it move decisively to the right. In the 1990s the Thatcher generation began to populate the Conservative constituency organisations and then the Conservative party in Parliament. Ever since Margaret Thatcher's Bruges speech in 1988 this ascendant force in the party defined Europe as the big issue. For them Europe represented 'socialism by the back door', an overly-regulated and protectionist market, and, 'foreign control' of our democracy – indeed these themes morphed into what became an anti-Europe ideology, one as powerful as the socialist ideology that overwhelmed Labour in the 1980s. For many Conservatives Europe and the EU became the perfect scapegoat and excuse for the continuing failures of neoliberal globalisation and the Thatcher revolution (which ended up with a huge banking crisis). In this environment every Conservative Leader since John Major – William Hague, Michael Howard and David Cameron – felt it necessary to run for the leadership of the party on a 'Eurosceptic ticket'. And, in a classic case of failure of leadership, the pro-European Tories, who were still quite influential right up to and including the Cameron coalition government 2010-2015, appeased the ascendant anti-Europeans rather than confronting them. Indeed it was this twenty year appeasement that set the stage for the weak and visionless pro-EU Remain campaign of 2016. For this reason the real 'guilty men' for pro-Europeans were the pro-European Tories, from John Major to Ken Clarke, who refused to take a stand for Europe until the referendum campaign itself when it was far too late.

The ascendant Tory anti-Europeans, often calling themselves 'Eurosceptics', were helped by the powerful mogul press, particularly *The Daily Mail* and *The Daily Telegraph*, which became a daily populist vanguard – issuing forth increasingly childlike xenophobic propaganda, endless pictures of the Royal family, references to the Second World War and Winston Churchill (*Telegraph* columnist Boris Johnson wrote a book on the wartime leader), the evocative 'Cliffs of Dover' syndrome, and on and on, day after day. A group of articulate neoliberal, anti-EU columnists (amongst them Roger Bootle, Ambrose Evans-Pritchard, Boris Johnson and Michael Gove) gave the increasing xenophobia of the anti-EU position a seemingly-intellectual carapace – for instance, Boris Johnson would lace his columns and speeches with show-offy clever Latin phrases that few understood but many were in awe of.

This shift within the Tory party was reinforced by the arrival on the British scene of the United Kingdom Independence Party (UKIP) and its populist leader Nigel Farage. The Poujadist origins of the party (Tory small-business right-wingers) over time morphed into a nationalist 'anti-establishment' party which placed opposition to mass immigration at the centre of its appeal – and the party made its political breakthrough in the European Parliament elections of 2009. Although it failed to establish a serious beachhead in the British Parliament (winning one by-election and one seat in the general election of 2015) it garnered millions of votes and consistently acted as a powerful pressure group calling for a referendum on British membership of the EU. It also, crucially, acted as a permanent threat to the pro-EU leadership of the Tory party, pushing it in an ever more anti-Europe direction. A very strong case can be made that without the rise of UKIP and the skillful manipulative skills of its Leader, Nigel Farage, there would have been no referendum and no withdrawal from the EU. In this sense, the 'real victor' of the 2016 EU referendum was UKIP and Nigel Farage. By comparison, Theresa May, a reluctant Remainer during the referendum campaign, was a bit player in the story of the road to Brexit. Her role in the story is of a careerist politician who switched sides, from 'Remain' to 'Leave', the very day after the referendum result in order to associate herself with the Brexiteer winners and thus seize the premiership from those who had actually campaigned for the 'Leave' campaign (none of whom, Boris Johnson, Michael Gove or David Davis, were considered fit for the premiership).

Of course, it could all have been different. In the road to Brexit seemingly small events were also decisive. Here the role of the Liberal Democrats remains important, because the 2010 decision of the Liberal Democrat leadership to go into coalition with the Conservatives represented an historic set-back (perhaps a fatal one) for the European cause in Britain. In this coalition the most pro-European party (the Lib Dems) aligned themselves in government with the most anti-European political party (the Conservatives). Such a coalition, in which the Lib Dems were as junior partners, ultimately served to destroy the Lib Dem party (and hence the pro-European cause), and at the same time opened the door to a pro-Brexit Conservative majority in 2015.

Had the Liberal Democrats played their role in 2010 differently Britain might not now be facing life outside the EU. For instance, in 2010 had they refused to go into coalition with the Conservatives and instead forced them to set up a minority government – allowing the Lib Dems to keep their critical faculties and bring down this minority Tory government on a popular issue at a time of their choosing – the resultant House of Commons might not have returned a Conservative majority. Also, any time during the 2010-2015 coalition government had the Liberals walked out of government and brought down the coalition government on a popular issue (as they nearly decided to do on the question of the NHS) then the Conservative party may have been denied a majority (and thus a referendum) in the subsequent general election. These points were made to the Liberal Democrat leadership during the 2010-2015 Parliament, but were consistently brushed aside by Liberal Democrat leaders and officials who were all too obviously enjoying the fruits of office – an enjoyment made even more enjoyable by the Liberal party's erstwhile long sojourn in the political wilderness.

However, just as culpable as the 2010 Liberal Democrats, perhaps more so, is the ex – Prime Minister David Cameron. Upon becoming Prime Minister in 2010 David Cameron still had the option of facing down his Tory back-bench Brexiteers by simply refusing to countenance a referendum on the EU whilst he was Prime Minister. Yet, such a principled and robust stance was simply not in his political character. After all, in an early manifestation of his decision to appease the anti-EU brigade in his own party he had secured the Conservative Leadership in 2005 as a proclaimed 'Eurosceptic'; and as Prime Minister he had continued to appease. The centre of gravity in his party had moved decisively against the EU, mainly under pressure from an insurgent UKIP (who had polled in first place in the European elections of 2009), and he was simply not in the business of going against the political grain. The most he was prepared to do was to preclude a referendum during the 2010-2015 Parliament, an easy option as he could validly blame this refusal on the Liberal Democrat coalition partners.

Nonetheless, so persistent was the pressure from the Brexit Tories during the 2010-2015 Parliament that in January 2013 in his now-famous Bloomberg speech he yeilded by promising a referendum by 2017 should the Tories win in 2015. He agreed to an 'In Out' referendum to be decided by a simple majority (50% plus one) and with no caveats about needing say a two-thirds 'Out' vote to leave the EU. (In an earlier Scottish referendum on devolution the Act establishing the referendum had stipulated that two-thirds was needed to change the constitution).

Of course, Cameron probably granted the referendum in the belief that he would never have to enact it as he may well have believed that he would not secure a Conservative majority in the coming 2015 election, and was as surprised as many others when his Conservative Party won outright. In the event on the morrow of his surprising victory in 2015 one of the very first political figures to enter 10 Downing Street was pro-Brexit Graham Brady the Chairman of the Tory backbenchers committee to call in his marker and ensure that David Cameron stood by his promise.

The result of the 2015 general election was therefore a real set-back for pro-Europeans, and a major milestone on the road to Brexit. But it was a close call nonetheless: for had the Labour or the Liberal Democrats won just a few more seats and secured another hung Parliament then Cameron would not have been able, even should he by then have wanted to, to hold a referendum.

Yet, even after the referendum date was settled the pro-European cause was not lost – for many pro-Europeans believed, right up to the actual vote in June 2016, that they would still carry the day. And maybe they would have done – had it not been for fortuitous events outside of their control. The main, most damaging, event occured when only months before the vote the Syrian refugee crisis broke. Nigel Farage and UKIP had already made immigration a major issue in the campaign and had skillfully linked it to the 'freedom of movement' policy of EU membership rather than to the broader immigration issue involving Third World immigration from the Commonwealth. Indeed, about 50% of the total number of immigrants in 2015 were from non-EU (largely Commonwealth) countries arriving during Theresa May's reign at the Home Office. UKIP Leader Nigel Farage was thus not wholly convincing when he sought to blame the EU's 'freedom of movement' principle for the unpopular immigration policy – for EU immigration was often short-lived as EU workers would contribute to the economy and then often go home. By comparison 'Commonwealth immigration' from, say, Pakistan, often bringing Islamic traditionalism – disliked by many Brexit voters – in its wake, had nothing to do with EU. That was, though, until the Syrian refugee crisis. It is quite possible that the referendum result could have gone the other way had the Syrian crisis not broken when it did in late 2015. When Angela Merkel opened Germany's borders to thousands of refugees from Syria Nigel Farage could then plausibly but speciously link the EU's 'free movement of labour' policy with Third World immigration – as he argued that once in Europe these 'new German citizens' would be free to travel to Britain.

It is becoming increasingly clear that the referendum result did not represent a national groundswell against the EU. Rather, Cameron's momentous decision to have a referendum was to do with the politics of the Tory party; and the result was largely to do with a generalised anti-establishment sentiment and the issue of mass immigration.

So, the question in post-referendum Britain remains: can the Brexiteer wing of the Tory party, now very much in control of the party and the Prime Minister, and with a referendum victory behind it, go on to finish the job – that is, to fulfill their vision? But, what exactly is their vision? A clue can be found in the fact that many of the leading Brexit politicians have been nurtured in what can be called the 'Murdoch' stable. (Many of them literally, as journalists paid by the Murdoch or Conrad Black empires). The 'Murdoch agenda' for Britain is to seek a separation from Europe in order to secure an 'England Alone' 'free market' offshore island; a low-tax haven with low wages, a small public sector with limited welfare, and freedom for the super-rich (including foreign oligarchs) to make even more money. It espouses 'free trade' and seeks to be 'competitive' (i.e. low costs) in the global economy. A sign that the Conservative government might wish for such a future was revealed when Chancellor of the Exchequer Philip Hammond stated, in January, 2017, that should Britain not get a satisfactory deal from its European partners, the country had the option of creating a 'competitive' offshore island economy to undercut mainland Europe – the so-called 'Singapore Option.

In principle, of course, such a vision of society and economy would demand free movement of labour (alongside capital). but, as with earlier Thatcherism, it is here that the Brexiteers face a contradiction and a dilemma. For many of them have ridden to power by appealing to nativist populism on the immigration issue – and Brexit's open neoliberal, 'global' economy with trade deals with, for instance India and Turkey, would increase, not decrease, non-EU immigration.

By the spring of 2017 the direction of travel of a Brexit Britain was becoming clear. There was no 'good deal' with the EU on offer. Many EU member state leaders were genuinely shocked that Britain could walk out of the club it had been a member of for over four decades, and could even threaten to walk out of the Article 50 negotiations, when there was no 'good deal' with the United States on offer who, in any trade negotiations under a new 'America First' administration, would only agree to a deal which would let American corporations have more power over our economy and society – for instance by giving the drug companies increased legal say in Britain's NHS system. Prime Minister May's 'Global Britain' was desperately seeking trade deals with India and Turkey but on terms that were increasingly unacceptable – such as freer migration rules. Thus, it was becoming clear that the country, post – June 23 2016, was in a very dangerous place – about to leave one of the world's most powerful trading blocs, espousing the vacuous mantra of 'Global Britain' and 'Free Trade' at the very same time that protectionist trading blocs were on the increase worldwide.

'England Alone' Nativist English Nationalism

Yet, even as it became clear that the British Brexiteer government had no serious strategy for the country following the exit from the EU, the pro-Brexit press was still giddy with nationalist euphoria. The British Prime Minister was winning Commons votes to trigger Article 50 and to start negotiations for leaving the EU, and there was a growing sense in the Brexit Tory government that the country, should it not get a good deal, might walk away from negotiations altogether; Mrs. May called an election specifically on an 'us' (Britain) and 'them' (Europe) platform, and was making statements, some of them filled with fake portentousness from the steps of Downing Street, about European leaders 'interfering in our [election] campaign' as though she was re-running the Second World War. It was a clear case of the Brexit drug of nativist, childish, nationalism still working its magic – more exciting obviously than the clear-eyed traditional nationalism based upon national interest that had guided earlier Tory Prime Ministers.

Interestingly, this peculiar and somewhat spurious form of nationalism – which both helped cause the Brexit vote and was further unleashed by it – was not about stirring up nationalist Britishness. Rather, it was all about 'England' and Englishness, about rousing the resentments and prejudices of many English people who felt England was not what it was and wanted a return to its glory days. It was built on a rather a false idea of 'England' perpetrated by an insurgent elite in politics and their friends in the child-like populist press media.

This strange form of 'English' nationalism – which amounted to a weird mix of superiority and resentment, and a longing for a lost world – had been building for many decades. Indeed, as I outlined in Essay Three, it goes back to the idea of 'Englishness', being English, that was constructed in the nineteenth-century as British imperial power was at its height – a notion and ideolgoly of superiority (often racial) based upon empire that, as time went on, was obviously increasingly threadbare. And as it became abundantly clear in the 1950s that America had taken over from the ruins of the British empire then a sullen resentment, just below the surface but covered by politeness, took hold amongst many elite English people – particularly from the public school products educated to run an empire – who began to see the reality of their country reduced in status and power. This resentful 'English' nationalism lay dormant and hidden for much of the postwar years as a realistic section of the British elite in both main parties attempted to carve out a future for the country first as America's junior partner and then as a member, awkward though it became, of the European Union. However, this dormant sense of 'Englishness' was unleashed as part of the appeal of Margaret Thatcher and Thatcherism and first appeared in its contemporary form during the 1982 Falklands war – unleashing a crude and visceral 'patriotic' mood whipped up by the popular nativist press.

For instance, the sheer coarseness and vulgarity of this new nationalist mood was such that the country's leading tabloid newspaper could feel free to refer to the sinking of the Argentinian cruiser Belgrano, in which hundreds of Argentines died, with the headline 'Gotcha'; and we saw it again in the mild hysteria of whipped-up support for the England Football team in the early 1990s – when, that is, they were worth supporting! – with the Flag of St. George fluttering from both front gardens and White Vans; and we saw it yet again, in more muted form, in the seemingly endless royal ceremonials before during and after the jubilee.

For some years before the June 2016 referendum, and then for months after it, the populist media – principally *The Daily Telegraph*, *The Daily Mail*, and *The Express* – played ruthlessly upon both the nostalgia and insecurity felt by large numbers of English people, a nostalgia and insecurity which had grown more powerful ever since the global financial crash of 2007-8. And in the run-up to the 2016 referendum the populist media outlets, often owned by 'super patriots' living abroad, bombarded readers on a daily basis with themes and images evoking the country's 'glorious past' – prominent were photos of the royal family, particularly the Queen, and references to 'the spirit if 1940' and the role of Britain in the Second World War.

The Break-Up of the Brexit State

And post-referendum the fires of 'nativist nationalism' were stoked yet again – so much so that seasoned observers of Britain were becoming alarmed. A post-Brexit analysis in the *New York Times* asked:

> So what's going to happen? These days, it feels like the worst-case scenario always prevails. If that happens this time, too, Brexit will mean that England, shorn of Scotland, Northern Ireland and maybe even Wales, contracts into a small, isolated, one-party state governed by schoolteacherly Conservatives who persist in wild-eyed delusions about the country's special grandeur...if what the Brexiteers want is to return Britain to a utopia they have devised by splicing a few rose-tinted memories of the 1950s together with an understanding of imperial history derived largely from images on vintage biscuit tins, then all of this [the 'England Alone' scenario] seems chillingly plausible.[1]

Thus although this nativist English nationalism may well have helped win the referendum for the 'Leave' campaign, and it may have served to bolster support for the May government in the 2017 general election and in its 'Leave' negotiations with the EU, it may also have unleashed another, and deadly, dynamic – nothing less than the break-up of the British state.

Scotland is the flashpoint. And on the morning of June 24th, 2016, it became clear that a long-dreaded 'nightmare scenario' had actually occurred: a majority in the UK referendum had voted to leave the EU whilst a majority in Scotland (and in Northern Ireland and London) had voted to remain. Thus, the pre-referendum claim by the SNP leadership that they would not allow Scotland 'to be dragged out of the EU against the will of the Scottish people' would now have real resonance, and would over time give fuel, perhaps decisively, to the mood for full Scottish independence.

Indeed in the days ahead of the Scottish referendum in 2014 the symbol of the UK union, the Queen herself, was reportedly so alarmed about the possibility of an independent Scotland that she had held 'talks with David Cameron amid panic at the prospect of the end of the 300-year-old Union'.[2]

As of writing the Scottish government, wary of Brexit, particularly a 'Hard Brexit', is trying to involve itself in the UK government's negotiating strategy for Brexit conducted with the EU. Should, however, the SNP conclude that the UK government is ignoring their wishes then a new clarion call for Scottish independence could issue forth – this time, should oil prices be off their floor, with some likelihood of success.

However, Scottish independence does not stand on its own as an issue roiling British political and constitutional life – a kind of one-off event that can be ring-fenced. For, Scottish separatism is, in my view, only but an example – a serious example – of how Brexit will lead to a broader long-term disintegration of the country and the state.

Irish Violence?

In fact, Scotland may not be the first of the Celtic countries to leave the Westminster UK state. As of writing it is touch and go whether Northern Ireland will upstage the Scots and be the first to break.

The root of the matter here – one consistently ignored by a complacent English establishment – is that Northern Ireland's historic troubles remain to this day just below the surface. The Anglo-Irish agreement (1985), the subsequent Good Friday Agreement (1998) and the 2007 St. Andrews Agreement – with the devolution and power sharing arrangements – is a story of uneven, slow, but real advance – at least in keeping the peace. But, in reality, these agreements are but a thick sticking plaster covering a still divided, tense and incipiently violent society – one that may not survive any serious change in the UK's structural stability caused by Brexit.

The fact is that Brexit will ineluctably create a border between Northern Ireland, whilst it stays in the UK, and the Republic to the south. Such a border can only stoke Catholic fears that the progress made with power-sharing and open borders will come to an end and cause them to feel trapped within the UK. On the other hand many in the Protestant community will tend to welcome a border. Such an impasse might well be solved by a border poll, but more likely will see a hardening of sectarian opinion and even a renewed outburst of violence.

More potentially destabilising still, the negotiations for Brexit between the EU and the UK may well, perhaps inadvertently, reopen in clear and stark terms the debate about a united Ireland. A majority of Northern Irish voters (including many Protestants) were EU 'Remainers', and the EU side in the negotiations may well cater to them by agreeing that Northern Ireland, although not a nation-state or a candidate member, can join the EU should the North join the Republic (which is a full member state of the EU). Such a development would create in all but name a united Ireland – the long-term goal of Sinn Fein. (There is a European precedent for an existing member state to enlarge its borders in this way – created when the 'Eastern Lander', the former East Germany, joined the German Federal Republic after German unification). Such a move, the direct result of Brexit, would set Ireland alight.

The border is one issue facing the Irish, but there can be little doubt that the effect of a Scottish exit from the UK union is another – as an independent Scotland will also unleash a pent-up sense of insecurity in the Protestant community about their place in the rest of the UK. Many Protestants will be asking urgent questions following an independent Scotland about the attitude of London to the continuing link of Ulster to the mainland. Protestant edginess about Scottish independence was on display during the September 2014 Scottish referendum campaign when the Orange Order intervened in the campaign, marching in Scotland in favour of a 'No' vote. In the period immediately after a decision for Scottish independence Protestant fears about their future with the mainland could be further exacerbated should the Catholic community – also anxious about their future status – start a new round of agitation to join the republic in the south. As tensions rise Northern Ireland could easily erupt again – with the return of violence not just in the province itself but also in some of the big cities of the British mainland where residual Protestant and Catholic communities still exist side by side – such as Glasgow and Liverpool.

The British Brexit government is thus facing some very difficult choices – each with their dangerous downsides. As power-sharing collapses the Brexit government in London could try a renewed bout of Direct Rule. Or the Brexit government could try to set up an independent new Northern Irish nation-state outside the UK. Or they could try to manage, in agreement with Dublin, the emergence of a united Ireland. Not one of these 'solutions' will secure a consensus within Northern Ireland, indeed the very opposite is the case. But such is the price that the Brexit government will have to pay for Brexit.

Contagion?

Of course, the disintegration of the UK may well come to a halt once new settlements have been secured for Scotland or Northern Ireland. It is possible that the British Brexit government might welcome 'England Alone' and be pleased to see England shorn of Ireland and Scotland. However, this highly complacent attitude, held by many an English Brexiteer, may well underestimate what could become a serious 'contagion' effect.

For instance, both Wales and the North of England would broadly-speaking be losers from a Scottish exit; and these two regions, without Scotland, will inevitably find themselves more and more dependent upon London, and may well resent it, and oppose it – just as has the SNP north of the border. Anti-London, or anti-Westminster, sentiment could take hold and find expression in increased support for Plaid Cymru in Wales and 'North Britain' parties in the North or parts of the North. It is not beyond reason to envisage a future in which a UKIP type populist party could win votes in large swathes of the North by playing on resentments against Southerners and London.

Alternatively, though, both Wales and the North could be propelled closer to London – as the only source of continuing financial support – and make their peace with southern England. In these circumstances the great dream of an English Parliament and government – an English nation-state no less – could well be born. And the aim of many Europhobes and Eurosceptics – that such an English Parliament would at last give representation to England's so-called 'common identity' and thus be a driving force for limiting immigration and multiculturalism – would be realised.

Independence For London?

Prospects for an English Parliament may, however, depend on how London and Londoners react to a Brexit economic crash and/or potential Celtic instability – for within days of Scotland exiting, a separatist movement for London could begin to stir. The fact is that London's fundamental economic and financial wealth is far greater than Scotland's, and its subventions to the rest of the England are considerable. The slogan that 'The UK is a drain on the capital' could easily apply to England being a 'drain' as well – a theme that could, over time, launch a movement in London for autonomy from the RumpUK state.

Once a debate gets underway then it will not take long for these powerful arguments to be deployed with some considerable effect. In the new circumstances created by a Scottish exit it is not overly-fanciful to envisage a future Mayor of London, the politician who possesses the largest personal vote in the country, making the case for 'this great world city-state' to break free from the shackles and subsidies of the declining welfare state in its hinterland. A 'London independence movement' will be able to ring some powerful bells in the City of London that London, like Northern Ireland and Scotland should try to do special deals with the Single Market to secure 'passporting rights' for its large global finance and investment companies – in other words 'that London should resist being dragged out of the EU by English nationalists' and that more autonomy for London might allow the great world city to negotiate its way back into the world's largest single market. Thus, Lexit (from the UK) could follow Sexit (from the UK). And it was instructive that in the very aftermath of the 2016 Brexit referendum vote the Mayor of London, Sadiq Khan, was reported to have had discussions with the SNP First Minister,

Nicola Sturgeon, about their similar situations within the UK. In reality, of course, such a campaign by London to re-join the Single Market will likely fall foul of EU rules and precedents. But increasing London's self-consciousness could become a major force for establishing an 'England of the Regions' rather than a centralised English Parliament.

A Perfect Storm

Such are some of the potential dramatic constitutional effects of Brexit upon the very stability and existence of the UK state. And as this growing instability becomes apparent then 'Remainers' and pro-Europeans will with credibility be able to point to an ironic truth: that membership of the EU, rather than threatening the existence of the UK as a nation-state, was, in fact, the glue that stabilised UK state, holding its various components together. Remove the EU and Britain breaks apart.

However, if these great constitutional fissures were all that Brexit had in store then, perhaps, just perhaps, they could be managed. However, it is here that the realities of global economic and financial markets come into play. For should the Scots or the Northern Irish ultimately decide to leave the UK no one should underestimate the effect on global markets of such a shock. One of the economic strengths of the UK has been its, largely undeserved, reputation amongst investors around the world for political stability. But, unfortunately there is no way that the break-up of an over 300 year realm can remain unnoticed around the world; nor is there a way that, with all the tensions not just between Scotland and England but in Northern Ireland as well, that the UK, or RumpUK, can be sold as a stable place to invest or indeed to do business. The only question remaining is clear: can this disintegration of the UK, swift or slow, be managed over time, or does it, at some point, lead to an immediate blind panic?

What is more, this potential high profile break-up of the country could easily coincide with the unofficial, or even official, collapse of the negotiations between the Westminster government and the EU. It is not beyond the realm of possibility that the British Brexit government could be faced with impossible negotiations on three fronts – with the EU over Brexit, with Scotland over a putative Scottish independence referendum and also with the Dublin government and the EU over the future of Ireland – all of this against a backdrop of an economic downturn, a run on sterling and further austerity measures. Such is the perfect storm that is in prospect as of writing.

'Hard' and 'Soft' Brexit

Yet, with a perfect storm brewing the debate in Britain – at least within and between the two major parties – was still about how best to leave the EU. By the early spring of 2017 the debate in Britain was coming down to one between a 'Hard' and a 'Soft' Brexit. A 'Hard Brexit' amounted to the country being outside the Single Market and Customs Union and possibly without any transitional arrangements or new trade agreements on the day of leaving – the so called 'cliff edge' option; and a 'Soft' Brexit meaning good access to the Single Market and membership of the Customs Union. As the EU leadership was making it clear that a 'Soft Brexit' would involve Britain continuing to accept the EU's 'free movement of labour' principle and also the jurisdiction of the European

Court of Justice, the 'Hard Brexiters' in the Conservative party were increasingly turning their backs upon the possibility of even attempting to secure a 'Soft' option.

By the early months of 2017 British politics the British Tory Brexit government under Theresa May's leadership was veering very decidedly towards the 'Hard Brexit' option. The British Prime Minister had declared that 'no agreement was better than a bad agreement' – an obvious tilt towards the 'Hard Camp'. And the Brexit supporters, mainly in the Conservative party, were seeking to push on with withdrawal from the EU, even should the negotiations prove difficult or even fail. They were increasingly seeking a clean break with the EU: in which new 'global' strategy for Britain which would involve a future in which the country could somehow manoeuvre 'independently' – and quickly – in the world.

As 2017 progressed it was becoming clearer that a 'Soft Brexit' was no longer a possibility as the position of the Brexit government and the EU negotiators had hardened significantly. In May as the country faced a surprise general election, called by Prime Minister May to secure a 'stronger hand' in the negotiations, the country was facing a 'Hard Brexit' – with little access to the EU Single Market – and the cold reality of a 'cliff edge' fall into competing in the world under the rule book of the World Trade Organisation, if the WTO would have us, or worse.

Thus, having walked out of one of the world's most prosperous clubs, the British people in 2017 were looking at a future as an offshore bargain basement society living precariously next to a hostile continent. It would indeed be the Brexiteers' dream of 'England Alone' – with a people luxuriating in so-called 'independence' and celebrating so-called 'Englishness' even as the country grew ever poorer, narrower and divided.

Reversing the Drive For Brexit?

Yet, although a majority of the public were seemingly still wanting to leave the EU there were some signs that a review was underway. In a YouGov poll published in April 27th 2017 those regretting the 2016 referendum result for the first time just outnumbered those supporting it. But in the early months of 2017 (as I write) the idea of 'Stopping Brexit' was a minority pursuit. However, as time went by, with a 'Hard Brexit' looking increasingly likely, the unthinkable was beginning to become the thinkable. Reversing the Brexit dynamic was slowly but surely entering onto the political agenda.

However, reversing Brexit would be a momentous decision that, if handled insensitively or at the wrong time, might well lead to an ultimate crisis of democratic legitimacy. Thus many 'Remainers' were fearful of finding themselves on the wrong side of the 'patriotic' and 'democratic' argument that was being ruthlessly deployed against anyone who sought to 'undermine the democratic process' of the referendum result. So fevered was the atmosphere post-Brexit that the judges on the Court of Appeal who in early 2017 had ruled that Parliament needed to approve triggering Article 50 were denounced in *The Daily Mail* as 'enemies of the people'. It was a chilling intervention that made its mark with many 'Remainers'.

Yet in early February 2017 47 Labour MPs, thwarting a three-line whip, voted against triggering Article 50 of the Lisbon Treaty, a move tantamount to voting against Brexit and the referendum result. They included Labour MPs Graham Allen, Chris Bryant, Neil Coyle, Stella Creasy, Maria Eagle, Paul Farrelly, Owen Smith and Ben Bradshaw, and they represented a growing body of opinion in Parliament and the country that wanted Brexit either delayed or stopped altogether (Owen Smith had suggested during his Leadership campaign against Labour Leader Jeremy Corbyn that the country should hold a second 'in-out' referendum after the terms of withdrawal were known). It is not impossible to believe that as historians look back on the Brexit crisis this grouping of 47 may well be seen as the core of a later growing revolt against Brexit. As one amongst them put it privately, this grouping could become the 'small acorn from which a great oak could grow'.

Options for 'Reversing' Brexit

But seeking the reversal of Brexit and achieving it are two very different things. By the spring of 2017, for anti-Brexiteers, the way forward was refining down into two alternatives. One, by far the most ambitious, was to stop Brexit altogether before the country leaves the EU in 2019. The European Commission seemed ready, should this happen, to allow the Article 50 process to welcome the UK continuing as a full member. The other way forward for anti-Brexiteers, at least in early 2017, was a refinement – that is, a 'reversal' in all but name by securing an agreement in which Britain retained if not membership then full access to the Single Market and full membership of the Customs Union. Of course, such a deal – essentially the softest of 'soft' Brexits would place us in something akin to Norway's position, entailing large financial contributions, acceptance of the European Court's jurisdiction over many matters and acceptance of many EU laws and regulations.

In early 2017 the 'Soft Brexit' supporters were biding their time, realising that reality would eventually actually bite – as the EU negotiations soured, as the country faced falling off the cliff edge of a trade limbo (no Single Market, no trade deals with anyone at all except, maybe, a WTO tariff system) and, on top of all that, when constitutional chaos beckoned in Ireland and Scotland.

And when Brexit fantasy-time finally fell away the anti-Brexit majority in the Commons could move to take control of the whole process and negotiate a very 'Soft Brexit'. Of course, all of this was dependent upon sufficient Tory rebels – Tory MPs like Ken Clarke, Anna Soubry and Nicki Morgan – deciding to put country before party by joining with the opposition Remainers. But looking at the history of careerism in the Conservative party this was a very tall order indeed.

Tory Xenophobia versus The British National Interest

The only problem was that the option of a 'Soft Brexit' was falling away – under pressure from home and abroad. At home the Prime Minister, Theresa May, had started flirting with a 'Hard Brexit' option – not least by saying that 'no deal is better than a bad deal'. More importantly, noises from the EU negotiators were sounding more and more hard-line, to the point where it was becoming possible that the Conservative government might well walk away from the negotiations, leaving the country to face leaving the EU without a trade deal or even a transitional arrangement – the so-called 'cliff edge option'. And a 'Hard Brexit' was looking more and more likely as the May government was souring relations with the EU leaders by stoking up xenophobia during the 2017 election campaign against a Labour party not really returning fire on the European question – as their Leader Jeremy Corbyn decided to fight the election on largely non-Brexit issues. So much so that on May 3 2017, during the election campaign Prime Minister May, accused un-named European leaders of 'threatening Britain' in the negotiations and 'interfering' with the general election – and adopted a tone outside Downing Street that echoed the 1930s and war-time. It was meant to sound as though the 1930s had returned with Britain standing up to Hitler. The Tory election campaign strategists obviously believed that stoking up xenophobia against foreigners would win them votes – and according to the initial polls taken before the 2017 result, it was.

Thus, by the summer of 2017, whilst a Tory government remained in place, the British people were faced with nothing less than an abrupt rupture with the EU with no transitional arrangements and without any signed trade agreements (including with the USA after the Trump White House let it be known that, as in President Obama's earlier warning, that the US would privilege the EU over Britain, who would indeed by 'at the back of the queue').

It seemed that the only circumstances in which a 'Hard Brexit' could be stopped would be for the British government to accept 'free movement' of capital and labour (and thus ceding control of immigration from the EU) and the legal sovereignty of the European Court of Justice over British law – two red rags to the Tory party bull.

And it was beginning to seem too that even should the crisis with the EU cause an economic emergency – say with house prices tumbling, mortgage costs rising, prices in the supermarkets soaring – the Tory party in Parliament most likely would still not change course.

And, even after the Tory failure to secure a majority in the June 2017 general election, it was conceivable (as of writing) that the unstable Tory government might yet simply decide to leave the talks with the EU, blame the EU 'foreigners' for the collapse of the talks, rachet up 'patriotic' sentiment whilst supressing opposition at home by 'enemies of the people' rhetoric from their mass media supporters. It could all turn very ugly, very quickly.

Notes

1. Tom Wyman, 'Theresa May's Empire of the Mind', *New York Times*, 15 Febraury 2017.
2. *The Daily Mail*, 8 September 2014.

Postscript
The End of Brexit

The result of the June 2017 general election has changed the whole dynamic of the British Brexit debate. It brings into question whether the UK can continue with a 'Hard Bexit, or even with a 'Soft Brexit'. And it places on the national agenda the possibility that the British Parliament could reverse the whole anti-European Brexit process by turning down the 'Great Repeal Bill' and passing an Article 50 Repeal Bill instead. In other words: Britain could stay in the EU. In the popular lingo 'Breturn' could yet become the 'Best Deal' possible.

Before the result of the June 2017 general election pro-EU, or 'remainer', supporters were becoming fatalistic. They believed that Theresa May would secure a huge majority in the Commons and that the enhanced Brexiteers would then force through the hardest of hard Brexits, placing Britain firmly on the road to a free-market, low wage, low tax 'Singapore future'. Thus, pro-EU supporters would need to start accepting the geo-political earthquake of leaving the EU and start thinking about the hard slog of a campaign to re-enter the EU after the country left the bloc. Such a campaign to re-apply for membership would only stand a chance of succeeding when life outside the EU no longer appealed to a majority of Britons; and any party or movement pledged to return Britain to the EU would need to overcome the likely bitter residual nationalism that will be arguing, in the face of all reality, for continuing to 'going it alone'.

All this changed as the election results came in on the morning of June 9th 2017. It became clear that the Johnson/Crosby/*Mail*/*Telegraph* Tory 'Flag Waving' xenophobic' campaign built around the Boudicea figure of Theresa May had fallen flat. Their central electoral strategy – that the huge UKIP vote in 2015 would return overwhelmingly to the Conservatives thus giving the party a landslide simply did not work. Instead millions of erstwhile UKIP voters, unsurprisingly, returned to their previous Labour loyalties – and, together with a large under-35 national vote, much of it in areas congruent to universities, it pushed Labour's vote up to 40%.

This result ripped the tried and trusted Tory Brexit playbook into pieces. Rule One in the playbook was that a xenophobic campaign built around a great national leader standing up for Britain would divert people from considering their increasingly difficult economic circumstances. Rule two was that a campaign to villify the Labour Party as weak on the national interest – particularly with a Leader like Jeremy Corbyn – would garner a decisive and winning number of votes. And rule three, developed during the campaign, was that terrorist attacks on Britain would increase support for the Conservative party. The Tory leadership was proved wrong on all three counts. In sum, so dire were the economic circumstances of millions of British households that there was limited popular support out there for the traditional xenophobic Tory drum-beating – and, by extension, 'foreigner bashing' as the default position in UK-EU relations. Instead it was the economic 'condition of Britain' rather than fake patriotism that determined the outcome.

Following the June 2017 general election, and the strategic position of Brexiteer Tories in tatters, those pro-Europeans who wanted to change the whole direction of travel of Britain's relationship with the EU finally had the wind in their sails. By comparison the Brexiteer Tories faced two, very bad, options. First, they could continue to back the wounded Prime Minister Theresa May and witness a European policy of drift and indecision; or, they could replace the May administration with another Leader who could go to the country on an 'Hard Brexit' line – and probably fail, taking down with them the failure of the whole Brexit project.

By contrast the ascendant pro-European forces were facing a different choice – either to go for a 'Soft Brexit', that is, remaining in the Single Market and the Customs Union, or alternatively go for a bold, but increasingly realistic, attempt to reverse the decision to 'Leave' and thus remain in the EU (by withdrawing the notification to leave made under Article 50).

In these circumstances the question was beginning to be asked: how exactly could such a change of direction come about? In other words how could Britain reverse Brexit, and keep Britain in the EU? Of course, the obvious course would be for one of the two existing big political parties – which, of course, meant Labour – to take the lead. Post June 2017 a plausible scenario was emerging in which the Labour party would become the unambiguous leader of a 'return to Europe' movement. And the party would campaign on a policy of staying in, or returning to, the EU via a second referendum or a general election. However, by mid June 2017 at least, the likelihood that the party under Jeremy Corbyn's leadership would adopt such a policy was uncertain. Corbyn himself, although supportive of EU workers rights, has a history of seeing the EU as an obstacle to creating the kind of socialist economy and society he is seeking – a kind of 'socialism in one country' approach – and, thus, Labour could be expected to remain somewhat ambiguous on the European question.

So, in the absence of Labour taking a strong pro-EU line then over the long run the only alternative is to create a whole new party or alliance dedicated to returning the country to the EU. Such a new party might initially be composed of an alliance between break-away factions from existing parties in Parliament – rather as the SDP was founded in 1981 as moderate Labour MPs broke ranks. It might also include some Tories who remain pro-EU, although the track record of Tory MPs breaking with their party and risking their careers is not good. In the spring of 1981 when the SDP broke away from Labour it attracted only one Tory MP, Mr. Christopher Brocklebank Fowler. So, as far as Tories joining in a new party is concerned, as the adage says, 'I wouldn't hold my breath'.

As in 1981 the MP members of this new pro-European party or Alliance would not stand against each other in future local, Parliamentary by-elections and the future general election. Thus, in every English (and Welsh) constituency there would be one anti-Brexit candidate pledged to re-apply for entry into the EU. So, for instance, the single anti-Brexit candidate in many seats would be the sitting rebel MP who would fight their own seat as an Alliance candidate, and in the many seats where the Liberals were second the Liberal candidate would become the Alliance candidate. Much would depend on the political mood prevailing at the time, but this Alliance, as long as it was sufficiently anti-establishment and willing to shake up the system, could, even in Britain, do surprisingly well. And together with Scottish MPs might well be enough to deny the Conservatives a majority at the 2022 or earlier general election.

Should Labour, under Corbyn or any other leader, ultimately accept Britain's fate as remaining outside the EU then, a new party could best be secured in the new Parliament elected in 2017 by sitting anti-Brexit MPs simply resigning their seats and running themselves, as independents or new Alliance candidates, in the subsequent by-elections. In by-elections voters love an independent standing on principle against the might of a party machine, and in seats with a large 'Remain' vote the resigning MP might well sweep back with a landslide majority; and the by-election, when other well-known anti-Brexit politicians would break ranks and support the independent candidate, could become the occasion for a new political force to be born then and there.

However, new party or old, any party dedicated to restoring Britain's relationship with the continent – through membership of the EU – would be facing an uphill task, particularly should the country actually leave the EU. However, life outside the EU in the WTO world could become so depressing – with living standards severely reduced – that reversing Brexit could become, very quickly, a popular cause.

What Mechanism for 'Breturn': Parliamentary Control or a Second Referendum?

As a pro-European, or 'Breturn', movement develops in Britain, one crucial issue that will arise is the thorny question of whether such a return to the EU should be secured through a second referendum. The arguments for a second referendum are powerful and centre around the seemingly 'democratic', simple and populist appeal that 'the people should have their say'. This tune resonates particularly if a reversal of an earlier referendum is contemplated.

Yet, defining 'democracy' can be tricky. And there are powerful and serious democratic arguments against the whole referendum process. Referendums are historically the tools of dictators, much beloved by authoritarians as a way of by-passing the checks and balances of a pluralist polity and solidifying their power; they are, or should be, anathema to a representative parliamentary democracy like that of the UK. What's more, in referendums, opinion is invariably swayed by populist tricks of the trade funneled through a biased media who possess their own agenda (in Britain's case, the decision to hold a referendum on the EU was tantamount to handing the decision over to opinion-forming newspaper moguls like Rupert Murdoch and Lord Rothermere). And, finally, and perhaps most important of all, the voters often cast their votes on other issues than that presented to them on the ballot – in the case of the 2016 referendum the evidence was that many, particularly Labour voters, voted on a range of other (than EU) issues such as immigration or dislike of the Westminster establishment or, ironically, opposition to Prime Minister Cameron (who led the 'Remain' campaign') and the Tories. All in all, in a parliamentary rather than a plebiscitary democracy the best course for reversing Brexit would seem to remain through the mechanism of a general election.

Whatever happens the question of Britain's relationship with Europe, and the underlying crisis of England and Englishness, will continue to determine British political, social and economic life for decades to come. And in the dangerous and unstable situation in the aftermath of the 2016 referendum, public opinion, which as long as the country remains a democracy may well change dramatically, will ultimately determine the final outcome. So it cannot be ruled out that the momentous decision to leave the EU taken in June 2016 could begin to look like a great mistake. Whether the British elite and its people, after all the xenophobic bombast following the referendum, have the maturity to admit this mistake, and put it right, remains the great question facing the country.

Lightning Source UK Ltd.
Milton Keynes UK
UKOW01f2228041117
312134UK00006B/297/P

9 781907 14406